DIVORCE CASUALTIES

DATE DUE

MAY 0 2 2013	
AUG 1 9 2015	
SEP 0 8 2015	

BRODART   Cat. No. 23-221

DIVORCE CASUALTIES

Understanding Parental Alienation

Second Edition

Douglas Darnall, Ph.D.

TAYLOR PUBLISHING COMPANY

Lanham • New York • Boulder • Toronto • Plymouth, UK

Published by Taylor Trade Publishing
An imprint of The Rowman & Littlefield Publishing Group, Inc.
4501 Forbes Boulevard, Suite 200, Lanham, Maryland 20706
www.rlpgtrade.com

Estover Road, Plymouth PL6 7PY, United Kingdom

Distributed by NATIONAL BOOK NETWORK

Library of Congress Cataloging-in-Publication Data
Darnall, Douglas.
  Divorce casualties : understanding parental alienation / Douglas Darnall—2nd ed.
    p. cm.
  Includes bibliographical references and index.
  ISBN-13: 978-1-58979-376-7 (pbk. : alk. paper)
  ISBN-10: 1-58979-376-5 (pbk. : alk. paper)
  1. Children of divorced parents. 2. Divorced parents. 3. Joint custody of children—
Psychological aspects. 4. Parenting. I. Title.
  HQ777.5.D37 2008
  306.89—dc22

                                                                    2008020576

∞™The paper used in this publication meets the minimum requirements of American National Standard for Information Sciences—Permanence of Paper for Printed Library Materials, ANSI/NISO Z39.48-1992.
Manufactured in the United States of America.

To mothers and fathers
for encouraging their children
to have loving and healthy relationships
with their other families

Contents

Acknowledgments

The success of the first edition of *Divorce Casualties* has strengthened my commitment to helping families manage the perils of high-conflict divorce. The second edition is possible because of the efforts of committed mental health and legal professionals, authors, and researchers who have since contributed to our knowledge about how to work with these families. Because of all that has been learned since the first publication, this revision is the first of two books: The second will address treatment and reunification. I cannot say enough about how grateful I am for the families that have shared their stories and experiences which have contributed to this offering.

Many of my dearest friends have helped me with editing and offering suggestions about the contents of the book. Words cannot express my gratitude. I wish to thank Barbara Steinberg, Ph.D. for her contribution on grief; Amy Baker, Ph.D. for her valuable critiques; Terry Heltzel, Ph.D.; Mary Geidner; Michele Hawn, M.S., L.P.C.C.; Marilyn Burns, M.Ed., L.P.C.C.; Deirdra Petrich, Ph.D., L.P.C.C.; Desiree Gomez, B.A.; Terry Smith, M.Ed., L.P.C.C.; Attorney Lane Harvey; Claudette and David Summers for their editing skills; Attorney Glennon Karr for his critique on the legal and ethics chapter; and, of course, my agent and friend Denise Marcil.

I am grateful to my parents, Paul and Jan Tanner, for sharing their wisdom and experiences. Paul, a retired professor at U.C.L.A., has published many books on music and was a member of the original Glenn Miller Orchestra. In addition, I am grateful to my mother for all her support and encouragement over the years. Their advice and support has been invaluable.

My wife, Jan, has sacrificed a lot, with my many late hours working on the revision and the second book. My daughters—Brianna, a law student at Duquesne University Law School; and Lindsey, a research technician at Cleveland Clinic Foundation—have been great and are always a source of support. I love them for standing beside me.

Introduction

The premise of the first edition of *Divorce Casualties* was to educate parents about the symptoms of parental alienation and teach them how to prevent the more severe consequences of parental alienation syndrome for their children. The first edition left the reader with very little hope for reversing the deleterious effects of parental alienation syndrome upon the children and rejected parent. The only hope offered was for the parent to understand parental alienation syndrome in order to prevent it. Much has been learned since the first edition. The original premise is still true today, but there is more reason for optimism in preventing alienation and repairing damaged relationships.

There were shortcomings to the first edition of *Divorce Casualties: Protecting Your Children from Parental Alienation*. The focus was on parental alienation, with little consideration of alternative explanations for severe parent/child conflicts. Parents feeling rejected and persecuted by the other parent sometimes do not take into account their own contribution to the parent/child tensions. Little was known about spontaneous reunification, the role of parent coordinators, and reunification therapy when *Divorce Casualties* was initially written.

During the past ten years since the writing of first edition, parental alienation and parental alienation syndrome have unfortunately become a political issue. The terms, and the very existence of the phenomenon, have been attacked in some courts and state legislative bodies by politically motivated parent groups and by angry parents feeling persecuted by the allegations raised against them. Just as there are false allegations of abuse, there are false allegations of parental alienation. No one with experience in domestic relationships denies the existence of parents who, consciously or unconsciously, attempt to alienate the children and would just as soon eliminate the rejected parent from their and the children's lives. Fortunately, this is a small number of cases, but these are the cases that continually reappear in court. They consume tremendous court resources, at great cost to the families. I have heard parents say many times, "The cost of litigation could have paid for my child's college education." This is, sadly, true. Then there are those who argue that parental alienation and parental alienation syndrome are nothing more than junk science and an attempt to protect an abusive parent from a protective parent. This second edition will clarity and refute these accusations. Whatever you want to call parental alienation and parental alienation syndrome, the phenomena are real. Arguing against their existence in court is nothing more than a damaging diversion to avoid facing the issue.

Children are often caught in the emotional crossfire when parents divorce or separate. Many couples continue to fight bitterly for years after a divorce, especially over such issues as child support and visitation (referred to in this book as "parenting time"). Yet research has repeatedly shown that children's adjustment and mental health depend directly on how well their parents protect the children from conflict. This edition expands the summary of research supporting the importance of both parents being actively involved in raising the children. Parents who, consciously or unconsciously, sabotage their children's relationship with the other parent for revenge on their ex-spouse will learn how their behavior can cause lasting damage to the children.

For ten years now, I have received thousands of messages on our site www.parentalalienation.com or by e-mail (Douglas900@aol.com). The feedback has been most gratifying. Parents have commented on how much they have learned about their own role in preventing alienating behavior and about feeling reassured that they were not crazy when they learned there is a name for the phenomenon. Knowing the phenomenon's name was, for many parents, very comforting. Perhaps it is ridiculous to think that parents who could not get along in a marriage should somehow be able to get along after the divorce. But as challenging as it may sound, parents have to put their personal needs aside and think about what is best for their children. For the children's sake, they must learn to get along, resolving disputes without involving the children. Many parents have learned this valuable lesson.

One problem with the first book remains the same in the second book: the language used to describe parents. I do not always know who my readers are. Families today are different from those of years past. Some readers are parents who are divorced or anticipating divorce and are struggling with their relationship with their ex-spouse. Other parents were never married. There are grandparents raising grandchildren, gay and lesbian parents, single mothers with children from more than one father, blended families with two sets of stepchildren, teenagers raising babies, and, more recently, babies conceived with donor eggs or sperm. Although I do not mean to exclude any of my readers, I have decided, for the sake of simplicity, to write as if my readers are two divorced parents. Thus, "ex-spouse" is used for parents who were never married as well as those who were. I have also tried to stay gender-neutral, because an alienating parent can be a mother, a father, a significant other, or even a grandparent. The assertion that only fathers are victims and mothers are the perpetrators is entirely false. In fact, there are many contentious divorces in which both parents actively alienated.

Writing the book required me to look at parental alienation and parental alienation syndrome from different perspectives. I want the book to be relevant both to alienating parents and the parent victims of alienation. The intent is to help parents from either perspective to work together for their children's welfare.

During the research for this revision, the amount of new research and material has grown exponentially. The organization of this volume differs from the first edition. To make the book more reader-friendly, the content is broken down into shorter chapters rather than long chapters covering numerous topics. After reading the first six chapters, you may want to choose from among the other chapters those you find most relevant to your situation. (Everyone, however, should read chapter 18, "Legal and Ethical Challenges to PA and PAS.") In addition, what began as a revision to a single book is now two books, the second of which will discuss repairing damaged parent/child relations, reunification, and spontaneous reunification.

I have tried to write in such a manner that will not cause the reader to feel defensive. Do not feel discouraged if you are not the perfect parent. No one can make that claim. All you can aspire to is to be a better parent. Parenting is a full-time job that takes a conscious effort on your part. Most of the parents I have worked with do more right than wrong, and I am sure this is true of you, too. Perhaps you will learn that much of what you have been doing is right, although there is more you can do to reduce alienation. While reading the book you will have an opportunity to complete exercises designed to stimulate your thinking and help enhance your awareness about your parenting during this trying time. I have used real-life examples to help you understand the issues more clearly and apply them to your own family.

Parents everywhere want the same opportunities: to share in raising their children in peace, to give them the love and protection they deserve, and to revel in their future successes. I sincerely wish you and your children all the best.

DOUGLAS DARNALL, PH.D.
MINERAL RIDGE, OHIO

A Cautionary Note

Going through a divorce is probably one of the most painful and guilt-ridden experiences you will ever encounter. Many of you have been through years of litigation and spent thousands of dollars with little to show for your efforts. This is an experience you were likely not prepared to face. Now you are in the difficult position of trying to remain an involved and loving parent while dealing with your fear and hurt from the divorce.

Reading this book will help you learn how to cope with your feelings while continuing to protect your children from the family crisis. You will learn how to recognize and minimize or prevent the damage caused by alienating behavior. You will learn specific strategies to strengthen the relationship between you and your children, your children and their other parent, and even you and your ex-spouse.

Before reading the book, a word of caution is necessary. It is possible to deliberately twist some of the information presented and use it maliciously against the other parent. Such vindictiveness is tantamount to child abuse and must be avoided. When reading, it is important that you believe in the value of your children having a loving relationship with both parents. If you cannot share in that belief you must honestly examine yourself and your motivation for interfering in the other parent's relationship with the children. Do you want to preserve the relationship between the children and their mother or father, or are you looking for further justification to stir your hate? Do you believe you have the right to make decisions about the relationship—or lack of a relationship—between your children and the other parent that will affect the rest of your children's lives? Keep in mind: alienation can backfire and in time destroy the relationship between you and your children.

If you are in any way tempted to inflict damage on the other parent, immediately stop reading. For your children's welfare, you should seek professional help to prevent doing them any harm.

1

Parental Alienation

You don't deserve to ever see your children after what you have done to me.

Barbara's Story

Barbara had had an uneasy feeling about her daughter, Emilie, for months. The normally spontaneous preteen had lost her smile and has since become evasive to a simple question: "Who was on the phone?" Then one day, Emilie, during one of her fits, let out her intention to live with her father. Barbara was stunned. Emilie began accusing her mother of breaking up the family and taking her father's money, making him live in a little apartment above her grandmother's garage. Then Emilie dropped the bombshell: Her father has her enrolled in Rosemount Middle School, not the school Barbara believed Emilie to be attending. Barbara had known nothing about this plan. At first she could not believe what she was hearing, but then some of Emilie's behavior began making sense. Emilie's cold stares, the new defiant tone in her voice, her refusal to be hugged, and her quick defense of her father—all should have raised suspicion that something was seriously wrong. Barbara began questioning in her mind about how Emilie and her father had been scheming. She questioned whether she was becoming paranoid. For reasons she could not explain, Barbara now felt compelled to visit Rosemont Middle School. She had to know what, if anything, was going on.

Barbara approached the unfamiliar stairs of the school with trepidation. She was unsure about what she would say to the school receptionist. How does it look for a mother to ask a school employee if her daughter is enrolled in the school? She felt stupid asking the question. The receptionist was very polite. She remembered Emilie and her father and directed Barbara down the hall to Miss Cleary's classroom. Barbara froze at the door when she saw her daughter's nameplate on an empty desk in the back of the room. Slowly, Barbara, not knowing what to say, scanned the room for any sign of her daughter's presence. Her gaze fell on a little white cutout snowflake hanging on the wall with Emilie's name. Barbara, confronting her worst fears, had to ask.

Barbara's story is true. Emilie and her father were conspiring to change custody and enroll her in Rosemount. Her father had successfully alienated or brainwashed Emilie to believe horrendous things about her mother. She became her father's mouthpiece for all of his anger and hurt. Emilie was now a true believer in everything bad about her mother.

Most parents agree that children of divorce should be raised in a loving family free from their parents' animosity and conflict. For a small percentage of families going through divorce or separation, however, peace between parents is only a dream, an aspiration, and far from a reality. Courts and mental health professionals refer to these family units as high-conflict families because of disparaging attacks among all parties, protracted litigation, and the resistance of the child to parenting time or visits. Custody is not always the issue. Instead, the noncustodial parent's limited or restricted access to the children often cause parents to return to court.

Although the number of divorces appears to be stabilizing in recent years, courts continue to have their dockets backed up with high-conflict litigants. Judges or magistrates know that whatever decision the court renders, they will see these same parents repeatedly. Courts have looked to mental health professionals for answers but, for a small group of parents, this has offered little help.

Many reasons explain why high-conflict divorces involving children occur. Social expectations, the parents' mental health, personality styles, deceit, the parents' misplaced values and beliefs, economics, family influences, family dynamics, political correctness, and the law all influence how parents respond to a divorce and the restructured family. For various reasons, some parents do not cope well with the stress caused by the interplay of all these dynamics. To cope with the uncertainty of a new family structure, one parent may begin a pattern of behaviors he or she believes will strengthen the relationship with his or her children. The parent tries to be closer to the children through these maladaptive behaviors, to the detriment of the other parent. Professionals commonly describe these behaviors as brainwashing (Clawar & Rivlin, 1991; Baker, 2007) and parental alienation (Gardner, 1998; Darnall, 1993; Kelly & Johnson, 2001; Warshak,

2001). An offshoot of alienation proposed by Turkat (1994) is Malicious Mother Syndrome, described as a mother feeling justified in punishing the father by interfering with visits and engaging in malicious behavior towards the father. Turkat's description poses a couple of problems. First, it negates the fact that both mothers and fathers are equally capable of engaging in alienating behavior; and second, the label has a strong sexist connotation that removes any hope for objectivity and balance.

TIP: PA and PAS are descriptive terms and not a clinical diagnosis.

High-conflict parents display a persistent pattern of animosity, hostility, and retribution towards each other. The children, and frequently significant others, are pulled into the battles and become the tragic victims of the hostilities. Frequently, the parents' battlefield is the allocation of parenting time and the children's minds, which become the spoils of the war. Over time, the children—the true victims—can display serious symptoms of depression, aggressiveness, social withdrawal, and other psychological problems. Considerable research (Amato, 1993) identified the adverse effects a divorce can have on children. Recently, Judith Wallerstein (2001) described the impact of divorce on children's lives years later into their adulthoods. Although professionals point out problems with her limited sample, which used only upper-middle-class Caucasians, Wallerstein's research made a dramatic point: that high conflict can cause lasting scars. Logic tells us that children deprived of a loving relationship with a parent can have significant consequences for the child later in life. They miss the affirmation of knowing they are loved and valued, the sense of family continuity, and the benefits of added financial resources and additional family support in later years.

In recent years, professional literature describes different models for working with high-conflict families. Recent trends advocate using mediators, parent coordinators, or special masters to work with these families to restore working relationships and head-off protracted litigation (Baris, et al., 2001; Baker, 2007).

During the course of the divorce or separation, problems between the children and parent may surface. The children may begin acting out, refusing to see a parent, withdrawing into the bedroom, mouthing off, throwing tantrums, or just being obnoxious. While looking for answers and resolution, everyone feels they are under a microscope. Worse, the propensity for everyone to behave badly during the course of a divorce is magnified. The rejected parent wants answers to why their child is acting so mean and angry, or withdrawn and uncooperative. Many parents search the Internet for answers and begin questioning if their child has been brainwashed by the other parent or that parent's significant other. The inquisitive parent reads about parental alienation (PA) and parental alienation syndrome (PAS), relieved to learn there is a name for what they are experiencing. The sense of relief, however, only leaves them wondering about what to do to prevent or repair the damage, especially when the alienating parent rebuffs and sabotages all attempts to talk and help solve the parenting problem.

The alienating parent may feel unjustly accused by the targeted parent of alienating behavior. The accused is now defensive and frustrated because his or her denials are not believed. This is one of the risks that come with a parent wanting to diagnose. Another risk is that it is possible to be wrong, causing unnecessary hurt and anger. The terms PA and PAS help with understanding behavior, and perhaps provide some insight about how to respond, but using the terms to strengthen accusations will make hostilities worse. Some of both parents' confusion is in the failure to understand the differences between estrangement, parental alienation, and parental alienation syndrome. Some parents also too quickly attach themselves to a label and use the words to attack the other parent, without fully understanding all that is involved making the distinction.

TIP: Parental alienation is not a gender issue. Either parent, regardless of gender, can alienate.

Parental Alienation

Parental alienation (PA) is not parental alienation syndrome (PAS). Failure to understand the difference is ignoring significant family dynamics that will hinder effective intervention by either the court or a therapist. The first edition of *Divorce Casualties* (1993) emphasized the importance of making a distinction between parental alienation and parental alienation syndrome because at the time the book was written, reunification or reversal of severe parental alienation was thought to be near impossible. The book's premise was to help parents recognize parental alienation to prevent the occurrence of parental alienation syndrome. This premise holds true today.

Parental alienation defined by Darnall (1993) is "any constellation of behaviors, whether conscious or unconscious, that could evoke a disturbance in the relationship between a child and the other parent." Dr. Gardner (1985), the physician who coined the terms, explained that PAS is similar to brainwashing except that the motivation for the alienating parent has a conscious as well as "a subconscious or unconscious" component.

Baker and Darnall (2006) conducted an Internet survey of ninety-six individuals to identify the most frequently reported alienating behaviors. These behaviors fell into particular categories, including:

General badmouthing	74.0%
Creating an impression that the targeted parent is dangerous or sick	62.5%
Moving or hiding the child	14.6%
Limiting visitation	29.2%
Saying the targeted parent doesn't love the child	44.8%
Confiding in the child about the marriage	29.2%
Confiding in the child about the court case and child support issues	45.8%
Badmouthing the other parent's new family or extended family	27.1%
Intercepting calls and messages	22.9%
Badmouthing the targeted parent to authorities	31.3%

The Baker and Darnall study was consistent with the results of Darnall's (1993) unpublished study also finding alienating parents to be extremely critical of the targeted parent's parenting skills. Targeted parents felt that the alienating parent undermined their parental authority (31.3 percent), coerced the child to reject the targeted parent (27.1 percent), and failed to provide school, medical, and activity schedules (18.8 percent). The results of Darnall's factorial study allowed for a more refined definition of PA: "A parent's purposeful campaign of vilification characterized by anger, resistant and inconsistent compliance with court orders, conscious or unconscious denigration of the child's other parent, and interference with the other parent/child relationship." The new definition took into consideration that severely alienating parents frequently ignore court orders, degrade the targeted parent, and criticize the other parent's parenting skills. These red flags help identify an alienating parent.

Baker and Darnall (2006) found that gender—of the targeted parent or of the targeted child—was not related to the frequency or type of alienating behavior. Girls were reported to be more alienated (55.6 percent) than boys (32.6 percent), and older children more severely alienated than younger children. Targeted parents who perceived their child as mildly or moderately alienated did not report differences in the number of alienating strategies employed. Targeted parents who identified their ex-spouses as "obsessed" in their desire to alienate reported having more severely alienated children. The point is that persistent alienation works, damaging what was once a loving relationship.

> TIP: A parent's persistent alienating behavior can adversely influence the child's long-term adjustment.

A parent's alienating behavior can be very subtle and not easily recognized by the targeted parent. Covert alienating is behind the unsuspecting parent's back until the child begins showing the telltale signs, usually by starting to resist parenting time or displaying a hostile change in attitude. An evaluation by a qualified clinician may be required to differentiate between alienating behavior and estrangement.

Alienation is not about a "bad guy" (the alienating parent) versus a "good guy" (the targeted parent). True, one parent is usually the initiator and the aggressor. However, the roles can rotate. The targeted parent, feeling victimized, may retaliate against the alienating parent with her own alienating tactics, thus becoming the alienator and the aggressor, to a degree, the victim. This repetitive cycle can continue well before PAS appears in the child. The true identity of the alienator is not difficult after ruling out the influences of estrangement.

The degree of parental alienation varies. The severity can be as minimal as a parent occasionally calling the other parent a derogatory name, or as overwhelming as the parent's campaign of consciously destroying the children's relationship with the other parent. Most children are able to brush off a parent's offhanded comment voiced in frustration about the other parent. On the other hand, children may not be able to resist a parent's persistent campaign of hatred and alienation.

Michelle's Story

Michelle, a young mother of three children, used a unique alienating tactic. She scheduled shopping trips with the children on the day that the support check was to arrive. The shopping day became a ritual and was greeted with great anticipation by the children. They knew their mother planned to buy them clothes or toys on this special day. If, for whatever reason, the check did not arrive on time, the children were understandably disappointed when they were told they had to cancel the shopping trip. Their father was blamed even if the check arrived just one day late. Michelle told her children the reason they could not go shopping was that their "deadbeat father didn't pay his support." She made no mention that the check was a day late. The shopping trip, along with the support check, became a weapon used against the father. Similar incidents taught the children to resent their father, when children should not be involved in matters of child support. Because he had no control over delayed mail delivery, the mother's accusations created an unjust and untrue backdrop for alienation. Sadly, for years their father was unaware this was happening behind the scenes. Had he known, he might have explained to his children that although he mailed the support check on time, they should not expect it on a certain date.

There are infinite examples of alienating behavior, all with the same result: harming the relationship between the child and the parent. The behaviors and tactics used may be intentional or inadvertent, conscious or unconscious. You may think of your own examples of alienating behavior. Consider these situations:

- **Allowing your children to choose whether to visit, knowing that the court has not empowered you or your children to make that choice:** "Billy is old enough to decide for himself. If he wants to visit, he'll tell me. Until then, I'm not going to force him."

- **Telling your children everything about why the marriage failed, and giving the children details about the divorce settlement:** "Billy, come here and look at these papers. This is why we don't have any money for you to take your girlfriend, Sherri, to the prom. If you want to go, ask your father for the money."

- **Refusing to give the other parent medical and school records, or schedules for school and extracurricular activities:** "If your father wants to see your soccer schedule, let him go to the coach and get it himself."

- **Being blamed by your ex-spouse in your child's presence for not having enough money:** "If your father wasn't driving around in a new car and taking his girlfriend to fancy restaurants, we would have money to go out once in a while."

- **Refusing to acknowledge that your children have personal property:** Children should have some control over where they want to take personal possessions. Parents should not restrict or dictate where a child can use certain clothing, shoes, toys, school supplies, or other items, even if one parent gave these as "gifts" or bought them; nor should parents punish a child for deciding where to take and use personal possessions, even if the child forgot or left the items at the other parent's home or in the car: "Sweetheart, you can't take your new doll home to Mom's. I bought you the doll and it should stay here." (Expensive gifts or family heirlooms are an exception and may have to stay at the giver's home, especially if the child is young and irresponsible.)

- **Becoming rigid about the visitation schedule for no reason other than getting back at your ex-spouse:** "The court order says you are to be here at six o'clock. That doesn't mean fifteen minutes *after* six o'clock. If you are early, you can wait in your car until six."

- **Assuming your ex-spouse is dangerous because he or she had verbally threatened you in the past during an argument:** "I'm not going to let that bastard take Jenny out of my house. How do I know that he won't hurt her like he said he was going to hurt me? I'll never forget him saying he'd 'smash my face in!'"

- **Making false or groundless allegations against the other parent about committing sexual abuse, using drugs, abusing alcohol, or doing other illegal activities:** "I know he's touching her. I can tell by her look when I ask her."

- **Asking your children to choose you over the other parent:** "Hon, just wait until you live with me; we'll be able to have fun like this every day. Wouldn't that be great?"

- **Reminding your children that they are justified in feeling angry toward their other parent:** "Billy, it's okay to let me know how you feel. I understand why you are angry with your mother after she left me for her boyfriend. You know how hard I tried to keep our family together."

- **Suggesting an adoption or change in the child's name should you remarry:**
  "Billy, after Jim and I get married, wouldn't it be great if he adopted you and became your real father?"
  "I didn't tell Billy to use Jim's last name. That's his choice."

- **Giving children reasons for feeling angry toward the other parent, even though they have no memory of the incident that would provoke such feelings.** Adults can rightly suspect that someone is

8

keeping the children's anger alive when they cannot personally remember, or couldn't possibly remember, the reasons for being angry: "I know you're too young to remember when your dad used to beat me, but I can never forget. He still scares me. Now you go off and have a fun visit with your father, but don't get him angry."

- **Having special signals, secrets, words with unique meanings, or plans for a private rendezvous, which suggest to your children something is wrong with the other parent.** These alienating behaviors encourage your children to lie, just to avoid telling secrets one parent has created:

  "Jenny, you know how much I love you and miss you. I'll tell you what: Why don't I meet you at recess by the playground so we can see each other? But you mustn't tell your mother, 'cause you know how angry she will get. This will be our little secret. Okay?"

  "I know you can't talk freely on the phone 'cause your mother is listening in. I'll tell you what: If you say 'I want to get a new CD,' that will be my signal to meet you at McDonalds. How does that sound?"

- **Using your children as a spy or to covertly gather information for the court:**

  "Billy, I need you to tell the judge about how Mom lets her boyfriend spend the night. Okay?"

  "Jenny, this is really important. I need your help. Could you go into the top desk drawer for Mom's checkbook and tell me the balance she wrote in the book? I need to know if she's paying the bills. Don't let her see you. You know how crazy she can get."

- **Talking about and planning for temptations that interfere with parenting time:** "I know you want to go with us to Cedar Point next weekend with Jim and his kids, but you can't. You're supposed to visit your dad that weekend. Why don't you ask him if you can go with us? But you know what he'll say. . . ."

- **Giving your children the impression that your feelings will be hurt if they had a good time with the other parent:**

  "Billy, how was your visit?"
  "Great, Mom. The Rock and Roll Hall of Fame was cool!"
  "That's nice," Mom says, with a dejected look.

- **Asking your children to tell you about your ex-spouse's personal life:**

  "Jenny, has your mother started dating yet?"
  "Where did your mom get the money for the home theater?"

- **Rescuing your children from the other parent when there is no danger:** "If your father gets angry or if you get bored, just call me and I'll come and get you."

Many of these examples probably sound familiar. The parent's statements are alienating. Notice that the child was not making the statements. If the child, rather than the parent, had made the statements, this would suggest parental alienation syndrome.

Parental Alienation Syndrome

In Gardner's second edition of *Parental Alienation Syndrome* (1998), he described PAS as "a disorder that arises primarily in the context of child-custody disputes. Its primary manifestation is the child's campaign of denigration against a parent, a campaign that has no justification. It results from the combination of a programming (brainwashing) parent's and the child's own contributions to the vilification of the targeted parent." Gardner emphasized the point that if "true parental abuse and/or neglect are present" and the child's animosity is justified, PAS would not be an appropriate explanation for the children's feelings. Gardner (1998) defined PAS as ". . . a disturbance in which children are preoccupied with deprecation and criticism of a parent—denigration that is unjustified and/or exaggerated."

Kelly and Johnson (2001) had a different description of the alienated child, as "one who expresses, freely and persistently, unreasonable negative feelings and beliefs (such as anger, hatred, rejection, and/or fear) towards a parent that are significantly disproportionate to the child's actual experience with that parent." There is considerable similarity in the two definitions, though Kelly and Johnson are not as specific in defining the syndrome. This is certainly understandable, because the specific behaviors Gardner describes have not been validated, though the Gardner behaviors have become a standard for identifying PAS.

When the child is subjected to persistent alienating tactics, they are at risk of becoming an advocate for the alienating parent by being the spokesperson for their parent's hatred. They become the soldiers to the alienating parent's general, directing the action against the targeted parent from the background. The children are frequently unaware of how one or both parents are using them.

Dr. Gardner (2002) also differentiated between PA and PAS. When referring to brainwashing the child in his definition of PAS, he is saying that parental alienation is a precursor to PAS. Gardner's "eight cardinal symptoms of parental alienation syndrome," focusing on the child's behavior, included:

- **A persistent campaign of denigration.** The campaign of denigration is heard when the child is relentless in name-calling, criticizing, and defacing the targeted parent. No amount of convincing can change the child's attitude or language.

- **Weak, frivolous, and absurd rationalizations for the deprecation.** The child will offer absurd excuses to hate, such as, "He made me eat my peas." "I have to go to bed by nine o'clock." "She looks at me strange."

- **Lack of ambivalence.** The targeted parent is all bad with no redeeming qualities. A common example is showing the child vacation photographs in which they are smiling with the targeted parent. When asked about the smile, the child will say, "I was faking it."

- **The independent thinker phenomena.** Some children understand when accusations of alienation are made against a parent: The alienating parent tells them, or they hear the arguments, or they simply are perceptive children who sense something is wrong and learn the words from one or both parents. In defense of the alienating parent, the child will insist that the feelings expressed are his own. There is reason to suspect alienation when a child proclaims, without being asked, that opinions about the targeted parent are independent of the alienating parent.

- **The tendency of the child to side with the alienating parent.** The child will jump to take the alienating parent's side after hearing an argument without hesitation or any thought. Whatever the alienating parents says is true and the targeted parent is a liar. The thinking is black-and-white, with no gray.

- **Absence of guilt over cruelty to and/or exploitation of the targeted parent.** The alienated child typically knows that her behavior and comments towards the targeted parent are hurtful. She does not care. She expresses no empathy, remorse, or guilt because she believes she is justified to feel the way she does. To an outside observer, the child appears to gloat about her hatred toward the parent.

- **Presence of borrowed scenarios.** The hateful child may justify his feelings from scenarios offered by the alienating parent. This isn't always done deliberately, but it can happen with devastating consequences. An alienated child may rationalize his hatred by saying he remembers his father abusing his mother when he was two years old. Two-year-olds will not have such memories. The rationalization comes from what is overheard from adults or told to them directly, and they believe the allegation must be true. Borrowed scenarios become especially dangerous when there are allegations of sexual abuse.

- **Spread of the animosity to the extended family of the targeted parent.** With no justification or personal experience, and without giving a reason, the child expresses hate and anger towards the targeted parent's significant other or extended family.

If you are a victim of PAS, you have likely heard your child say many hurtful statements to you or even about your family. You probably were shocked by what you heard. You want to blame your child for the disrespect shown you, but you also realize your child may have been influenced by what other adults (likely the other parent) have said that fuels anger and prevents healing from the divorce.

The existence of parental alienation syndrome is not black-and-white, where it either exists or not exists. There are degrees of severity. Gardner differentiates between mild, moderate, and severe degrees of PAS. His criteria are arbitrary and have been criticized because of the lack of valid studies (Kelly & Johnston, 2001). Using Gardner's criteria, it is reasonable to assume that a severely alienated child may not exhibit all the symptoms; also, there may be some behaviors consistent with PAS that Gardner did not identify in his description of PAS.

Baker and Darnall (2007) conducted a second Internet study to examine the relationship between PAS and the eight cardinal symptoms Dr. Gardner described (2002). The reported frequencies of PAS symptoms or behaviors reported (mostly and always) by sixty-eight targeted parents are:

Campaign of denigration	87.8%
Weak, frivolous reasons	98.4%
Lack of ambivalence	96.9%
Independent thinker phenomenon	95.0%
Expresses no guilt or remorse	88.9%
Sides with alienating parent	100.0%
Borrowed scenarios	79.7%
Rejects extended family	76.6%

The percentages are very high for all the reported behaviors, suggesting a strong interrelationship between the reported behaviors. The study also found that length of time spent with a targeted parent did not prevent PAS: "Joint custody is not a de facto protective mechanism against PAS" (Baker & Darnall, 2007). A second finding, of a more positive note, was that all but one alienated child had something positive to say about the targeted parent, suggesting a window of opportunity for reunification with even the most severely alienated child. All but the one child exhibited some degree of attachment and affection towards the targeted parent.

The PAS Child

Parents ask what an alienated child looks like. The statements below are examples of what you may have heard from your child or had conveyed to you by the other parent that may indicate parental alienation syndrome. When reading the examples, keep in mind that if the child has been abused or there are serious parenting issues, the statements may not be indicative of PAS.

- **Refusal to give reasons for not wanting to visit:** "I don't want you to see me play soccer. You don't deserve to watch me play."
- **Rejection that includes the extended family:** "I don't want to see grandma. She always takes your side."
- **Inability to express reasons for hating targeted parent or their family:** "I don't know." (How often have you heard that?)
- **A tendency to parrot the obsessed alienator, even when they cannot pronounce the adult's words:** "I know you are crazy. You have narcissistic personality disorder."
- **Relentless hatred towards the targeted parent:** "I hate you! You're mean. I will never forgive you for breaking up our family."
- **No desire to visit or spend any time with the targeted parent:** "I don't want to see you ever again."
- **Beliefs that are enmeshed with the alienator, thinking often mirroring the alienating parent's:** "I know you abused my mom. She would never lie to me."
- **Beliefs that can be delusional and frequently irrational:** "I hate you! You make me brush my teeth."

- **Failure to be intimidated by the court:** "I can't wait to tell the judge what you did to me."

- **Reasons for wanting nothing to do with the targeted parent that are not based on personal experiences but reflect what they are told by a parent obsessed to alienate:** The children often cannot, or have great difficulty, distinguishing their personal experiences, thoughts, feelings, and beliefs with the targeted parent from what the obsessive parent has told them: "I remember you dropped me when I was a baby. You never cared about me."

- **No ambivalence in feelings towards the targeted parent; it's all hatred with no ability to see the good:** "I will always hate you. I will never talk to you again."

- **No capacity to feel guilty about their behavior towards the targeted parent or forgiveness for any past parenting mistakes:** "I will never forgive my mother for having a boyfriend. It's all her fault for breaking up the family."

Outside the chaotic world of divorce and court, severely alienated children are hard to detect. Often they are bright and do well socially and in school. They can appear like normal, healthy children until asked about the targeted parent. When questioned about the targeted parent, their rage and irrational behavior are ignited like an explosion. Once triggered, they are eager to tell their story to anyone who will listen, especially to the court or someone they perceive as an authority. This reaction can be different than that of children who were physically or sexually abused. While abused children fear telling secrets, the PAS child is eager to malign the parent. Abused children may feel shamed about themselves and fear the abusive parent, while the PAS child has no shame about attacking or lying about a targeted parent.

Dori and Mike's Story

Mike's problems began when his ex-wife, Dori, learned of his engagement to Christina, his girlfriend for two years. Dori and Mike had two children, Joey and Jimmy.

Mike explained, "The boys came home from their visit from their mother's with an attitude. Joey was sort of smug, almost sneering. When I said hello to Joey, I caught him from the corner of my eye

---

> shooting a disgusted look toward Jimmy. Then I went to hug Jimmy and caught Joey making retching motions behind my back. I was surprised by their behavior because our visits usually go fairly well. I know this must be their mom's doing. She must have had one of her fits and bad-mouthed me the whole weekend. The other day Joey said that I 'obviously didn't have his best interests at heart.' How would a seven-year-old know to say that unless he heard it from his mother first?"

Mike is rightfully suspicious of his children's behavior. They had lost their typical spontaneity with him and are now secretive and hostile. He suspects Dori's boyfriend's is having a negative or alienating influence on his children, causing a change in their attitude. Mike knows something is desperately wrong but feels powerless to do anything about it. What he sees in his children is characteristic of what many parents see when the children are under the powerful influence of an actively alienating parent.

There is considerable controversy about Gardner's use of the term "syndrome" and over the fact that PAS is not a recognized diagnosis by the American Psychiatric Association (2002). In time, this may change. Because of the controversy, some courts and clinicians refuse to use the term "syndrome" or acknowledge PAS, and instead favor the more general term parental alienation. Though this may be more politically correct, using a single term for both parental alienation and parental alienation syndrome only adds to the confusion because both are distinct constructs, each requiring its own unique intervention. More important than the terms, however, is the pattern of behavior that hurts children and families. Ignoring the behaviors while attorneys argue over the terminology only makes matters worse for the children.

How Common Are PA and PAS?

Because there have been no empirical studies conducted, nor studies with a sufficiently large sample, it is impossible to determine how common PA and PAS are among parents. Part of the difficulty also arises because of the lack of agreement about how to define the terms and lack of knowledge about which behaviors form a cluster that are descriptive of PAS.

Clawar and Rivlin (1991) published the results of a twelve-year study commissioned by the American Bar Association looking at the issue of high-conflict divorces. They used the term "brainwashing" rather than PA and PAS. These researchers found that parents' various attempts to program the children occurred with about 80 percent of the parents. The statistic does not reveal the percentage of children who are successfully brainwashed or display behaviors similar to PAS.

The biggest challenge for parents and the courts is knowing whether the child's immediate reactions against a parent are caused by the child's legitimate fear of the parent because of past abuse, maltreatment, or intimidation. If abuse occurred, then the child's reactions can be reasonable or appropriate and not indicative of parental alienation syndrome. Estrangement due to poor parenting and failure to bond can also be viable reasons for the child's reaction. Making the distinction between estrangement, factual abuse, PA, and PAS is not always easy.

The Parental Alienation Scale

You may be asking yourself if you are engaging in alienating behavior. That is a fair question, given what you have already learned. If you want more awareness about your behavior, go to the Appendix and complete the Parental Alienation Scale. There are two forms: Form C for custodial parents and form N for noncustodial parents. The scale is not for you to make a diagnosis. You should not do that. Instead, take your total score and then look at the specific items on which you scored a 4 or 5, and then reflect on how these behaviors can cause harm and what you can do differently.

Types of Alienating Parents

Blaming me for alienating our children is nothing more than a bogus attempt to take my children from me.

Learning how to recognize the three types of alienating behavior helps prevent or stop alienating behaviors. How to respond to each type of alienation is different. Parents should not consider the terms for alienation as a diagnosis, but only descriptions of parental behaviors. These terms should not be used as an excuse to label an ex-spouse. Angry parents are frequently heard describing their ex-spouse as an obsessed alienator. Saying this undermines the relationship with the ex-spouse and may not be accurate. Only a thorough evaluation by a qualified clinician can make that determination. Furthermore, courts do not want to hear name-calling. Instead, the court wants to learn how the parties can repair a damaged relationship. After reading this book, you will have some idea how to intervene with each distinct pattern of behavior.

Types of Alienation

Naïve Alienators

Naïve alienators are parents who acknowledge the value of the children's relationship with the other parent but occasionally inadvertently do or say something to alienate. All parents will occasionally be naïve about how they alienate because they are not conscious of what they are doing until after some reflection.

Active Alienators

Parents who *actively alienate* know better about how to behave with the children. If the parent's old marital hurts and anger are unresolved, circumstances from the divorce or exposure to the ex-spouse can periodically trigger intense feelings. The triggers cause an emotional swell that provokes a temporary loss of control and judgment. After calming down, the parent may feel remorseful about the behavior and worried about how the child felt after witnessing the parent's meltdown.

Obsessed Alienators

Obsessed alienators have a fervent cause: to destroy the targeted parent. They rationalize their behavior by believing they or the children are a victim of abuse or betrayal. Personality disorders or mental illness can contribute to the obsessed parent's irrational thinking. Rarely do obsessed alienators have enough self-control or insight to contain their rage when confronted with the prospect of having to interact with the targeted parent. Sadly, the children exposed to the alienating manipulations are often exposed to the rage. Reasoning rarely works with these parents, because any questioning or challenge is perceived as an attack, which reinforces the delusion. The behavior of obsessed parents can often be seen in other aspects of their life, outside the scope of the divorce. The irrational or intense emotions may be a manifestation of a pervasive dysfunctional personality.

Parental alienation or parental alienation syndrome fails to explain all the reasons for parent-child hostilities. Most targeted parents want to believe that alienation by the other parent is the only viable explanation for the rejection. They don't stop and think about how they may contribute to the conflicts.

Estrangement

Estrangement must be considered as a possible explanation of an impaired parent-child relationship. Kelly & Johnson (2001) defined estrangement "as a child having a rational reason to reject a parent because of neglect, physical or sexual abuse, abandonment or domestic violence." For our purposes, a broader definition of estrangement may better help differentiate between problematic parent behavior and alienation. Simply put, estrangement is any parent-child problematic behavior, excluding alienation. The cause of a child's rejection or parent-child conflicts may be a combination of a parent's alienating behavior and the targeted parent's estrangement. Understanding how each contributes is difficult and requires evaluation. Although it is difficult to look at your own behavior, you must be honest and ask yourself if your behavior is part of the problem. Examples of estrangement that must be considered when trying to understand a parent/child relationship problem are:

- The lack of an attachment or emotional bond, characterized by the parent's inability or failure to provide acceptance, emotional availability, sensitivity, and responsiveness to the child, particularly when the child is in need (Cassidy, 1999)
- Family violence and abuse
- Mental illness or substance abuse that exposes the child to frightening or confusing behavior
- The absence or minimal presence of the parent in the child's life during formative years that prevented or hindered an adequate attachment
- Ineffective or overly punitive parenting
- The lack of warmth and affection
- Marked cultural and/or value differences
- A parent's inability to control the intense expression of emotions: children and adults will want to avoid yellers.

Dr. Reading's Story

Dr. Reading accused his wife of alienating his two children against him. He described how he had worked long hours for many years to provide a well-to-do lifestyle for his family. He admits to spending little time with the children because his sixteen-hour days caused him to arrive home after they were in bed. Now he is hoping to spend more time with his family after retiring at the age of forty-six. To his surprise, his wife almost immediately served him with divorce papers. The children were now refusing to spend time with him. Understandably, Dr. Reading is angry and hurt. He explained that he was raised with old-fashioned beliefs and traditions. He expected that his wife would run interference for him while he was working long hours, telling the children how much he loved them and how hard he was working for their benefit. He believed that his wife's support and encouragement would make up for his lack of involvement with the children. The thought never occurred to him that his wife's pep talk to the children would not make up for this absence or failure to bond. He instead believed that she reinforced the alienation by supporting the children's feelings that they did not have to see their father because he did not deserve their affection.

Dr. Reading's story—the father's failure to bond with the children and the mother's alleged alienation—is very common. He contributed to his own estrangement by keeping his distance from the children and maintaining the irrational belief that his wife would make up for the shortfall. What is learned from Dr. Reading's account is that a parent cannot expect a stand-in parent to take his or her place in creating a bond. Parents have to do this themselves. Sometimes busy parents have to make a difficult choice: more money or a loving relationship with their children.

The Naïve Alienator

Tell your father that he has more money than I do, so let him buy your soccer shoes.

Most parents have moments when they are naïve alienators. These parents mean well and recognize the importance of the children having a healthy relationship with the other parent. They rarely have to return to court because of problems with visits or other issues relating to the children. They encourage the relationship between the children and the other parent and both families. Communication between both parents is usually good, though they will have their disagreements much as they did before the divorce. For the most part, they can work out their differences without bringing the children into it.

Children, whether or not their parents are divorced, know there are times when parents argue or disagree. They don't like seeing their parents fight, and may feel hurt or frightened by what they hear. Somehow the children manage to cope, by talking out their feelings to a receptive parent, ignoring the argument, or trusting that the skirmish will pass and all will heal. What the children see and hear between their parents is not typically damaging to the children. They trust in their parents' love and protection. The children learn that each parent has a distinct personality, set of beliefs, and feelings. No one—children or parents—feels threatened by the others' feelings towards them or the others.

The Characteristics of Naïve Alienators

- They are able to separate their children's needs from their own: They recognize the importance for the children to spend time with the other parent so they can build a mutually loving relationship, and they avoid making the other parent a target for their hurt and loss

- They feel secure with the children's relationship with their grand-parents and their other parent

- They respect court orders and authority

- They can let their anger and hurt heal and not interfere with the children's relationship with their other parent

- They are flexible and willing to work with the other parent

- They are able to feel guilt when they have acted in a way that hurt the children's relationship with their other parent

- They are willing to allow the other parent to equally share in the children's activities

- They allow the other parent equal access to medical and school records.

Naïve alienators usually don't need therapy but will benefit from reading this book because of the insight they gain about how to keep alienation from escalating into something more severe and damaging for all. These parents know they make mistakes but care enough about their children to make things right. They focus on what is good for the children without regret, blame, or martyrdom.

The Active Alienator

I don't want you to tell your father that I earned this extra money. The miser will take it from his child support check so we won't be able to go to Disney World. You remember he's done this before, when we wanted to go to Grandma's for Christmas.

Most parents returning to court over problems with visitation are active alienators. These parents mean well and believe that the children should have a healthy relationship with the other parent. The problem they have is with controlling their frustration, bitterness, or hurt. When something happens to trigger their painful feelings, active alienators lash out in a way to cause or reinforce alienation against the targeted parent. Children hearing the screams may withdraw in fear. They are unable to effectively communicate with the targeted parent to work out their differences. After regaining control, such parents usually feel guilty or bad about what they have done and stop their alienating tactics. Vacillating between impulsively alienating and then repairing the damage with the children is the trademark of the active alienator. They are prone to blame. These parents have trouble separating the ex-spousal issues from the parenting issues. They are quick to feel personally attacked when the other parent has no intention of hurting them.

The Characteristics of Active Alienators

- They tend to lash out at the other parent in front of the children: This problem has more to do with loss of self-control when upset than any sinister motivation

- They are able to realize, after calming down, that they were wrong: At this point these parents usually try to repair any damage or hurt to the children and can be very comforting and supportive of the child's feelings in the process; during an evaluation, they have good insight about their behavior and may admit their shortcomings

- They, like naïve alienators, can differentiate between their needs and those of the children by supporting the children's desire to have a relationship with the other parent

- They allow the children different feelings and beliefs from their own (During the flare-ups of anger, however, the boundary between the child's and parent's beliefs can become very blurry. For the most part, older children have their own opinions about both parents based upon personal experience, rather than what they are told by others. To keep peace, older children usually learn to keep their opinions to themselves. Younger and more trusting children feel more confused about and vulnerable to their parents' behavior.)

- They respect the court's authority and, for the most part, comply with court orders. However, they can be very rigid and uncooperative with the other parent. A common example is rigid adherence to the time when an exchange is to occur. Being so much as fifteen minutes late is reason to refuse an exchange. This is usually a passive attempt to strike back at the other parent for some real or perceived injustice.

Active alienators are usually willing to accept professional help when they or the children have a persistent problem. They are sincerely concerned about their children's adjustment to the divorce. Harboring old feelings continues to be a struggle, but active alienators continue to hope for a speedy recovery from their pain.

The Obsessed Alienator

I love my children. If the court can't protect them from their abusive mother, I will. Even though she's never abused the children, I know it's only a matter of time. The children are frightened of their mother. If they don't want to see her, I'm not going to force them. They are old enough to make up their own minds.

The obsessed alienator is a parent, or sometimes a significant other, with a *cause*: to align the children to his or her side and, together with the children, campaign to destroy their relationship with the targeted parent. These parents feel driven by strong beliefs. They will solicit a cadre of family, friends, teachers, attorneys, and even mental health workers that supports their cause and even their delusional beliefs. Failure to offer support is reason to fire the attorney or counselor. They vehemently argue that their behavior is just and rational. For the campaign to work, obsessed alienators enmesh their children's personalities and beliefs into their own. This process takes time, but the children, especially the young, are completely helpless to see or combat it. The behavior usually begins well before the divorce is final. Obsessed parents are angry, bitter, or feel betrayed by the other parent. The initial reasons for the bitterness may actually be justified. Alienating parents who are truly victims of abuse consider their behavior a sincere reaction to protect the child, even when there is no reason to believe the child was ever abused. Obsessed parents may continue to harbor hatred because of past or ongoing verbal and physical abuse, betrayal from an affair, or because they believe they were somehow financially cheated. They sincerely believe they are victims and believe that their children, too, will become victims, if they are not already. Just having to see or talk to the other parent reminds them of the past and triggers the hate. They feel trapped with nowhere to go and heal. In other instances, obsessed parents alienate out of maliciousness, revenge, or greed for reasons that sound to others totally irrational or unjustified.

The Characteristics of Obsessed Alienators

- They are obsessed with destroying the children's relationship with the targeted parent

- They hold beliefs that can become delusional and irrational: No one, especially the court, can convince obsessed alienators that their beliefs are wrong, and anyone who tries becomes the enemy

- They ascribe irrational or unsubstantiated motivations to the other parent's behavior

- They attempt to enmesh the children's personalities and beliefs about the other parent with their own: This is evident in such statements as, "You don't have to talk to my son. I know what he wants and what's best for him," which suggests the likelihood that the parent is projecting his or her irrational delusions on the child

- They actively gather support from family members, quasi-political groups, or friends who share and reinforce their belief that the other parent and the system have victimized them (These supporters often appear at the court hearings even though they haven't been subpoenaed. The battle becomes "us against them." Targeted parents will also seek support from others because they frequently feel victimized by the system, complaining that no one believes what they say.)

- They have an unquenchable anger—exaggerated when stressed— and have very poor coping skills. They behave impulsively in a variety of circumstances. This can be a long-standing pattern of behavior witnessed outside the scope of the divorce

- They desire the court to punish the other parent with court orders that interfere with or block the targeted parent from seeing the children, thus confirming in the obsessed alienator's mind that she was right all the time
- They are not intimidated by the court's authority: They interpret the court's threats to sanction as a bluff (which, unfortunately, is frequently true)
- They believe in a higher cause than the law: protecting the children at any cost
- They refuse to read this book, or similar books, because the content makes them angrier.

A targeted parent who has felt victimized for months, if not years, who has appeared numerous times in court with no resolution, and who struggles with thoughts of giving up may appear to be an obsessed parent when, in fact, he is not. The difference between these parents is in how they relate to the children. Targeted parents avoid engaging in alienating behavior. Their behavior and attitudes consistently advocate for a strong relationship between the children and the other parent. This is contrary to what obsessed alienators say or how they behave.

Summing Up

An off-handed criticism of your ex-spouse, a look of disgust, or a slip of the tongue can all have an alienating effect on your children. None of these behaviors, which most parents do at one time or another, will have a devastating affect on your children. In fact, most children just brush off comments as meaningless, or they think, "Mom's just in a lousy mood" or "there goes Dad again." However, over time, such comments (usually made by a naïve or an active alienator) can have a cumulative effect on how your children feel towards their other parent. Obsessed alienators are typically more blatant in their comments and actions against the targeted parent. Either way, an important step in preventing alienation is being able to recognize alienating behavior, whether subtle or blatant.

High-conflict families are thought to make up approximately 5 percent of the cases brought to the court's attention. The cases can range in severity from a loving relationship between the parents and children, to the other extreme, in which the children have been subjected to alienating behavior and presently display severe symptoms of parental alienation syndrome. The severely alienated child outside the divorce arena can appear normal or well-adjusted by all accounts. This makes the rejected parent's argument that the child is severely alienated seem implausible. After all, how can a child who unjustly hates a parent appear normal? However, they can. Within the world of divorce, the severely alienated child will appear to:

- Display an unjustified hatred towards the rejected parent with no ability to see any good
- Show no capacity for guilt or remorse towards the rejected parent
- Maintain thinking or beliefs in lockstep with the obsessed parent to denigrate the rejected parent: Their irrational beliefs come from what they are told by others, especially the alienating parent, rather than personal experience
- Feel generalized hatred towards others (family, friends)
- Act normal in all other aspects of life
- Parrot the language or phrases of the alienating parent
- Remain unaffected and unintimidated by the court
- Feel relentless hatred and an inability to forgive
- Demonstrate an enmeshed relationship with the alienating parent.

The child's behavior is similar to Gardner's description of parental alienation syndrome (1998). The confusion about parental alienation syndrome comes from the difficulty in distinguishing between parental alienation syndrome and estrangement. The exercise below has real-life examples of behavior and should help you distinguish between the behaviors of parental alienation syndrome and estrangement. Complete the exercise by identifying the below behaviors as examples of alienating behavior or estrangement. Place an "A" in the space provided identifying alienating behavior and an "E" for estrangement, then compare your answers at the end of the chapter.

EXERCISE: ESTRANGEMENT VS ALIENATION

1. Refusing to take the children to court-ordered counseling. _____
2. Badmouthing the other parent in front of the children. _____
3. Asking the children to find the other parent's old cell phone and bring it to you. _____

4. Yelling at the children because they won't obey you. _____
5. Avoiding or missing your children's activities because of your busy schedule. _____
6. Missing school conferences. _____
7. Asking your children about the ex-spouse's new friend. _____
8. Neglecting your child's request to help with homework or school projects. _____
9. Asking your child to keep a secret from the other parent. _____
10. Pressuring your children to warm up to your new friend. _____
11. Threatening to punish your children for refusing to visit. _____
12. Insisting your children talk to you on the phone at your convenience. _____
13. Asking your children to spy on the other parent. _____
14. Showing your child divorce papers. _____

The answers are: Estrangement (1, 4, 5, 6, 8, 10, 11, 12); alienation (2, 3, 7, 9, 13, 14).

If you think your problems with your children stem from estrangement, you may want to consider therapy. Though this book briefly discusses estrangement, the primary focus is on how to respond to alienating behavior.

A Word of Caution: Making a Diagnosis

Many parents victimized by an alienating parent are very passionate about wanting to learn all they can about the other parent's behavior. They report being surprised to learn that there is a name for what they observe in the other parent. They look for answers that will provide them direction. Too often parents diagnose the alienating parent as an obsessed alienator or having a personality disorder without sufficiently understanding the meaning of the terms. A diagnosis made by a layperson is not helpful; in fact, it can make matters worse. Diagnosing is another way of blaming or attacking the alienating parent. Though the feelings are understandable, diagnosing only reinforces the targeted parent's anger and sense of helplessness. "Obsessed alienator" is not a diagnosis but a descriptive term describing a pattern of behavior.

Parents in search for answers have turned to the Internet. In recent years there has been a proliferation of new Web sites and organizations on parental alienation and parental alienation syndrome. The sites offer the rejected reader reassurance that they are not crazy and what they experience is a real phenomenon. Many of the parents report feeling reassured knowing there is a name for the phenomenon.

During the parents' pursuit for answers, they read that alienating parents are frequently described as having a personality disorder. This is another opportunity to place blame: suggesting that the alienating parent has a personality defect without necessarily understanding what a personality disorder is. To make such an unqualified diagnosis is to risk being wrong, and this name-calling only perpetuates the alienating behavior.

TIP: Do not diagnose or label the alienating parent as having a personality disorder. You are not qualified to make the diagnosis, and doing so only creates further hostility.

There has been a lot of discussion about the role a parent's personality contributes to high-conflict divorces and severe alienation (Eddy, 2006; Baker, 2007). Many evaluators would agree with this premise, but there has yet to be any supporting studies finding the relationship between a personality disorder and an alienating parent. Many therapists or court evaluators will offer anecdotal examples of an alienating parent having a personality disorder. Conducting such a study would be very expensive and difficult because of the problems in getting a large enough sample to make the results meaningful. Before describing an impaired personality, we need to define and look at the characteristics of a healthy personality. A personality is the individual's approach or style, and how they perceive, interpret, and respond to the world around them. The characteristics of a healthy personality are flexibility, empathy, good adaptive skills when facing stress, and a willingness to accept personal responsibility for one's own behavior. Individuals predisposed towards a pattern of thinking and behavior that adversely affects their adaptive skills and who are thought to have a personality disorder can be described as having:

- A rigid and narrow perception of the world
- An attitude and perception that is very self-centered, with minimal ability to empathize or understand another's perspective
- A tendency to become overly emotional when confronted with beliefs contrary to their own
- A tendency to avoid taking responsibility for their behavior; instead, they are quick to blame others or circumstances
- A tendency to view as positive attributes what others consider personality flaws: "I have good reason to not trust anyone." "I live by my rules. The court doesn't know what it's talking about."

When parents with a personality disorder are exposed to excessive stress—for example, a court appearance—their pattern of behavior becomes more fixed because they see these behaviors and beliefs as positive attributes. In other words, being more suspicious, rather than less suspicious, is good. The specific criteria for the more frequent personality disorders associated with an alienating parent are not provided here because of the temptation to diagnose yourself or the alienating parent. Again: making a diagnosis will only make matters worse, and should be left up to qualified professionals.

Understanding the different degrees of alienating behavior is helpful because the distinctions allow you to better relate to these individuals and perhaps learn something about yourself. Preventing or minimizing the damage caused by alienation begins with understanding.

3

False Allegations

I know he touched my daughter. She would never lie.

Children complain all the time about their parents. When children describe behaviors that could be a sign of alienation, the listener has to sort out three possibilities: complaints that sound reasonable; preposterous complaints; and complaints that suggest alienating behavior. This is perhaps one of the more difficult tasks for an evaluator.

There are three perspectives when discussing false allegations. There are the child's allegations, the alienating parent's allegations, and the targeted parent's allegations. Most damaging is an allegation of sexual abuse. Courts typically stop all contact between the child and the alleged perpetrator until an investigation is completed. The rationale is to protect the physical safety of the child and prevent the targeted parent from influencing the child's testimony. In the meantime, a targeted parent may lose all contact with the child for months, if not longer. At most, the targeted parent may have supervised visits. At issue is the validity of the allegations. The investigators may include a team of professionals (in this chapter, "professional interviewers" can include police detectives, child service workers, medical personnel, psychologists, and social workers). Depending on the results of the investigation, the case may be referred to the district attorney for prosecution.

If you have questions about your child's allegations, or you believe you are a victim of a false allegation, you will question what you should or should not do after hearing the allegation. The material in this chapter will give you direction. As much as you want to know the truth, this chapter will not answer your questions. The material presented should cause you to pause and think about what is happening in your situation, but will not qualify you to make any determination as to the validity of the allegations.

Children and parents often have many reasons to complain about the other parent. Complaining or badmouthing is part of parenthood and of being a child. The nature of the children's complaints changes as they age and mature. Some complaints are valid reasons for not wanting to spend time with a parent. Others are ridiculous. Most have nothing to do with alienation or parental alienation syndrome or even ineffective parenting. They are just children complaining, perhaps only to satisfy their narcissism and desire to get what they want. Some complaining is healthy, though a pain for the parent. As children mature, they develop their own values and views of the world that are not consistent with the parent's view of the world. During their maturation, older children or teens are conflicted between being dependent and staunchly independent. The vacillation between extremes is normal. Frequent reasons children give for not wanting to visit that have nothing to do with alienation are:

- **"He/She is always angry."** Children are like anyone else in that they want to avoid people who always sound angry. Worse than walking on eggshells is not knowing when to expect the next explosion.

- **"She/He yells and screams at me."** For whatever reason, some parents cannot just talk calmly to their children when they do something wrong. They yell and expect the child to just take it; to listen and change behavior. Any rebuttal is viewed as disrespectful.

- **"He/She breaks promises."** From the child's perspective, promises mean more than parents realize. A parent may say he is going to do something with the child without realizing that the child believes the parent made a promise—even though he never used the word "promise." The child may be hurt or angry when Dad breaks a date or fails do something he said he would do. Children can be very sensitive, and unforgiving when a parent breaks a promise. Parents cannot always prevent breaking promises. What becomes a serious problem is when parents make a *habit* of breaking promises. In time, the excuses mean nothing. You should not make promises to your child to pacify them when you do not mean what you say. They will learn to not trust you, and in time, will write you off. In addition, you can expect the other parent to resent making excuses for you while they try desperately to help relieve your child's disappointment. Your child may refuse to see you because of broken promises. The other parent may genuinely try to help gloss over your irresponsible behavior and encourage your child to forgive. The other parent rightfully feels enraged if you then come back and accuse him of alienation because of a problem you created. It is not fair to put the other parent in this position.

- **"She/He doesn't spend time with me."** Parenting time for the child should be precious because most parenting time is limited. Every parent wants to believe that her children are looking forward to the time they spend together. When the children anticipate your visit and later learns they are going to be farmed out to a babysitter or another relative, it is very disappointing. The rejection hurts. After all, they want to see *you*. It is true that grandparents also want to see the children, and they should. But take the children's lead on this. Ask them, "Do you want to visit your grandparents this weekend?" If they say no, respect their wishes for another day. If there is a family outing, do not drop off the children at the grandparent's home so you can go play golf. If the children are not okay with this, they will interpret your playing golf as more important than spending time with them.

- **"His/Her girlfriend/boyfriend is always around."** I cannot tell you how many times a parent has said, "If they can't accept my girlfriend, they can't accept me." What a selfish statement! Children want to be with you, not your significant other. In time, if the relationship is serious and your relationship with the children is strong, the significant other should be introduced—and then only after you prepare the children. Do not surprise them with, "Guess who's coming to dinner?" You may think this is cute, but your children will learn to distrust you.

- **"I can't trust him/her."** (**Because younger children lack the vocabulary, they may only say, "I don't like him; he's mean."**) Trust means the ability to predict another person's behavior. It has little to do with liking a person. An example is liking a car salesperson but not trusting what is written in the contract because of the little surprises that are in small print or not knowing if the salesperson is truthful about the quality of the vehicle. Trust is not something that the other person bestows upon you. It is earned. To earn it, you must be predictable: meaning you do what you say you are going to do. You risk losing your child's trust and the other parent's respect if you create surprises with unscheduled cancellations, secret appointments with doctors, or unannounced trips out of town. To regain trust, you must develop a new history of predictability. Since regaining trust takes a long time, it is easier to avoid losing trust in the first place. Do what you say you are going to do. Be trustworthy with your children and with the other parent.

- **"We always go where he/she wants to go."** Some children complain about having to go places that are of no interest to them. True, sometimes parents must take children where they do not want to go, but parents should seek their children's input if possible. If there is more than one child, they might take turns choosing. A common mistake is the belief that children must share a parent's interests. "If I love hockey, I know my son can't help but to share my excitement." Your son or daughter may have very different interests and may not share your passions. Their lack of excitement is not a rejection of you, so do not take it that way.

- **"I'm bored."** A parent can create financial burdens trying to make every weekend more exciting that the last. Kids do get bored. Part of the problem with boredom is the child's limited use of language. Frequently they complain of boredom when they really mean they are not in the mood. Children tend to think in terms of black-and-white. For example, you serve your children a dish that they absolutely love, and the next week they say, "I don't like that." Confused, you ask, "How can you not like this dish when last week you loved it?" The answer is simple. The child does not understand the concept of not being in the mood for something, so they say, "I don't like it." This can happen with visits. When a child says, "I don't like visits," it may be because your child is not in the mood, or from their perspective, would rather be doing something else.

- **"He/She always says mean things about my mother/father."** Nothing reminds children more about being caught in the middle than hearing one parent complain about the other. This is a common example of alienating behavior. Immediately they may feel like defending the other parent, and yet they have learned that it does no good, so they keep their mouths shut and their feelings to themselves. Children do not want to hear negative comments. Parents should not think their children would automatically agree with these comments. Frequently they do not. Instead, the parents' alienating behavior actually causes their own estrangement.

- **"He/She used to hit us."** While children can remember some past events well, that does not mean their memories are always accurate. Consider Roger's dilemma: Roger had always prided himself in being a stern but fair disciplinarian. He, like his father before him, would pull out the belt to make his point. At the time, people thought corporal punishment was responsible, loving, and excellent parenting. Roger did learn that using a belt was no longer socially or legally appropriate, and his children learned at school that "beating" a child with a belt was physical abuse. Today, Roger would not think of using a belt. However, the children have not forgotten. They now believe that their father was an abuser and they were victims. Some children are not very forgiving and continue to harbor their fears and anger years later.

- **"He's/She's mean to my sister."** Though children often yell and scream at their siblings and fight as though they hate each other, they can also be very protective of each other. A child who perceives you as being "mean" to a sibling can vicariously learn to fear you, even though you have not done anything to that child personally. Consequently, the child, believing he is protecting his brother or sister, does not want to see you.

Elaine's Story

Elaine, a few years younger than her brother, was bright for her ten years. She understood that her brother had learning problems and was socially awkward. Often she would come to his defense when teased by others. Her maternal ways were very comforting to her brother, who submitted to her guidance. Always protective, Elaine ran interference for her brother—except when it came to their father. Though Elaine had no personal reason to fear her father, she saw how he treated her brother. She described controlling her rage when she witnessed her father's tantrums directed towards her brother. She wanted to flip the dining room table over when her father unmercifully raged. The only way she knew to protect her brother was refusing to visit her dad. Of course, she would never tell her dad why she refused. She just made up one excuse after another. In all fairness, their father had no understanding why his children were refusing to visit. After he learned about parental alienation, he came to believe that Elaine's mother allowed the insubordination. He did not understand his role in the problem.

- **"We have nothing in common."** People like to be with people who share common interests, beliefs, and values. This is equally true for children. Children not interested in sports will rebel or withdraw if they feel pressured to participate by an overzealous parent. Someone standing at a distance would question, "Whose need is the parent trying to satisfy, the child's or his own?" Parents must listen to their children and negotiate how they want to spend time together. Just because you like sports (or music, or cooking, or reading) does not mean your child will share your interest. Try to have a little empathy for how your children feel.

- **"I can't be like you."** Parents frequently imagine "the ideal child." The image is of a bright, athletic, attractive, and socially confident child. In a short time, they realize the difference between the image and reality. Our children are not perfect. They cannot and should not have to live up to all our expectations. A physician's son may hate science, or a coach's son may be physically inept. Children can be very sensitive to a parent's subtle ways of communicating their displeasure. If your children believe they are displeasing you or cannot live up to your expectations, they may want to avoid spending time with you, especially if you are pushing an activity that they believe they will fail or in which they have no interest. Parents need to foster their children's interests and abilities, not their own interests and fantasies of success.

Many of the excuses children give for not wanting to visit have nothing to do with alienation. An alienating parent or a parent's estrangement can influence children's excuses. For a parent and an evaluator, the issue is how to discriminate between the two. There is usually no definitive answer, but we can get some guidance from the research and literature.

The issue is not just whether alienation exists; the issue is how the information is gathered. The evaluator relies on the child, parents, and sometimes significant others as sources of information to make a determination. The process for assessing alienation and parental alienation syndrome is similar to a custody evaluation. A court order to conduct the evaluation is necessary. The assessment involves extensive interviews, observing parent-child interaction, collaboration with family members, and sometimes testing. Testing by itself cannot identify parental alienation or parental alienation syndrome. The evaluator must also rule out all alternative explanations for what is happening in the family, such as the parent's or child's mental health, substance abuse, or personality disorders. A clinician cannot determine the existence of alienation unless all parties are interviewed. Without interviews and a review of all supporting documentation, the most the clinician can do is talk hypothetically without making any specific recommendations for custody, visitation, or parenting time.

TIP: Not all reasons a child gives for not wanting to visit are caused by the divorce or the other parent's alienating behavior.

Estrangement

You are familiar with what a severely alienated child looks like. The targeted parent will accuse the other parent of alienating the child; the other parent denies the allegation. The challenge for the evaluator is to learn how alleged alienation and estrangement contribute to the parent-child problems. The evaluator cannot make a judgment about the role of alienation without examining the role of estrangement. Frequently, the complaining parent is unaware of how they may be contributing to the problems. A skilled interviewer will gather information from the parents and children without introducing the clinician's own biases or manipulations of the party's statements. This process may have to occur over a number of sessions. Avoid an evaluator who appears to only have a social cause or the desire to prove a point. Taking a phrase from *CSI*, the evaluator should "follow the evidence" wherever it leads, instead of looking solely for alienation and then trying to prove or disprove its existence.

Assessing the Validity of the Child's Allegations

Children can adapt their behavior and what they say depending on who is present. Some alienating parents insist upon sitting in on their child's interview. An evaluator should never allow this to happen if she expects candid statements from the child. An evaluator strives to build a rapport with the child, without the parent's participation or interference. Ideally, the child should tell his story in a "stream of thoughts," rather than answering "yes" and "no" questions. Children feel more relaxed to tell their stories without a parent present.

The child should be told the limits of his confidentiality. A signed release for older children is a good idea. The child should not feel manipulated by either the parent or the evaluator. The child should also be explicitly told that he does not have to answer a question.

The alienating parent may argue that the child does not want to meet with the targeted parent and hates the targeted parent. However, the evaluator observing the interaction between the child and each parent separately may observe otherwise. The child's interaction with the rejected parent may be very positive and nurturing. This would help refute parental alienation syndrome, but not alienation.

In severe alienation, the alienated child consistently hates with no ambiguity. Any reference to the targeted parent typically incites anger and rage.

Conversely, some behaviors may refute alienation or parental alienation syndrome. For example:

- The severely alienated child consistently hates with no ambiguity. The alienating parent will support this view. Any reference to the targeted parent incites anger and rage. Estrangement should be considered if the child is able to give rational reasons for the anger based on first-hand experiences. Physical and sexual abuse would certainly justify the reasons for the anger and fear. On the flip side, there are occasions when the evaluator observes tender feeling towards the targeted parent. He may see the child climb on the targeted parent's lap, give a hug and laugh during the play. This is the reason that multiple observations may be required. These behaviors would refute parental alienation syndrome. The evaluator will make a judgment about how rational are the child's reasons.

- The child's past memories of alleged indiscretions by the targeted parent are not supported from other objective sources. The child's reasons for the denigration are attributed to events that he could not possibly remember because of his age at the time of the alleged incident, or because the event was never personally witnessed by him. Siblings of severely alienated children will use their brother or sister's alleged experiences as reasons to hate the targeted parent.

- The child is able to give accounts of having a good time or fond memories with the targeted parent, which tends to negate parental alienation syndrome.

- The child complains about both parents, though perhaps for different reasons.

- The evaluator who observes the parent-child interaction identifies ineffective parenting skills, personality traits, and other factors contributing to the parent-child problems. The evaluator may observe punitive or overly critical parenting, the inability of a parent to control anger in the child's presence, a lack of empathy or warmth, and a general insensitivity to the child needs. The child's response to the targeted parent is a realistic response to mistreatment. This is not parental alienation syndrome.

- The child expresses dislike of a new significant other after the new partner was pushed on the child. This is not parental alienation syndrome.

- The child reacts negatively when exposed to drinking, drug use, inappropriate sexual conduct, or the parent's loud and obnoxious friends. Some children strongly object to cigarette smoke. This is understandable, and not parental alienation syndrome.

- The child is willing to spend some time with the targeted parent, such as at holidays when she would receive a gift, or attend a special social event like a concert.

- The estranged child will not defend the alleged alienating parent's behavior, instead focusing criticism towards the targeted parent.

- The alleged alienating parent is willing to look at alternative explanations of the other parent's behavior or the parent-child problems, rather than continuing to accuse the targeted parent of wrongdoing.

- The alleged alienating parent displays some capacity to empathize with the targeted parent and can admit some value of the child having a relationship with the other parent.

Assessing the Validity of Allegations of Sexual Abuse

Assessing the truthfulness of the child's complaints against the rejected parent can be very difficult, particularly when the allegations are of physical and/or sexual abuse. No one knows with certainty what percentage of children's allegations of sexual abuse is false. The figure is probably very small. The confusion comes from the differences between substantiated abuse, unsubstantiated abuse, intentional false allegations, and innocent false allegations. (An example of an innocent false allegation is a child saying the other parent touched her private parts but the evaluator later learning that the child was given a bath. Helping a toddler with a bath is appropriate.)

Most jurisdictions do not make these distinctions between the type of allegations when compiling statistics because there is no consensus of the definitions. Why? The percentage of intentional false allegations of sexual abuse in the context of custody litigations ranges from 23 percent (Bala & Schuman, 2000) to 4.7 percent (Faller & DeVoe, 1995). Poole and Lamb (1998) claim approximately 5–8 percent of sexual abuse allegations are false. Many judges are very skeptical when they learn an allegation of sexual abuse was first raised in the context of the custody litigation. Herman's study (2005) stated that "... the available evidence indicates that, on the whole, these substantiation decisions currently lack adequate psychometric reliability and validity; an analysis of empirical research leads to the conclusions that at least 24 percent of the decisions are either false positive or false negative errors." The study suggests that a reasonable probability exists for an evaluator to wrongly conclude that a child made a deliberate false allegation of sexual abuse. A judge's skepticism is understandable.

Knowing how to discriminate between valid and invalid reasons is, at best, difficult and challenging for the clinician and the court because the investigator always risks being wrong. No one wants to risk the children's safety or see an abuser get away with criminal acts. On the other hand, there are innocent people in prison.

Discriminating between true and false allegations is difficult, but research and literature supports some assumptions (Bruck, Ceci, & Hembrooke, 1998; Poole & Lamb, 1998) that evaluators must consider when conducting the assessment.

- The more interviews with the child, the more likely the child's account will become distorted or adversely biased. This includes repeated questioning by parents seeking "the truth." Though most parents want only to protect their child, parents can accidentally alter a child's story and invalidate professional investigations later. If you have reason to believe that your child was physically or sexually abused, immediately report the allegation to the proper authorities. Have experts interview your child. As a side note, normal police procedures can include multiple interviews, a tactic that can cause problems because of the risk of an interviewer's bias being introduced in the questioning. The rationale for multiple interviews is to determine if the child's account is consistent, as a consistent account helps validate the allegation. But if you notice too many professionals interviewing your child after an allegation of abuse, you should mention your concern to your attorney.

- The interviewer should avoid leading and repetitive questions.

- Intentional lying about abuse is more likely to occur with older, rather than younger, children. Misinterpretation of events is more likely with younger children than a deliberate fabrication, even when the allegation first occurs in the context of custody litigation.

- Children can be very suggestible. They become less vulnerable to suggestion as they get older. Children *are* capable of lying.

- Memory or recall of events is a complex process. Because of the complexity, *how* the child is interviewed is as important as *what* the child has to say. Many children's testimonies are deemed unreliable and inadmissible because the child was interviewed by an unqualified examiner. That includes you. If your child speaks of abuse, listen, but do not ask questions. Questions can introduce a bias and distort the child's recall. Just reassure your child that you will listen and get help. Look into the allegation. Avoid telling your child you will "make it stop" or that abuse "will never happen again." Though parents want desperately to protect their children, you cannot guarantee no one will ever abuse your child again. Do not promise your child the abuser "will pay" or "will go to jail." First, you may trigger within the child feelings of guilt or protectiveness towards the abuser (a normal reaction), causing the child to change his story. Secondly, you cannot guarantee what the police, the prosecutor, or the court will do about the alleged abuser. Always remember, the way you respond to your child can affect how he feels today as well as years from now. Listen, and then let professionals ask the questions.

- When a child spontaneously initiates the allegation without any coaxing or unjustified inquiry, it is more likely a true allegation.

Studies (Trocmé & Bala, 2005; Ceci & Bruck, 1995) have identified methods for helping to discriminate between false and truthful allegations of physical and sexual abuse. Some behaviors should be considered that can raise questions about the validity of allegations:

- The child should be the initiator of the allegation, rather than responding to parent's questions, such as "Has Daddy ever touched your privates?" The interviewer must be careful when asking questions. Children may try to answer a question without much deliberation, in order to please the adult. They may answer a question with "I don't know" if they do not understand the question or if the question makes them uncomfortable.

- A judgment is made about whether the child's account of the abuse is improbable and absurd, or whether the descriptions sound plausible and reasonable. An example of an improbable account would be, "Grandma put a broomstick up my butt." A more probable event would be "Daddy promised me a present if I didn't tell anyone."

- The child's inconsistent account of painful events over time suggests an unreliable report. This is more of an issue with younger children because they have difficulty staying focused on the central theme of the interviews. Young children can accurately recall painful events, but the details can be distorted with repeated interviews. The inconsistencies are more likely an unintentional distortion or confusion, and not a fabrication. Inconsistent accounts by younger children do not necessarily mean that the essence of the account is untrue.

- A child who describes events that supposedly occurred when he was too young to recall suggests a fabrication. Professionals disagree about how young is "too young" for a child to remember an event. Most agree that younger than three is too young, though some research contradicts this view. Very young children can recall painful events, but will forget events faster than older children or adults.

- A severely alienated child making a false allegation of abuse is generally not afraid of the consequences after making the allegation. She may say to the court that she would rather go to jail than see the rejected parent.

- Usually, an untruthful child does not hesitate to tell his story to anyone who will listen. By contrast, abused children are usually private and frequently are afraid to tell their story. They may be embarrassed.

- Children giving a false allegation require few or only a single session to feel comfortable enough to tell their story. Abused children may require more sessions to develop a rapport. Most children, when properly interviewed, will disclose the details of the abuse in three or more sessions.

- When the interviewer has established good rapport and the child is able to verbalize a stream of thought, yet the circumstances of the act of abuse remain vague and not very descriptive, a false allegation must be considered.

- A child describing a physically painful act of abuse is more likely telling the truth, provided the account is plausible.

- A child whose recall of major events about the abuse is inconsistent is likely to be fabricating. Inconsistency with minor events is normal.

There are no hard-and-fast rules for discriminating between a false or true allegation as seen from the child's eyes. There are protocols for how child victims should be interviewed. Any conclusion the evaluator may draw must allow for the possibility of error. Remember these points and be very cautious when you hear a mental health professional or evaluator emphatically conclude allegations are true or false. An evaluator should always acknowledge room for error.

Investigators will look for physical evidence of abuse: bruises, vaginal or rectal tears, broken bones, sexually transmitted diseases, or lacerations. The difficulties with physical evidence include knowing what caused the physical injuries and the fact that the absence of physical evidence does not rule out abuse. Qualified experts must make these determinations, taking into consideration the child's testimony, physical evidence, the alleged abuser's statements, and other potential evidence supporting or refuting the allegations.

An evaluator's conclusions obviously elicit different reactions from each parent. Some alienating parents use the *possible* supportive findings of abuse as more ammunition against a targeted parent, even though definitive conclusions are lacking. Some parents refuse to accept any doubt that the allegations may be false, and instead continue dragging their children to evaluators until they find one who agrees with their assertion. Many targeted parents accused of false allegations are quick to believe the other parent maliciously fabricated the allegations to destroy their parent-child relationship. Although this does happen, this is not always true. Many allegations are reports by parents who sincerely misunderstand their child's suspicious behavior and do not want to damage the parent/child relationship.

Amy and Jill's Story

Amy has a lovely five-year-old daughter, Jill. When Jill alleged that her father had sexually abused her, the court ordered both Amy and the father for a custody evaluation. Of course, the father was indignant and denied the allegations. The Child Protective Agency's investigation was inconclusive. Amy was angry and, understandably, very protective of Jill's safety. At the same time, she did not want to believe that Jill's father would have abused Jill. During the evaluation, Jill was alone during the interview. She and her mother gave permission for the interview to be taped. Jill was spontaneous and, with minimal prompting, described what had supposedly occurred with her father. She appeared comfortable and was very matter-of-fact when describing the alleged abuse. At one point the interviewer asked, "Was anyone with you when your father did this to you?" With enthusiasm in her voice as though she had received a gift, she said, "Oh, my mom. She was sitting on the couch." At this extraordinary revelation, the bewildered evaluator asked Jill if her mother could listen to the audio tape. With the same enthusiasm, Jill agreed. Amy sat beside Jill with an inquisitive look on

---

her face. She listened to Jill's story about what supposedly had happened with her father, and Jill's statement that her mother had been in the living room where the alleged sexual abuse was to have occurred. Amy was shocked by what she heard. She said, "That couldn't have happened." Amy then realized that Jill's allegations were false. Equally important, Amy felt relieved that nothing had happened and that Jill's father was not a risk to Jill's safety.

When an allegation of abuse comes before the court, the attorneys want to know who interviewed the children, including the parent (or other family members). They want to learn how many times the child was questioned and under what circumstances. For professional interviewers, the defense attorney will ask about the interviewer's qualifications and methods used to conduct the investigation. As described before, repeated interviews by numerous well-intentioned investigators increase the risk of inaccurate reports and the risk of tainting the child's account by a biased interviewer with his own agenda (Ceci & Bruck, 1995).

Differentiating between parental alienation and a child not wanting to visit for just causes is a multi-faceted process. Both parents, the children, significant others, and anyone else who can corroborate the allegations should be interviewed. The evaluator must assess the alleged perpetrator for any attitude or behavior that would cause or reinforce alienation between the child and the targeted parent. Interviewing the child is another matter. The evaluator will look for:

- **An adult coaching the child:** "My daddy knows I can't remember bad things, so he helps me remember."
- **Alternative explanations for the child's broken relationship with the rejected parent:** "My mother always screams at me for nothing I did."
- **The child describing his personal experiences with the targeted parent, rather than someone else's story:** "No! My mother wasn't there when my father hit my brother with a spoon."
- **Whether the child's resistance is a reasonable or proportionate reaction to the complaint about the rejected parent:** Not reasonable is, "I don't want to see my mother 'cause she made me eat my carrots."

The evaluator must be open to the idea that the parent's alienating behavior is not necessarily the reason for the child's resistance. All possible explanations must be explored.

Much is lost when a parent and child become estranged. Nothing can make up for the lost years. Children lose that valuable bond, knowing their parents are out there, yet missing their support and love. Parents forever have an empty place in their hearts for the memories lost of their children growing up.

It is hard to imagine how parents who profess to love their children can lead them to believe for the rest of their lives that they were sexually abused. When parents deliberately set out to ingrain into their children's minds that their other parent sexually abused them, when in fact they were not abused, *this* is abuse and should be punishable by law. West Virginia (2008) recently passed a law criminalizing a parent's deliberate false allegation of abuse in the context of custody litigation. Other states should follow suit.

4

Your Child Comes First

You want to raise a child to be patient, compassionate, forgiving, loving, and honest. Well, children learn those things from parents who are patient, compassionate, loving, and who tell the truth. The qualities you want passed onto your children can only be passed along by those of you who show you have them yourself.

Referee Alex Savakis
Trumbull County Family Court, Ohio

Divorce puts extreme strain on parents and children. Parents, particularly custodial parents, complain about not having enough time between work, housework, and child care. Children are more active than ever with school activities, sports, and homework. All the demands truly require a team effort.

Since the inception of the best interest doctrine and the proliferation of working mothers, there have been dramatic changes in the family structure after divorce. There are more mothers working, grandparents raising grandchildren, single parents having children, and fathers more involved with parenting. "This generation of fathers is more involved in child care than ever" (Braiker & Dy, 2007). The change in family roles does not negate the child's basic need to feel secure, attended to, and nurtured. How this is accomplished is not always easy with warring parents. Contentious litigation has actually made matters worse for children. During the decade of the tender years doctrine, there was little hope for a father to have an active parenting role, much less custody. Fathers passively accepted their minor role as parents. Ironically, with the women's movement and changes in the laws, many fathers are more vocal about wanting a voice with parenting. Like social change in the past, groups that felt oppressed actually became, when given hope for change, more vocal and militant. This was true with the civil rights movement and the women's movement, and is now seen with fathers' or parents' rights groups. While parenting has sadly become a political issue with advocates from opposing views attacking each other, children's needs have not changed.

PA and PAS are two concepts used to explain the reasons behind parent/child conflicts. The concepts have been criticized for failing to address the child's needs and the child's rights because they focus more on the parents' interests than the child's needs. The assumption still being debated is how much weight should be given to the child's preference. What are the children's rights? The answer to the question is difficult, because many factors come into play. There can never be a prescription that fits all because of differences in the children's ages, maturity levels, and verbal skills, all of which influence what the children say. Then there is the question about the degree of the parents' influence. Getting to the truth about how the child actually feels over time is difficult. Courts may seek guidance from custody evaluators, parent coordinators, or mental health workers. Evaluators may explore the possibility of PA or PAS as a explanation for the child's preference. Blank and Ney (2006) argue against "these formulations of conflict" and the legal system because the child's feelings are ignored, implying that a child's resistance is pathological, suggesting a disease or illness and warranting a medical diagnosis, or implying that the child's behavior is unreasonable. Many would argue against Blank and Ney's premise, but they raise a good point shared by many: What are the child's rights to choose where to live? A child's right to choose must come after someone determines that the child's opinion is her own and not someone else's. Blank and Nye offered no answer. Children need to be heard, but a child's preference will carry more weight if:

- The child initiates an opinion to someone that is impartial and has no special interest in the outcome.
- The child's preference is consistent.
- The child's reasons reflect maturity. Emotional reasons carry more weight than what a parent promises the child.
- There are no enticements or rewards from anyone to encourage a child's preference. An honest preference cannot be expected if a car, a cell phone, or some other highly desirable object has been promised by one parent.
- The child understands that the court, and not the child, makes the decision.

Patsy and Robert's Story

"Excuse me. Excuse me!" The school psychologist practically had to shout to get Robert and Betsy's attention. They had been arguing viciously since they walked into his office ten minutes before. After tossing off a final barb or two, the couple, who had been divorced for eight months after a nine-year marriage, finally turned their attention to the psychologist.

"I asked you here to talk about Tommy," he said. He had already explained that their eight-year-old son's teachers were concerned about changes in their son's behavior and frequent requests to go to the nurse's office.

Both Robert—a thirty-four-year-old small business owner—and Betsy—a thirty-seven-year-old office manager—looked confused. "I thought that was what we were doing," Betsy commented.

"Well, then, maybe I missed something," the psychologist quietly proposed. "I heard you two mention child support, each other's spending habits, and who's responsible for Melanie's coat that turned up missing. Hardly a word was mentioned about what Tommy feels or needs."

"Are you sure?" Robert asked.

The school psychologist was certain about what he heard while they were arguing. "I am sure. I don't hear the two of you trying to understand each other's perspective about Tommy's problems at school. I felt frustrated and powerless," he explained. "I was afraid that you would get violent right here in the office. I was feeling somehow responsible for bringing you together and causing this fight. Most of all, I wanted to stop you, but I felt helpless to do so. And," he pointed out, "I'm an adult. So I must ask you if you two fight like this in front of your kids."

Betsy wanted to deny it, but the truth was that they did. Robert wanted to blame Betsy for the fights. They fought when Robert picked up the kids for visits, and when he dropped them off. They fought over the telephone, with the children near enough to overhear. And, Betsy admitted, just last week she had allowed Tommy to stay up past his bedtime because Robert was stopping by with some tax papers. She thought she and her ex-husband would be more likely to control their tempers with their son in the next room. They argued anyway.

Fights with Robert often reduced her to tears, Betsy told the psychologist, and Tommy would try to comfort her. "It's okay, Mommy. I love you," he'd say. On more than one occasion, she had replied, "I know you do, honey. It's your father who's going to be the death of me." According to the psychologist, Tommy seemed to have taken that statement literally.

"Children don't always realize when you're exaggerating or using clichés," he said. "I know Tommy worries about you. And I have a feeling that he sometimes pretends to be sick and goes to the school nurse hoping she'll send him home where he can keep an eye on you."

Betsy was beginning to feel sick herself as she thought about the other signs of stress Tommy had been showing: falling grades, difficulty concentrating, going off by himself during recess, and occasional bed-wetting. She began to see the connection between their incessant fights and Tommy's deterioration.

Robert was less insightful. He knew there was a problem but had difficulty seeing his role in the fights. His solution was, "If Betsy would keep her mouth shut, all would be fine."

"I'm always telling Tommy that I love him and won't let anything bad happen to him," Betsy remarked, her voice quivering. "But something bad happens every time his father and I speak to each other. It has to stop." Robert agreed. They both could agree that Tommy should not be exposed to the fights, and the fighting had to stop.

This realization hit Betsy like a bucket of ice water, dousing her anger and forcing her to take action—positive action this time. She began to monitor her behavior, to be more aware of the nuances in what she said, and to recognize when her words or actions were adversely affecting her child and her child's relationship with his dad. Robert also recognized that he had to maintain self-control and calm down before reacting to Betsy's triggering comments.

Regaining Perspective

Your child's post-divorce adjustment begins before the divorce or separation. Children are sensitive; they are influenced by what you say, even the tone of your voice. They know dissension. Responsible parents recognize the impact their words and actions have on their children. Words are powerful, whether spoken in anger or meant only in jest.

You may believe that you have no influence or control if your ex-spouse is determined to alienate your children. Your fears are understandable, but you are not totally helpless. Prevention begins by understanding and empathizing with your children's needs during these trying times. You must focus on strenthening your relationship with the children well before the separation and the divorce. This begins by understanding the influences affecting your children's adjustment and future well-being.

Preventing parental alienation syndrome or minimizing the affects of alienation begins when you recognize the impact your words and behavior have on your children and you make a conscious effort to address the unique needs and feelings the children have because of your divorce. This will require sensitivity, and a more charitable attitude towards your former mate than you've had in some time. To understand this attitude, try to remember the frame of mind you were in when you were first dating the person who is now your ex-spouse. Way back then, you paid attention to almost everything your new love said or did. You noticed his reaction to your comments. He, in turn, kept a mental record of the things that pleased you. And you both chose not to behave in a way that might adversely affect, or completely derail, your budding relationship. Although you no longer *feel* the way you did then, for your children's sake, you can behave with the same sensitivity towards your children and the other parent.

You are no longer lovers or even sparring spouses. You are divorced parents with a mutual interest in your children's welfare. Although you may have had some trouble adapting to those roles up until now, by remaining attuned to each other's feelings and negotiating when behavior changes seem to be called for, you and your ex can make your new co-parenting relationship work.

Of course, you may not feel ready or willing to do that. You may still be too angry or hurt. The memories of infidelity, verbal abuse, or violence may be too fresh in your mind. Perhaps you're thinking, "That bastard doesn't deserve to be treated sensitively," or "I'm not the one who should be monitoring and changing my behavior. *She* walked out of our marriage. Let her change," or "He's a nut case. We'd all be better off having no contact with him ever again." And you may be right, but that attitude does not help your children.

A Reality Check: What Does the Research Say?

There is frequent reference in later chapters about reunification therapy and the realities parents must accept. One reality is that *protracted litigation and parents fighting hurts children.* Unless the fighting stops—or, at minimum, stops happening in the children's presence—the risk of the children being harmed is great. If you don't believe this, read a sample of studies addressing the impact of high-conflict divorces on children's adjustment.

Parental conflicts harms children (Sarrazin & Cyr, 2007; Emery, 1982), leading "to damaging lifelong effects on the children's wellbeing." Fighting parents affect all members of the family, particularly defenseless children, making them more susceptible to harm. It has been shown that high conflict is more damaging to children than divorce itself (Amato, 1996; El-Sheikh, Harger, & Whitson, 2001). The degree of the parents' hostilities is related to childhood illnesses (El-Sheikh, et al., 2001). Cummings and Davies (1994) learned that children repeatedly exposed to conflicts between parents "often showed cardiac rhythm, higher blood pressure, lower body temperature as well as frightened and anxious facial expressions."

Slater and Haber (1984) concluded in their study that teenagers who experienced high levels of anxiety caused by the divorce often later suffered from lower self-esteem. Forcing children to pick their allegiance to a parent contributes to the stress. This is understandable when we look at different models of child development. The social learning model would argue that children witnessing intense parental conflicts find it difficult to enter into a healthy relationship when they get older. They learn, personally or vicariously, about how parents should relate to each other. They may come to believe that what they see is the appropriate way to fight or resolve interpersonal conflicts. Plutchik and Conte's (1973) study of high-conflict families learned that the gender of the child and the dominant parent influenced the child's adjustment. The results showed that boys with a dominant father had fewer problems, as did girls with a dominant mother. This may explain why latency-age boys (seven- to twelve-year-olds) adjusted better living with their father (Guidubaldi, Perry, & Nastasi, 1987). This is not true for the other age groups. The gender of the child and parent is not related to adjustment. Amato (1993) claimed that a girl's self-esteem is less affected by parental conflicts than that of younger boys. Boys exposed to high conflict are more likely to have behavioral problems and poor reading scores (Hetherington, Cox, & Cox, 1979).

Children need both their mother and father in their lives, particularly boys. It appears from the research that boys have more problems adjusting to divorce than girls (Hodges & Bloom, 1984). Younger children were reported to act out more, while older children displayed more depression. Adolescents of either sex exposed to high conflict performed more poorly in school and were more likely to be socially withdrawn (Forehand, McCombs, Long, Brody, & Fauber, 1988) than children from low-conflict divorces. This could be a result of the fact that most boys end up living with their mothers and have less contact with their fathers. Growing up in an all-female household without a male's influence can be hard on some boys because they don't get affirmation of their own masculine behavior. Many boys feel insecure about growing up to be what society thinks of as manly. Unresolved conflicts between parents is associated with greater insecurity, anxiety, and distress in children of both sexes (Cummings and Davies, 1994). There continues to be some question about how a child's adjustment is influenced when there is no father contact, compared to exposing the children to high conflict. Amato and Rezac (1994) found that sons, and not daughters, having frequent contact with fathers had greater adjustment problems when the parents are involved in high conflict. This and other studies (Hetherington, 1999) suggest that sons have greater problems than daughters when exposed to parental turmoil. The children of mothers who expressed dissatisfaction with the father's frequent contacts with the children were not as well adjusted as those with mothers who did not complain. It is not known if the reverse would be true, though fathers are usually more accepting of noncustodial mothers' involvement with the children. Most mothers want fathers involved with the children (Hetherington, 1999).

A Caveat

If your ex-spouse is truly dangerous, incapacitated by a mental illness or addiction, or for some other reason is completely incapable of caring for your children, the recommendations in this chapter won't always apply. But in all other cases, you owe it to your children to at least try to heal, forgive, and parent cooperatively.

Parents usually have good instincts about what their children need to grow into healthy adults. Unfortunately for all, divorce often derails parents just when their children's needs are the most intense and heartfelt. As Robert and Betsy discovered, it's easy to lose sight of what is happening to your children even when you know they are probably going through the biggest adjustment of their young lives.

Children of divorced parents have essentially the same emotional needs as children from intact families. However, when children of divorce turn to their parents for nurturing, attention, or reassurance, they are often turning to two people who are overwhelmed by their own problems and no longer available to each other for mutual support.

If parents have to adjust to new roles, time may be a precious commodity. Their struggles to make ends meet financially or pull themselves together emotionally may leave them too drained to deal with their youngster's demands. Yet, even in the midst of all this chaos, it is possible to refocus and, if it seems necessary, to revamp what you're doing to help your children through a difficult time of transition.

Neglected Needs

Children need you to provide an environment in which they can feel secure and thrive. You may think this is common sense, but separation and divorce create new challenges, some of which you may not have considered. When you read the suggestions, think about how well you meet your children's needs and ways you can improve your parenting.

- **Be emotionally available to your children, willing to answer questions, and able to show affection without going overboard.** They do not expect you to devote every waking moment to them; however, they need to know they can get your attention when they need your comfort or help.

- **Give your children your approval and encouragement.** They look for clues that you cherish and feel proud of them. It reassures them to see that you carry pictures of them in your wallet, or to hear you brag to friends and family about their accomplishments (think about how good it feels to overhear someone bragging about you). Compliments and congratulations from you have a big impact on how they feel about you.

- **Recognize that your children are unique individuals with their own personalities, perceptions, and preferences, and treat them accordingly.** They need you to remain sensitive to their adjustment to the divorce and listen to their feelings, even if they are different from your own. Children experience more success in general and find it easier to adapt to the divorce when parents' expectations are realistic. So be aware of where they are developmentally and try not to ask more—or less—from them than they are capable of giving (for example, don't expect a ten-year-old to be a confidante).

- **Encourage your children to have a positive relationship with their other parent; or at least don't stand in their way.** Like many custodial parents, you may see your ex's presence as an intrusion, a privilege forfeited by the divorce, or a potential hassle you'd rather avoid. It may be more comfortable and convenient for you if your former mate stayed away from your children's activities, but what feels good for you is not always what's best for your children.

- **If you are the targeted parent, insist that your child continue to call you Mom or Dad, not by your first name. If you are the other parent, insist that your children call both you and the other parent Mom or Dad, not by first name.** Mom and Dad are titles that have considerable symbolic significance in our culture. The title represents an emotional bond that should not be threatened by calling a parent by a first name.

- **Assure your children that they do not have to choose sides, that it is possible to love both their parents, and that they are not hurting you.** Your children want to feel free to have a good time during a visit or to invite their other parent to watch them in school plays or other activities. Children don't want to feel they are betraying a parent by having fun with the other, or as if they were prizes in a tug-of-war.

- **Show your children how to respond to stressful situations in emotionally healthy ways.** You are a role model for how to behave. They count on you to cope, without using drugs or alcohol and without becoming violent or verbally abusive. Your children need to know you won't fall apart under pressure; they need to see you express anger without losing control. This ensures that they won't be afraid of you when you're angry.

- **Demonstrate that your hurt and anger can heal.** Your children will feel safer and more secure once you have gotten beyond the initial pain and confusion of your divorce. In the meantime, they need you to be honest about your feelings (while exercising a reasonable amount of self-control) and to let them know that it's okay to feel sad or angry. By watching you manage your emotions, they can learn to manage theirs.

- **Maintain as many family or community ties as possible.** Although you might like to pack up, move away, and start a new life far away from everyone you know, making such a major change soon after your divorce is rarely advisable. Your kids have already "lost" one full-time parent and a family life as they knew it. They need the comfort of familiar surroundings and ongoing contact with their network of grandparents, cousins, friends, neighbors, scout leaders, doctors, and teachers. Encourage them to accept support from these people, and accept some yourself, especially if you are a working parent.

- **Make every effort to peacefully resolve any differences of opinion with your ex-spouse on how to raise your children after the divorce.** Your children need examples of flexibility and two people working together rather than of rigidity, backstabbing, and one-ups-manship.

- **Be sensitive to how your children are feeling during the exchange.** Children do not want to dread the times when you and your ex are together. The moments immediately before and after a visit when they are "exchanged" from one parent to another are among the most stressful. Keep everything calm. Exchanges are not the time to discuss emotionally charged issues.

Many children react to fights between their parents by blaming themselves. They think, "If it weren't for me, there would be no visitation and nothing to fight about." And they look for ways to prevent future arguments. Many will keep the peace by wanting to avoid visits or keeping their mouths shut when they would like to ask for a change in the parenting time. Knowing that there will be an argument if they are late getting home, they don't dare ask to stay at Mom's until the end of a movie on television. And they won't risk starting a fight between their parents by letting on that their best friend's sleepover party falls on a parenting time weekend. Instead, they just don't attend. They sacrifice their desires to make life easier for their parents. Does this sound fair? If sacrifices must be made to bring about some semblance of family harmony following a divorce, parents ought to be the ones making the sacrifices. Swallowing some pride, passing up opportunities to argue, and uttering a kind word now and then doesn't hurt anyone. It can do wonders for your kids.

Stuart and Mary Beth's Story

"It's the same argument over and over again," Stuart complains. "I call to ask for a change in visitation and she goes nuts." To prove his point, the forty-three-year-old investment counselor produces a tape recording of a recent telephone conversation. It begins with his ex-wife, Mary Beth, reacting to his request to take the kids for the upcoming weekend instead of the one after it.

"You'll never change," Mary Beth says with disdain. "You're the same selfish, self-centered bastard you were when we were married."

"And you're still a controlling bitch," Stuart retorts blandly. He's been down this road before. "Can I see my children this weekend or not?"

"You don't care about your kids. If you really loved them, you'd stop disappointing them. Don't you think they're sick of you not showing up when you're supposed to? Why should they change their plans when-ever it suits you?"

"What kind of plans?" Stuart attempts to ask. But Mary Beth goes on as if she has not heard him.

"I thought you'd be different once you stopped drinking, but you're just as inconsiderate and unreliable as ever," the thirty-seven-year-old registered nurse says.

Stuart cuts in angrily, "This isn't about my drinking. There's a con-vention in Vegas next weekend."

"Right. And it will be something else the weekend after that," Mary Beth snaps. She lists the out-of-town meetings, camping trips, busi-ness dinners, and once-in-a-lifetime Super Bowl tickets that have interfered with parenting time over the past few months. "You've got some life, Stu, running all over creation having a good time while I'm here working double shifts, taking care of your kids, and trying to explain why Daddy can't fit them into his busy schedule again."

Although the conversation continues and escalates into a loud exchange of insults and accusations, Mary Beth had hit the crux of the matter here. After enduring more than a decade of Stuart's alcoholic binges, week-long disappearances, and inability to hold onto a job, she had finally divorced him. But she was still struggling. He was now sober and had landed a high-paying job with lots of perks and adopted an exciting, carefree lifestyle that Mary Beth alternately envied and resented.

"It isn't fair," she thinks. "Not after all he's put me through." She feels he owes her something, some courtesy, some consideration, or at the very least, some predictability so that she can manage her time. Instead, he repeatedly asks to change the parenting time schedule.

At first, Mary Beth tried to accommodate Stuart. But his excessive requests disrupted her routine, interfered with her plans, and left the children uncertain about when they would next see their dad. Over time, she became more resentful about his requests, his carefree way of life, the years she "wasted" on him, and more.

"I'll show him," Mary Beth decided, and began to refuse Stuart's requests regardless of the circumstances, igniting his anger and leading to bitter confrontations. Now, each sees the other's actions as spiteful and malicious. From their entrenched positions, they get into what Stuart originally referred to as "the same old argument again and again."

When this occurs, Stuart and Mary Beth appear to be arguing about parenting time schedules. But visitation is actually the battleground for a war that began before Mary Beth and Stuart were divorced. They are struggling for power, control, retribution, or the resolution of some old, personal business between them. And once these ex-spousal issues get mixed up with the parental issues they set out to discuss, their children's interests or desires are completely lost.

How Can I Tell Whether My Child is Adjusting to the Divorce?

Parents are usually good about knowing how their children are adjusting to stress or trauma. Though children may not talk about their feelings, their behavior will give some idea about how they are coping. Your experience with your children tells you if their behavior is out of the ordinary. A sudden drop in school grades, frequent fights with friends, or retreats for hours at a time are hints that something is wrong. You will want answers now so you can come up with a game plan to help later.

Rather than just reacting to how your child is behaving, approach your child by trying to understand the reasons for his hurt or changes in his behavior. Begin by closely watching your child's behavior and think about what has happened during the past few weeks that may help explain the changes. Then plan to make a conscious effort to take time to talk and listen to what your child has to say. Talk to him alone with minimal distractions. Sometimes children are more talkative if they are also playing a game. You are better off if you can focus your attention on your child and be sure you have enough time to complete the conversation. Having to say to your child that you are out of time, just when he opens up, can be a big let down, making it more difficult for him to open up later.

TIP: Plan on having enough time talking to your child without interruptions when you know the issues to be discussed are emotionally charged and complex.

The game plan to help your son or daughter must begin with effective communication. The ability to help your child and to improve the quality of your relationship with your friends, colleagues, and even your ex-spouse depends on sound communication skills.

Developing good communication skills is difficult. Relating to others is impossible without "fully hearing" what they have to say. This means that sometimes we should be listening to what is said rather than talking to justify our point. One way of knowing that you are not listening is when you think more about what you are going to say next than about what the other person says. Frequent interruptions are a clue that someone is not listening.

For children to talk freely, they must feel physically and psychologically safe. Listening for how your child is feeling, rather than debating the merits of his feelings, will bring the two of you closer. Children, like anyone else, don't want to be feeling judged as wrong, stupid, and silly. Instead, they want someone to recognize what they are feeling and why they feel the way they do. Once your child knows his feelings are understood, you may be able to clarify any misperceptions or offer comfort. But don't rush to do this or he will feel cut off.

Learn from listening to what your child has to say. Let your child know that you understand why he feels the way he does. This is done by repeating back to the child, or paraphrasing, what you just heard. Resist any temptation to defend yourself when it is not necessary to do so. Instead, be patient and listen. Your child's spontaneity will give you an idea about how you are doing as a listener. When your child pauses and appears to be watching his words, it indicates that he is not yet comfortable or that, for whatever reason, you have lost him. You must be patient and let him set the pace of the conversation. You do not have to finish the conversation in one sitting.

When your child starts to get restless or distracted, this is the time to stop talking. You can come back later to talk. End the conversation by telling your child how good you felt talking with him. Do what you can to reinforce that talking together was a positive experience. Also, be aware that how the conversation ends is what the child will remember next time.

If the conversation ended badly, he will be hesitant to open up and talk with you later.

What Should I Do if My Children Do Not Want to Talk About Their Feelings?

Don't push them. Most children will adjust fine to the divorce even if they don't want to talk about it. Usually you will know what they think by various comments they make. Remember, the problem with most kids—particularly male teenagers—is that they try to avoid talking about anything uncomfortable. When you raise an open-ended question such as, "How are you feeling about . . . ?" they go blank or say, "I don't know." This response can be confusing. The only choice you have is to take your children at face value and believe everything is all right. Be patient, open the door by giving them permission to talk, and then back off and let them take the initiative.

Should I Ask My Children Where They Want to Live?

No. Don't ask your children to make decisions about custody or visits when they obviously don't want to. In fact, the decision is usually not up to them anyway; it is the court's decision. Be patient with your children. If they have something to say, let them spontaneously tell you when and if they are ready. Usually, the parent prods the children to reduce their own anxiety rather than out of concern for their children's welfare. Children have been known to tell both parents on different occasions they want to live with them as a way of getting temporary relief from persistent questioning. A precocious five-year-old gleefully said during an interview that she "drove both Mom and Dad nuts because when I am with Mom, I say I want to live with her; and when I am with Dad, I say I want to live with him."

> TIP: Asking your child to make a custody decision is asking your child to reject a parent.

Do not trust what your child says about custody. If your children have strong feelings about custody and want you to know, they will spontaneously tell you in time. Many children want to be left alone and have the adults make the decision for them. In this way, your child does not have to be responsible for hurting or rejecting someone they love. Children need to rationalize that the decision was the court's rather than their own. In this way, the children are not rejecting anyone. To children, rejecting one parent over the other can be equated with "not loving" a parent. This belief might be used by an alienating parent to influence their children's feelings.

How Long Will It Take My Children to Adjust to the Divorce?

There is no simple answer because children are different. Like adults, some children recover quickly, while others can take years. You must be patient. Adjustment is a process that takes time. The issue isn't whether your children are adjusting, but whether their behavior says they are accepting the divorce and getting on with their lives. Children should be doing better a year after the divorce, and even better after two years. This is also true for parents.

How Important Is It for My Children to Have an Active Relationship with Both Parents?

Sadly, a lot of fathers have psychologically abandoned their sons and daughters for various reasons, having little or no contact with them. This can be devastating to children, particularly to boys, who need a role model and a mentor to teach them how males get along in this world. Boys need the assurance that their dad isn't rejecting them and is available to show him how to play sports, hunt, or do those other "male" things. It's true that sometimes the father is not the healthiest influence for a boy. In this situation, the mother needs to encourage her son to get involved in activities that will give him the positive affirmation he needs to build his self-esteem. Kelly (2000) found that the reason most fathers stop paying support and abandon their parenting role is not because of problems with the children, but because of problems with the mother.

Girls also need their fathers. Dads give their daughters appropriate male role models who teach them how to understand and relate to the male culture. He is the one who tells her how pretty she is, raves about her successes, guides her social values, and later offers her insight about what males think and feel. Dad helps to affirm girls' femininity.

Children having access to both parents is important, but there is more to the story. Contact is one thing; what you do with the time with your children is another. The quality of the time and the bond you create is more important than just sitting on the couch and directing traffic. Parents who help the children with homework, assist with projects, attend sporting activities, praise achievements, listen to what their children say, and teach life skills are going to see better-adjusted children.

What Can I Do When My Child Is Moody?

There is a lot you can do. Begin by accepting the fact that children, particularly teens, get moody. Kids get cranky, complaining that they are bored. When asked to pick up their socks, hang up their jackets, or turn the music down, you may be confronted with a smart comment or a whiny, "I'll do it later." They will talk back, acting as if you know nothing or you're nuts: "*Fine*, I'll do it; I don't care," or, "It's a free county and I don't have to." You may think to yourself during these trying times that your child is "going through a phase," or "it's the hormones kicking in." This becomes even more complicated with children of divorce because the parent may not know whom to blame for the children's problems. Resist the temptation to blame your ex-spouse or the stressful parenting time schedule. Parenting never stops. Once you think you have one problem worked out with your child, another surfaces. If you are lucky, you will get a rest between problems.

> TIP: Do not blame all the problems with your child on the divorce. Many behavioral problems are part of the child's normal development.

I Know My Children Hear Our Fights. Will This Hurt Them Later?

It sure can. Hearing their parents fight scares children. To help them make the best of the divorce, your goal should be to keep your hostilities towards your spouse under control and away from the children. You must control your feelings. This is the most important point we have learned from multiple studies on divorce.

Children hearing their parents yelling, cussing, and threatening each other are terrified. While sitting on the floor watching television, they may act as if they don't hear you, but don't believe it. Think back to when you were a child: how you would lie in bed and strain your ears to hear what your parents were saying if either mentioned your name. Kids, like adults, are nosy and will eavesdrop.

How Can I Help My Children Adjust to the Divorce?

There are number of ways you can help your children adjust. Begin by resolving the conflict and anger between you and your ex-spouse. Keep in mind that children learn by observing their parents' behavior. If you and your ex-spouse need counseling to regain control, then please get counseling. Next, continue your parenting role and responsibilities. Your children need you to maintain the structure and routine in your home, and that includes appropriate limits and expectations about how they behave. Do not blame your children when they complain about the other parent setting limits, or their discipline style. When your child violates limits or your rules, administer appropriate discipline. This is also true during visits. Visits are not the time to throw out the rule book. Once the rules are gone, it is difficult to ever get them back without a major revolution. It is easier to set limits on a five-year-old than on a teenager who has rarely heard a "no."

Children respond well when you make a conscious effort to share activities together. Take time to play with your children without distraction. That means turning off the cell phone or television. Don't forget that your children are fun to be with. Find mutual interests and enjoy them together. A mutually satisfying relationship between you and your children will do wonders for both of you.

Children need family and family traditions. Let your children know the importance of loving relationships with all members of the family. Encourage them to participate in family traditions with both sides of the family. Let family and friends be a source of support for both you and your children.

Children want to be prized by both parents for who they are and for what they achieve. Make it clear to your children that you enjoy spending time with them. Brag to your children and others about their accomplishments. They need to hear excitement in your voice when you tell them they've done something well. Reassure them that they are loved and that you will do what you can to keep their lives stable. Children become anxious over changes they do not understand or cannot predict.

Can Children Love Both a Stepparent and Biological Parent?

TIP: A word of caution: Having your child use a stepfather's last name is usually asking for serious problems.

Occasionally children have the mistaken belief that if they love one parent, love for the other parent or a stepparent will diminish. They feel torn between wanting to express their love for one parent while not wanting to hurt the other. One adolescent said it well: "I hate to hurt people's feelings and disappoint them, but when you are in the middle, trapped, you got to go to someone's side." This child does not understand his capacity or his parents' capacity to love. His mistaken belief is forcing him to choose between his parents. Children need to be continually reassured that they can love both parents and stepparents.

Is It Important to Display Physical Affection Towards My Children?

Yes, but there are exceptions. You must be sensitive to how your children feel about physical affection. Many older children are uncomfortable and will pull away if you try to hug or kiss them. Don't take this personally. Respect their boundaries and find other ways to show your love. As for the children, they may be uncomfortable initiating affection to you in the other parent's presence. Explain to them that there are other ways to express their feelings, like writing a letter, sending a card, buying a special gift, continuing a family tradition, or acknowledging birthdays and holidays. Older children may rationalize their hesitation by saying, "I don't need to do that. Dad knows I love him." Even though your children are teens, they need continual encouragement and guidance in helping them express their positive feelings.

How Can I Protect My Children from Being Hurt?

Often you can't. Divorce has tremendous potential for hurting children, and often the hurt cannot be avoided. What you can avoid is exposing your children to the hostilities between you and the other parent. You may remember the hurt on the children's faces the first time their father did not show up for a visit, or when their mother didn't come to a recital. You understandably felt angry and protective. Perhaps you tried to make excuses for the other parent to lessen the hurt. The fact is that you cannot keep making excuses for the other parent's behavior. In time, the children will form their own opinions about both parents, based not on excuses but on their own personal experiences. Dad's relationship with the children will depend more on how he behaves towards them than what you or he tells them. In time, the children will no longer believe excuses. After your children have learned to draw their own conclusions, they usually will not be honest and express how they truly feel to the offending parent. They may act as if everything is fine, when it is not. Their behavior towards the parent will give you some clue about how they actually feel.

> TIP: If you are chronically late or disappoint your children, do not expect your ex-spouse to always cover for you. The problems you create with your children are your responsibility to prevent and repair.

What you should have learned from this chapter is that a child's positive adjustment to divorce is best served by both parents being actively involved in their lives, void of parental hostilities. If you care more about your children's welfare than your own agenda, you will listen to what the studies say and align your beliefs accordingly. The consistent results of the numerous studies on children's adjustment to divorce is the reality you must accept, or your children will pay the price. A "parentectomy" removes your child from important opportunities in life: a resource to lend support during a crisis, unconditional love, financial support, a grandparent for his or her children, and sources of self-esteem.

If you want to bring stability and tranquility back into your children's lives following a divorce, you will need to focus on their needs more than your own. That won't always be easy to do. The most effective parents are able to consciously put their personal needs aside in deference to their children's needs. They find a balance between the time they need for themselves and the time they give to their children, and they do not feel bitter about the sacrifices involved in parenthood. Less effective parents are frequently resentful when their children's needs infringe upon their own.

Reflecting back on your behavior since the marriage ended may have been both enlightening and discouraging. At times you may feel you cannot do anything right. You may lose all hope of being a "perfect" parent. But remember, no one can make that claim. All you can do is aspire to be better. A great start is taking what you learn and committing yourself to do what's best for the children.

5

Why Parents Alienate

It's only a matter of time before your father will hit you like he hit me.

Parents obsessed will not admit to alienating the children. Most will deny the allegation or say they are only trying to protect the children. For whatever reason, they are angry, bitter, or frightened about the prospect of losing control of their children's affections. Wanting to control the children's feelings and attitude towards the targeted parent is a common feature. On occasion, the alienating parent may feel gratified knowing they are hurting the other parent. Alienating parents act under the assumption—conscious or unconscious—that many of their problems about access with the other parent will simply go away if they can convince the children to hate that targeted parent until the targeted parent gets discouraged and disappears. Their grasp of reality is distorted by irrational beliefs that paralyze their seeing any point of view but their own.

Parents who are naïve or active alienators are more insightful about their alienating behavior after learning about the behavior. They may not understand the underlying reasons for their behavior, and may sometimes lack sufficient self-control when triggered, but they are receptive to learning new behaviors. Insight into why a parent alienates does not always lead to change, especially if the parent has an entrenched personality disorder. For parents with good self-control, understanding reasons for their feelings may help alleviate some guilt and provide a rational reason to change their behavior.

Understanding what motivates an alienating parent is very complex. There is no simple explanation. The alienating parent may not be conscious of their motives. Some reasons are irrational, while others appear to some as justified. Whatever the reasons, the result for the children, and usually both parents, is hurt and bitterness that can last for years, if not forever. Studies (Amato, 1993; Clawar & Rivlin, 1991; Sarrazin & Cyr, 2007) consistently document the adverse influences high-conflict divorces have on children's long-term adjustment. However, not all high-conflict divorces are due to alienation.

The motivation for a parent to alienate can come from social influences as well as characteristics inherent in the individual. No one lives without being influenced by the society in which we live. Your cultural values and your community help define how you see your role as a mother or father, how you expect to be judged by others, and provide a context for judging yourself. Intrinsic characteristics are simply about who you are as a person, your personality, your mental health, feelings about the divorce or separation, and your beliefs and values. All of these influences define who you are and serve as a driving force that motivates your future behavior.

Social Change

The rise in divorce rates has leveled off, but contentious litigation continues unabated. This is partially because social change has not kept up with legislative changes. Some parents voice resistance towards shared parenting, and fathers' more active participation in raising their children conflicts with the sustained belief among many subscribers to the tender years doctrine that a mother has an instinctive biological bond and innate love with the child that fathers are unable to share. Schepard (2004) made the point well that "the drive for legal equality of the sexes spurred by the women's movement also undermined the tender years doctrine." Now mothers and fathers are legal partners, though both sexes will agree that equality is in name only and not in their family roles. Mothers will rightfully argue that the distribution of household responsibilities and parenting is not equal in most families. In the past, the presumption was for the mother to have sole custody unless the court found her unfit. Many judges to this day do not believe in their hearts that a father is as capable as a mother, or even a grandmother, to raise and care for their child, particular if the child is a baby or toddler. The change of the doctrine to the best interest of the child in the 1960s is a good example of how legislative change cannot alone change social attitudes and beliefs. However, legislation has shifted from the tender years doctrine to the best interest of the child. (Each state has its own definition of best interest, though there is considerable similarity in the criterion among the states.)

Stereotypic parenting roles continue to influence court decisions. Genders are not equal in the court. Fathers are perceived as workers and mothers as nurturers. Many believe fathers are incapable of nurturing in the same manner as mothers. I remember a judge expressing disbelief that his adult son was capable of changing a diaper. Marveling, he said, "I am going to have to change my thinking about fathers."

Sexist Attitudes

Our society continues to adhere to many sexist beliefs that in turn contribute to beliefs that spur alienation. One example is a mother feeling stigmatized for not choosing to seek custody or, for whatever reason, losing custody. She knows that she has more to lose than the father. She expects to be harshly judged by both men and women for her apparent abandonment of the children or her loss of her maternal responsibilities. If a mother loses custody, she is looked at with suspicion. People will wonder, "What's the matter with her?" or even ask the dreaded question, "Where are your children?" One mother said, "I hide behind the curtains when a neighbor kid comes to the door asking my son to come out and play." These questions remind her of the stigma of not having custody of her children, which threatens her self-esteem and sense of competency as a mother. When the divorce is not their idea, mothers often feel betrayed and angry, and frightened and vulnerable at the prospect of losing custody of their children. Their hurt is contained until their anger becomes too intense, at which point they may express their outrage and sense of ownership of the children: "That's my baby. He has no right to have her!" Though conscious that more fathers are being given custody, most mothers deny the possibility of their not being the custodial parent.

When the father seeks custody and loses, he is disappointed, but admired by others as a loving parent for his effort. Fathers rarely struggle with feeling stigmatized if they do not get custody. In fact, fathers can use society's sexist attitudes to protect their ego and self-esteem. They are able to rationalize losing custody by arguing that the mother always wins. Many fathers vehemently argue that they have done nothing wrong to deserve having their children taken from their lives. They do not believe they are entering the court arena on equal footing. In recent years, these fathers have developed a strong conviction for their right to be active parents. The role of a part-time, weekend father is not enough. They are willing to fight the mothers and the court to assure their active and shared relationship with their children. Many fathers have joined support or political groups to vent their frustration with the legal system. They are fighting for both legal and social changes that support their position: namely, that they have the same rights as mothers to be custodial parents.

Ironically, no-fault divorce has inadvertently heightened animosity between the parents. One parent may feel betrayed when the court does nothing to protect his or her rights. Betrayed parents seeking retribution from the court are often disappointed and angry when they learn that the court will not champion their causes. This can contribute to ex-spousal issues dragging on for years to come.

TIP: Courts will not use the children to punish a parent.

Social attitudes and prejudices are slow to change. Frequently, states' legislative bodies and the courts are slow to respond to society's demands for change. Nonetheless, change is occurring. Courts are responding to fathers' demands for more active involvement with their children and mothers' concerns over the inequities of child support. Both men and women are becoming more conscious of the unfairness of stigmatizing mothers for not having physical custody of their children. Unfortunately, it is still easy to feel impatient and frustrated because change is slow.

Sexism plays a role in alienation because traditional attitudes influence both self-image and the perception of how we will be judged by others. Parents take these attitudes into the court and back home to their children. Social attitudes about what constitutes a competent mother or father can motivate a parent to alienate. Parents sensitive to the judgment of others may, under the guise of being a loving parent, alienate to maintain the integrity of their self-esteem and social appearance ("I will look like a loving parent to my children if I can make the other parent appear inept and maybe even dangerous"). Parents appearing to protect children from the throes of the other parent's incompetence answer all questions in the parent's mind about who should have custody. This phenomenon is similar to what is described as Munchausen syndrome by proxy, in which a caregiver consciously or unconsciously fabricates or causes illness or injury in a healthy child, later rescuing the child by getting the child health care. This behavior is intended to reinforce the idea, to the parents and others, that the parents are loving and responsible.

Entitlement

I'm his mother. You aren't the one who gave birth.

Being a parent is a special status to be worn proudly. I still get more of a thrill being called "Daddy" than being called "Dr. Darnall." I am sure this is also true for most parents. Motherhood and fatherhood are both very special.

Some parents are motivated to alienate because they hold the mistaken belief that they are entitled to their role as a custodial parent because she gave birth, because he paid the bills, or because her personal identity and sense of self-worth is dependent upon the parental role. Unfortunately, courts inadvertently reinforce this belief because custodial parents usually do have more rights and privileges than do weekend visitors.

Feeling entitled is different from believing you are the better parent to raise your children. The difference is knowing that your children are truly better served by what you give them rather than what the children give you. Your children's interest must come before your self-interest, even if the realization hurts.

Your Children Are Not Your Possessions

You may think you are entitled to your child's custody much as you are to any other prized possession. Losing custody is tantamount to losing your identity: "After all, if I am not a mom, what am I?" The prospect of not having the primary responsibility of raising your children is personally threatening. You may complain about your ex-spouse being less deserving and "only seeking custody to hurt me." Perhaps your assertion is correct. However, usually such a statement is shortsighted because it reflects a belief that your ex-spouse has fewer rights than you do, or is a less competent parent. Neither of these beliefs may be true. Instead, the beliefs may be a reflection of your insecurities or arrogance.

Neither you nor your ex-spouse owns the children. They are in your temporary care. The children are no more your possession than your ex-spouse's. If your ex-spouse makes statements suggesting ownership, ignore what is said. Such statements are meaningless and only incite an argument.

Sometimes a parent—usually the mother—fears that the ex-spouse will challenge the children's custody, so she vehemently defends her position while attacking the ex-spouse's claim to the children. Both parents consciously or unconsciously strive to align their children to their side, thus reinforcing the belief that they are winning the custody war. The children struggle from being pulled in opposite directions by their parents. Wanting to avoid the conflict and tension, they feel they have no choice but to emotionally withdraw. When a parent raises the question of preference, the children look away, avoiding eye contact and speaking softly. Some children admit to telling both parents they want to live with them, knowing they are lying to avoid rejecting either parent. What children say to the inquisitive parent should not to be trusted, as they are likely to say what the inquisitive parent wants to hear. One child was heard to say, "When I am with Daddy, I tell him that I want to live with him. When I am with Mom, I tell her that I want to live with her. I drive both of them nuts." In this way, the children avoid feeling disloyal or fearful of the parent's rejection.

Avoiding Entitlement

If the expression "they are *my* children" is more comfortable than the expression "they are *our* children," perhaps you need to rethink your reasoning. If your motivation for returning to court is entitlement, you are probably already fueling alienation. The reason is that "entitled" parents usually sound angry when discussing the idea of the ex-spouse sharing custody and are typically overly protective and defensive when questioned about their parenting.

Overcoming entitlement must begin with the recognition that you are holding on to beliefs that are both false and damaging to your children. These beliefs are heard in your self-talk. Your words are important because you will emotionally react to them as if they are true. If you expect your feelings to change, you must begin by identifying the irrational beliefs or self-talk that provokes the feelings. Take the belief that women are always better parents: If you believe this is true, you cannot help but feel threatened or offended by the idea of the father having custody or being a co-parent. Another example is the belief, "I'm the parent and I always know what's best." Any suggestion to the contrary will anger the entitled parent.

To eliminate feelings of entitlement, the parent must begin by recognizing that the irrational belief is damaging to the children and that he or she must change self-talk to a more rational belief. For example, the belief "I'm the parent and I always know what's best," could be restated to "I'm one of my child's parents and I would like to think that *sometimes* I know what's best." Believe it or not, consciously changing the self-talk will help change the feelings. If this is awkward, rehearse the words for the time being. It takes practice and requires patience.

Avoiding Guilt

Your father wouldn't have left you if he really cared.

Guilt is a terrible feeling that everyone tries to avoid because it is painful and can linger for years. In fact, that is the purpose of guilt. Guilt, or the fear of guilt, is intended to keep you from misbehaving. The problem is that you may not know why you are feeling guilty; and if you know, you may not know how to rid yourself of the guilt. Guilt implies that you did something wrong. Some parents think that they should be punished for their sins. One mother's assertion "I know I'm getting what I deserve. How else can I explain why I feel so miserable?" is a typical statement from a parent struggling with guilt. If you are a newcomer to divorce, you know how easy it is to find reasons for feeling guilty. All you have to do is think about what you did wrong, even vague generalities like "I know I could have tried harder to save my marriage."

Parents feeling depressed or betrayed are often driven to absolve their guilt and regain their self-esteem in the most irrational ways. Some parents believe they will be exonerated from their guilt if they reinforce, in their mind, the belief that they care more for the children than their ex-spouse. Alienation is the strategy. Guilt-ridden parents look for opportunities to prove their point to themselves, their children, and their ex-spouse by rationalizing their reasons for denigrating, among other strategies, the targeted parent. A common rationalization is "I am only trying to protect my children." They do this by cutting down the other parent, reminding the children of the other parent's faults, or leaning on the children for comfort and reassurance of their self-worth.

TIP: Absolving your guilt by attacking the other parent's worth does not work.

Parents deal with guilt in many ways. They can either blame others for their problems, overcompensate by being the "super-parent," make excuses, or just feel depressed or angry and do nothing. Obsessed parents typically feel no guilt. Most of these tactics do not work. True, time sometimes helps the pangs of guilt fade, but usually the feeling is just pushed aside or masked by stronger emotions such as resentment or self-loathing. Learning to understand and resolve guilt is absolutely necessary in order to adjust to divorce, go on with life, and be a more effective parent.

Playing "supermom" or "superdad" is a good tactic because you look good to others. After all, how can a super-parent think any bad thoughts that would hurt the children? The problem with many alienating super-parents is that they strive to look good to others while aggressively degrading the other parent's competency (Darnall, 1993). They are usually critical and, often unconsciously, look for every little fault in the other parent. They play upon the other parent's faults by focusing on the bad, instead of the parent's positive attributes. The targeted parent cannot win because she can never live up to the alienating parent's standards. The guilt-ridden parent believes that the worse the other parent looks, particularly in the children's eyes, the more likely he will appear as the loving and competent parent. If he can somehow carry this off, his hope is for the guilt to stop. Unfortunately, the tactic is doomed for failure because the hurt will fester even if he successfully alienates the children.

If you are able to identify the source of your guilt, you can take action to absolve yourself. The fix is changing your behavior. What can you do differently now because what you have been doing is not working? If you cannot change your behavior and your guilt continues to eat at you, consider getting professional help.

Terri and Robert's Story

Terri divorced Robert because she just couldn't take his verbal abuse and putdowns any longer. There was not a day without yelling and screaming "over the stupidest things." Survival was all Terri was able to think about. During a rare moment when she wasn't paying any attention to the children, Terri let Robert have it with both barrels. She lost all control, pounding Robert's chest with her fist, yelling for him to "get the f—- out of this house!" Reflecting years later, Terri still felt guilty about the terrible scene she had caused in front of the children. She never said anything to either Robert or the children because she had hoped that the feeling would just fade away. Any time the topic of the divorce came up in conversation, Terri felt embarrassed and fearful that someone would say something about what she had done. Subtly, she would steer the conversation in another direction.

Terri's guilt may not be earth-shattering. Do not confuse her behavior as alienating. In fact, hitting Robert in front of the kids may be just one of many things that has occurred over Terri's life that caused her guilt. What is important is that Terri's guilt is still not going away. Instead, it influences how she behaves and feels around her children. If Terri is to rid herself of guilt, she must change her behavior and do something different. She must take action. Terri could begin by honestly talking with her children, sharing her regret and guilt about what she did to their father. She could assure them that it is understandable if they were hurt and disappointed by what she had done. If Terri asked, the children might even forgive her. This way, her action will help the guilt to fade away.

Both alienating and targeted parents can feel guilty, because neither is perfect. If you suspect that your guilt is from alienating or poor parenting, you must begin by owning up to the truth and changing your behavior towards your children and your ex-spouse. To do this, identify the specific behaviors causing your guilt. Look back at chapter 1 ("Parental Alienation") and your results of the Parental Alienation Scale in the Appendix. The items that you rated a 4 or 5 will give you some ideas about what you are doing that may explain how you feel, and provide direction about what you can do to feel better.

Take, for example, item 21. Suppose you rated the statement a 5, acknowledging that you always have good reasons to be critical of your ex-spouse. Though you may believe in your heart that this is true, your attitude can be a source of your guilt. Try an experiment to see if you can reduce your guilt. Start with the notion of being less critical and recognize that the other parent has some positive attributes as a parent, though perhaps different from your own. As abhorrent as it may sound, giving the other parent credit for what he does well and stopping the critical comments to the children will help absolve your guilt. I know this is hard to believe, but if you can keep from getting sick to your stomach, try it. You may be surprised. Forgiving and saying kind words, especially to your ex-spouse, can take you a long way towards feeling better.

Often, super-parents criticize targeted parents about parental issues even though their bitterness has more to do with ex-spousal issues. This is confusing for the targeted parent, who asks, "What's the big deal?" Of course the "big deal" for the super-parent is "How can you let the children outdoors without a coat?" or "Shouldn't they be in bed by nine o'clock?" or "How can you let Johnny use his roller blades in the street?" The tip-off that the super-parent is probably still dealing with unresolved ex-spousal issues is the intensity in the accusing parent's voice. The rage is usually out of proportion to the offense. These parents cannot talk about what is troubling them; they have to yell, demean, or scream. The intensity of their rage can be a carryover from feeling betrayed by their ex-spouse, bitterness caused by the drop in standard of living, and so on.

To find peace, try to stop being critical and identify any ex-spousal issues that may explain your feelings. Chapter 7 ("Obstacles to Change: Parental vs Ex-Spousal Issues") may help you with this. Then, maybe with therapy, you can find a way to heal. As with entitlement, this is usually done by finding new ways of thinking about the past and by changing your self-talk. For example, instead of saying to yourself, "That bastard can't be trusted with my children," change your self-talk to something like, "I need to get him to understand the importance of not bringing the children home late on school nights." Changing your self-talk and behavior will help lessen your guilt and add some much-needed peace to your life. Be patient and give yourself some time to change: Saying something nice to your ex-spouse once is not enough to absolve years of guilt. Keep trying.

TIP: Admit your mistakes.

Worrying that others will discover your mistakes will add to your guilt and anxiety. Rather than fearing that your mistakes or shortcomings will be discovered, openly admit them when you are wrong. You will be surprised how much better you feel.

Sometimes parents find themselves faced with an allegation that is true. Even so, they get defensive and start arguing for no rational reason other than to hold on to a belief that they must never acknowledge to the other person that they might be wrong. Admitting mistakes is an easy and effective way of avoiding these meaningless arguments. This also does wonders for reducing guilt. For example, let's say you are accused of not caring for the children because you are always late picking them up after a visit. Hearing the accusation, you feel defensive and want to attack. The fact is, you usually *are* late. What is not true is that you do not care for the children. Now you have to make a choice. You can either counterattack with your own accusations, or admit that you are usually late. Admitting your lateness will defuse the attack. After all, how can you be hurt by admitting what is true? Defending your actions in this example will only incite more fighting. Instead, by taking responsibility for your actions, you and your ex-spouse can begin discussing how to solve the problem of your tardiness.

Don't Play the Blame Game

TIP: Avoid blaming; it only leads to a fight.

Blaming is another common tactic for trying to avoid guilt. "Successful" blaming, assuming you believe your accusations, is a way for blamers to maintain their sense of self-worth. The purpose of saying "it's your fault" is to absolve the alienating parent from taking any responsibility for what is wrong. Unfortunately, it is easier to find fault with others than to admit our own shortcomings. Nevertheless, blaming only makes matters worse because the blaming parent will get angrier while waiting for the other parent to fix the problem or change the annoying behavior.

Now the tensions build and the accusations fly. The blaming parent will rally around the parental role and accuse the ex-spouse of causing all the troubles. The allegations against the ex-spouse are intended to protect the ego and strengthen the blaming parent's self-worth. Degrading the targeted parent, particularly in the eyes of the children, helps assure the blaming spouse of her value as a parent. However, like the alienating super-parent, the blaming parent is using a tactic that never works. The irony of this tactic is that you actually empower the other parent at the expense of your own power. When your ex-spouse fails to respond to your satisfaction by fixing the problem, you will again feel victimized, even though your ex-spouse usually doesn't understand what is happening. Believe it or not, it is common for the blaming parent to become depressed. After all, depression is akin to helplessness, a victim's unwelcome companion.

Avoid Spoiling

> TIP: Don't spoil your children to make up for the past or relieve your guilt.

Some divorced parents try to align themselves with the children by giving them extra attention, taking time to play games, frequently taking them to the mall, and so on. This can be a strategy to diminish guilt and make up for past neglect. The parent finds solace from "buying the children" while the ex-spouse is passively excluded from the activity. Though the exclusion is usually unconscious, the activity with the children is a subtle form of alienation. It sends the children the message, "I bet your mother isn't this nice." Of course, give your children the attention they need. But overindulging will only spoil them. It will not resolve your guilt.

Avoid Irrational Fears

> He abused me. I know it's only a matter of time before he abuses our children.

It is natural to want to protect your children when you believe their physical or psychological safety is threatened. You will do whatever is necessary to safeguard your children from any perceived threat, even if the threat comes from your ex-spouse. But this is where you must be cautious. There is a difference between what you think is a threat and what you know is a threat. You need to *know*, rather than just react to what you think; otherwise, you're heading for big problems. If you react to your belief by getting angry and threatening the other parent to withhold visits or return to court, she will naturally prepare to retaliate. To avoid this dilemma, first realize that you do not know the reasons for the other person's behavior or your child's accusations. You may instead be reacting to wrong information. Recognize when you are hypothesizing about the other's behavior. Secondly, you must ask your children to clarify what they are feeling, rather than guessing at their feelings. The act of asking for clarification will help restrain your emotional reaction to your interpretation because you now have to listen rather than react. Be careful not to interrogate your children, however. Leave that to the experts.

Parents sometimes make assumptions about their ex-spouse's behavior because of history. Certain facts—he once pushed me, she was sexually abused as a child, he once forgot the car seat—may be sufficient reasons to be concerned, but not to stop or restrict access to the children. You must keep your fears under control. Stop and think about the difference between what you know is true and what you believe to be true. If you have a laundry list of reasons to fear the other parent, consider talking to a counselor to help sort out fact from fiction.

An alienating parent can teach his children to fear the targeted parent. A parent was heard saying to his son, "When your mother starts raising her voice, run out of the house and go to the neighbor's and call me. I will come and get you." The fear can become so intense that the child goes into hysterics just at the mention of the parent's name. Any thoughts of visiting send the youngster to the floor having a fit. The fear is usually irrational and requires professional intervention to desensitize the child to the targeted parent.

Alcohol and Drug Abuse

Alcohol and drugs alone do not motivate alienating behavior. The problem lies in the abusing parent's impulsiveness and poor judgment while under the influence. Parents under the influence will do and say things they later regret. Alcohol and drugs are no excuse. What you say to your children or the other parent is still hurtful. When the drug—and alcohol is a drug—is more important than your children's welfare, you have a serious problem. You need to get help.

Parents enter the divorce arena knowing each other's history and habits. Information once entrusted to your spouse may now be used against you in a contested custody case or when your ex-spouse tries to restrict parenting time. You could have a serious problem in court if you used illegal drugs during your marriage. An angry parent will sometimes bring this up in court in a custody dispute. (What I find interesting is that the parent making the accusation usually admits to having also used drugs with the ex-spouse.) To play it safe, you must assume that courts will never tolerate using illegal drugs in a child's presence. This includes marijuana.

TIP: Whatever your beliefs are about marijuana, domestic court is not the place to take a political stand.

Regardless of whether you are accused of abusing drugs or concerned about your ex-spouse's use of drugs, you must understand what an abuser is before taking the issue to court. Alcohol, by itself, is legal unless it causes illegal behavior or behavior that jeopardizes the safety of others. The most obvious example is drinking while driving with children in the car. This behavior is inexcusable and illegal in all states. Excuses are meaningless if caught.

Alienation is common when a parent is abusing alcohol or drugs. When one of the parents is abusing, there are usually allegations going back and forth: One parent making the allegations and the other defending or blaming others for why they drink. What you now have is a power struggle in which one parent is angry because the other parent is telling how the other should behave or disclosing a family secret. Denigrating attacks fly back and forth. This is alienation.

TIP: Don't abuse alcohol or drugs in front of your children unless you want to lose parenting time or custody.

To help clear up any confusion about alcohol and drug abuse, it may be helpful for you to know something about what constitutes alcohol and drug abuse. The criteria are not listed for you to make a diagnosis but instead to alert you of the warning signs. Some of the generally accepted criteria (American Psychiatric Association, 2000) of abuse include these factors:

- Significant life problems because of using alcohol or drugs, such as failure to fulfill major role responsibilities at work, home, or school
- Legal problems such as domestic violence, disorderly conduct, and driving under the influence

- Recurrent use in physically hazardous situations like driving or operating machinery
- Evidence of physical withdrawal when the individual stops using
- Continued use despite ongoing interpersonal or social problems like arguments with family members or physical fights.

The criteria assumes that abusers do not have sufficient control over their alcohol or drug use to use good judgment. The substance is causing serious problems in their lives though they still continue to abuse. To learn more about alcohol and drug abuse, contact your local help hotline or an appropriate agency listed in the Yellow Pages.

Drinking in front of your children is not illegal. On the other hand, sometimes a parent's drinking causes children distress or puts their safety at risk, such as with drinking and driving. For example, Robert, an inquisitive seven-year-old, complained that his father always has a can a beer between his legs when driving. In these cases, the court can order you to have a drug and alcohol evaluation and order you to not drink in your children's presence. If you violate the court order and risk your children's safety, the court can change custody or stop visits. You have to decide what is most important.

A history of alcohol or chemical dependency will not necessarily hurt you in court, providing you can show that you are recovering and managing your life successfully. Steady attendance at Alcoholics or Narcotics Anonymous will help tremendously. Many recovering parents win custody and do well raising their children. Problems arise if you currently abuse alcohol or drugs, the symptoms are apparent to everyone (particularly your children), and you do nothing about it. This is a serious problem, because the court's first commitment is to protect the children, even if that means keeping them from you until you get treatment. For example, would you want your children driving around with a parent who is drinking and doesn't see that it is a problem? Yes, parents have problems, but there is little excuse for not getting help. At least that is the way the court will see it.

Mental Illness

A mentally ill parent may have a tainted perception of what is happening during and after the divorce. Divorced or separated parents after twelve months (Chatav & Whisman, 2007) were compared to married couples and found to be at greater risk of a mood, anxiety, and substance abuse disorder. The authors found no differences in the prevalence between gender and length of the relationship. The stress from a divorce and separation, and especially custody litigation, increases the risk that the symptoms of an existing mental disorder or personality disorder will get worse. A dependent father will become more frightened at the prospect of being alone. A paranoid mother becomes more suspicious and volatile, believing that others are plotting to deliberately hurt her or take away her child. The narcissistic father loses all capacity to empathize with or distinguish between his and the children's needs. Both parents may easily become an obsessed alienator. The added strain of the litigation itself will magnify the severity of the symptoms. These parents become vulnerable, struggling with the stress from the divorce and having to rebuild their lives.

A parent's mental illness may have contributed to the breakup of the marriage and may continue to be a problem during the separation or after the divorce. There is little doubt that some of the symptoms of mental illness can contribute to alienation. However, mental illness alone does not cause alienation; how the parent behaves is the issue. If you suspect that your ex-spouse's irrational behavior is causing a problem between you and the children, consider talking with your attorney about getting a professional psychological evaluation of both of you. The evaluation should be unbiased and not an attempt on your part to have a "hired gun" come to court and blast away at your ex-spouse. Instead, the evaluation could help assess the seriousness of the mental disorder and make recommendations to the court about the need for treatment, custody arrangements, and parenting time schedules. A good evaluator will always consider what is best for the children in making the recommendations.

If you have a history of a mental disorder, you may need additional counseling or medication to get through the stress from the divorce. Prior symptoms can return during this stressful time.

Nearly everyone will have moments when they question their sanity. To cope with these difficult times, remind yourself of your capacity to heal. Spend time relaxing with friends or in surroundings you enjoy whenever you can. Make a conscious effort to do things that are fun and refreshing. If you feel truly overwhelmed by problems, you may want to consider seeking qualified help. Therapy can help you understand yourself better and teach you how best to handle stressful circumstances. Perhaps you will feel reassured knowing that many of your feelings are normal and you are coping fairly well.

As with recovering alcoholics and drug abusers, parents with a history of mental illness can win custody and do a good job of raising their children. However, the same logic applies: they must show that they are getting treatment for their problems, responding well, and managing their lives successfully. The court will look skeptically at a parent who is too depressed to get out of bed in the morning and see the children off to school and who does not actively participate in the children's lives.

Hurt and Anger

Your mother's a tramp. She doesn't deserve to see you.

A betrayed parent feeling hurt after a sudden pronouncement of divorce often has no place to vent feelings. Trying to keep composed, the parent suppresses the suffering. The children may see the parent shutting off his feelings and interpret this as his not caring about them. In time, the suppressed hurt turns into anger. Since the parent feels victimized by the ex-spouse, he directs the anger towards the ex-spouse, using the only issue they have left in common: the children. He feels justified in his anger and unkind, uncaring behavior because of some rationalization or a distorted belief that attacking will offer relief.

> *TIP: An angry parent can wear the other parent down with their nagging and complaints—but this "victory" comes at a high cost. Avoid nagging your children and your ex-spouse.*

Anger changes a parent and the children. Anger and hurt are powerful motivations for alienating the children against the targeted parent. At the same time, angry parents estrange themselves from the children. Many parents have no interest in resolving the anger; instead, they are driven to show the world how they have been wronged. They believe they have been wronged, and their retaliation is justified. They focus more on ex-spousal issues than on what is best for the children. The children may hate seeing a parent browbeat the other parent. Children do not want to hear this, regardless how justified the parent feels. One parent expressed her feelings of bitterness well when she said, "I have all the responsibility but none of the power."

Alienation is suspected when a parent cannot give a direct answer to questions. For example, a mother is asked, "How would you encourage your children's relationship with their father?" Instead of talking about the children, she responds with a diatribe about her ex-husband. She vengefully attacks him for his infidelity or lack of concern for the children.

Forgetting the original question, she cannot stop talking about what she has suffered from her ex-husband's behavior.

An active alienator's troubles have more to do with his sense of self, who he is, as well as fear of losing the children. The alienator's sensibilities are set off when his self-esteem or integrity is attacked. We know this because after the parent calms down, he is able to understand the issues and see the other parent's point of view. Obsessed parents may calm down but refuse to see another perspective.

Saving Face

I don't care what he says. I'm a good mother. My kids think so, and all the neighbors do too.

Like it or not, everyone worries about what other people think of them, which influences behavior and self-image. Everyone has an ideal of how they want to be perceived by others, especially as parents. This is even more an issue for most women because our society places more emphasis on their role as parents. For example, when you see a mother and father at the store and their child has a tantrum, which parent is expected to get the child under control? Usually the mother is the first to intervene. The father may be waiting and hoping that his wife will get things under control, or he may appear oblivious to the problem. Meanwhile, the mother is embarrassed and desperate. Perhaps the father eventually intervenes with his stern authority to subdue the child. His intervention may not be any more effective than hers. Nonetheless, in most marriages, the responsibility for initially subduing the crisis still rests with the mother.

There are variations in attitude from one part of the country to another, but in general, our society is usually a harsher critic of mothers than of fathers. So when there are problems with the children, which parent has the greatest risk of losing self-esteem? Self-esteem develops from a history of successful accomplishments. The accomplishments must have been challenging and had personal value in order to be meaningful. For example, the initial success from painting a room may enhance self-esteem, but as more projects around the house are completed, each task that contributes to self-esteem lessens. If no personal value is placed on painting a room, then the accomplishment may be nothing more than just getting another thing done.

TIP: The greater the challenge of the task, the greater the potential for building self-esteem. This involves taking risks.

Parents may try to protect their self-esteem by attacking the other parent's competencies. This is alienation. Many parents' self-esteem is dependent upon their personal perception of their competency as parents. This is particularly true for women because they are looked upon as the primary caretakers in our society. Fathers are typically less dependent than mothers on their parental role for their self-esteem. In our society, fathers usually have a number of other resources for building their self-esteem, such as their paid work, recreational activities, hobbies, and the friends they meet through these activities. Mothers who stay home with young children have fewer resources outside the family. Working mothers have more resources.

Parents are typically unaware of their strengths and weaknesses. Even incompetent parents who lack sensitivity and effective parenting skills will believe, contrary to the evidence, that they are competent and caring parents, that they have more strengths than shortcomings. They will defend and rationalize their incompetent behavior, often blaming the children or others for their personal failings. Any challenge from their ex-spouse as to their competency in fulfilling their parental role is seen as a threat to their self-esteem. These parents will react to the threat with anger and vengeance to protect their favorable self-perception. This is why custody litigation is so painful. The court proceedings afford the opportunity to publicly attack parents' competency while they have to sit back and listen, depending on their attorneys to defend their character.

Parents with good ego strength and self-confidence are not easily threatened; parenting is only one of many resources for building their self-esteem. Those who are dependent on the parental role as the exclusive source of self-esteem are more quickly threatened by any suggestion that someone else could effectively assume their parental responsibilities. If you find yourself with parenting as your only source of self-esteem, start doing other things. Many divorced parents find it difficult to schedule a lot of hobbies and activities just for themselves, but it is important to add activities in your life that will give you more meaning. Remember, in some ways you have an advantage: every other weekend, you have time for yourself.

EXERCISE: WHO AM I?

Being an active parent is one of the most important—and hopefully satisfying—things you can do with your life. But being a parent is not *all* of who you are. You represent other valuable things to other people. You may be a teacher, a good friend, or a skilled craftsman. These other roles are also who you are. Take a moment and write down on a sheet of paper as many of your roles, skills, and attributes as you can that other people see and value. If you have trouble making the list, consider enriching your life by getting involved in new interests, making new friends, or finding new ways of having fun that don't involve parenting. I hope you find making the list easy.

Fathers merely babysit, while mothers parent.

Have you ever heard of a mother who has an appointment and asks the father to "babysit"? Why would the father taking care of his children be considered babysitting rather than parenting? No one thinks of mothers as babysitters. This different sexist message our society communicates to parents influences their self-esteem. Mothers may feel less entitled to a life outside their role of a parent, while fathers feel relegated to the subservient role of babysitter. The terms "visitation" reinforces the subservient role and undervalued feelings as a parent. That is the reason in recent years that the term "parenting time" is used, acknowledging that *both* parents have a responsibility to parent.

Today's parents are less accepting of traditional sex roles handed to them by society. In the 1990s more mothers had full-time jobs and assumed more household tasks that were traditionally considered "man's work." Fathers, too, are changing their interests by becoming more involved in their children's activities: school conferences, ball games, dance recitals, and open houses. The decrease of rigid sex roles is a healthy trend that allows both sexes more choices and opportunities to involve themselves with their children. Though changes in traditional gender roles continue, true equality in most households has not yet been achieved. Neither parent should be excluded from any of their children's activities because of their gender. Sharing activities with the children encourages bonding and enhances the children's security.

Parents want to believe that other people see them as loving and competent. Even the opinion of their ex-spouse is important. Parents need their ex-spouses' support and reassurance that they are doing a good job parenting. Comments made by grandparents are also important, because the parents' confidence is usually weakened by divorce. Parents are sensitive to even the perception of a criticism. They do not want to hear about what they are doing wrong or have their motivations questioned. Instead, they want to be reassured that they are doing a good job.

> *TIP: Parents are more sensitive to criticism during a divorce. Keep your critical comments to a minimum. Instead, offer suggestions rather than make demands about how the other parent should parent. Pay attention to the tone of your voice.*

If you suspect that your ex-spouse has poor self-esteem and this is a cause for her defensiveness, consider what you can do to help. Remember, people get defensive if they don't feel safe in the relationship. If you are critical or demanding, your ex-spouse will either yield to your demands or retaliate. Either way, you and the children lose. Instead, help build your ex-spouse's confidence. Give praise when it is due. Remind your ex-spouse that you are available to help, and then help without criticism or wisecracks. Suggesting that you praise your ex-spouse may stop you in your tracks. Your first thought may be your ex "can't do anything right." It is important to see that you are wrong. Complete the exercise below and then take the opportunity to share these comments with your ex-spouse. You will be amazed by the reaction. If you keep giving sincere compliments, in time your ex-spouse will feel safer and less defensive.

EXERCISE: WHAT DOES MY EX-SPOUSE DO RIGHT?

Write down five specific examples of when your ex-spouse displayed good parenting skills. It makes little difference how significant these skills are. If you find it difficult to come up with examples, be patient and take time to think.

_____

_____

_____

_____

_____

The next time you notice your ex-spouse displaying these skills, give a sincere compliment without any critical innuendoes. In time, the results may surprise you.

Mary and Jim's Story

Mary, a loving and devoted mother, had long hated her ex-husband, Jim. Though Jim had custody of the children, he always cooperated with parenting time and encouraged the children to spend time with their mother. Jim reasoned that if he were going out for an evening, he would give Mary first choice to babysit. She wanted to babysit but could not reconcile in her mind the idea of helping her ex-husband. Mary felt she would be "giving in" if she accepted Jim's offer. Mary stated during an interview that she refused to babysit because she resented Jim telling her what to do. She misunderstood Jim's intentions. Jim was not *demanding* that Mary babysit. Regardless, Mary refused Jim's request, believing that she had won the power struggle. Mary inferred too much from Jim's request. She had the mistaken belief that saying "no" was punishing Jim and reminding him of her bitterness.

Mary's thinking is irrational. She is allowing her suffering and bitterness to interfere with good judgment and the opportunity to spend more time with the children. Whom is Mary really hurting by refusing Jim's request?

Avoid Power Struggles

I'll show her that she can't tell me what to do.

Some parents can't tolerate the idea of losing anything, particularly losing a battle to a person by whom they have been hurt or betrayed in the past. Losing is humiliating because, in their mind, it implies to all around that they were wrong and the other person was right. Of course, this is not true. But the mere thought of losing control and having to bow to the other parent's demands ignites a rage that is felt in every muscle of the body. It is all they can do to keep from exploding.

Mary's rationalization was flawed because her stubbornness and need to win caused her to lose valuable time with her children. Other than the inconvenience and the children missing time with their mother, Jim was not hurt by Mary's rejection. His hurt was nothing more than Mary's fantasy. She and the children would have been winners if she had put her resentment aside and accepted Jim's invitation.

TIP: Children always lose in the parents' power struggle.

Some parents get so wrapped up in their own anger and power struggles that they can't see what they are doing to their children. They can't see how they are hurting the children by their actions because they insist, "No one is going to tell me how to raise my kids." Some parents fight for longer visits or seek custody with no reason other than to prove that they are in control. These parents are not concerned for the children. Instead, they are compelled to push on for what they want because they have the irrational belief that winning is the only hope of ridding themselves from their awful feelings. What these parents fail to realize is that winning does not heal the wounds.

Little things can incite a power struggle. Forgetting to return a jacket, returning Johnny from a visit ten minutes late, or Sue outside playing and not wanting to take a phone call can trigger a fight because the behavior—whether the child's or parent's—is seen as an act of defiance. Even when the child's behavior is causing the problem, the angry parent will challenge the other parent: "Why can't you control Sue? You know she should be waiting by the phone for my call." Such statements reflect a parent's irrational belief that his needs or desires are more important than those of the child. However, once Sue finally comes to the phone, her father will sound loving and gentle.

A power struggle occurs when one parent wants to control the other parent's behavior and the targeted parent refuses to be controlled. It is not always easy to recognize a power struggle. The most obvious sign of an impending power struggle is when someone gets angry at any suggestion or demand. Any suggestion—good or bad—triggers the anger. It doesn't usually make much difference if the suggestion or demand comes from the court or the other parent. Either way, the parent is angry and wants retaliation.

When parents believe their motivations are challenged or a critic is closely watching their behavior, they get defensive, fight back, or withdraw into secrecy. Withdrawing becomes a matter of self-protection. Letting someone know how they feel is thought of as too risky and an open invitation for an attack.

A parent is heading for a power struggle when they say, "I know what's best for my children. What do you know about raising kids?" This is a common attack that implies to the receiver that she knows nothing about child rearing and should just do what the attacking parent says. You can see examples of items on the Parental Alienation Scales that reflect the likelihood of a power struggle. You can head off a power struggle if you listen to what the other parent is saying. When the occasion arises, listen for the statements below. These are but a sample of what you may hear suggesting the possibility of alienation and an ensuing power struggle.

Guidelines for Sidestepping Power Struggles

- Stay calm and try not to make demands. Instead, make suggestions and negotiate. If you can't keep down the tension, agree to come back and discuss the issue later.

- Be specific in stating what you want. You should be able to describe it in a way that the other person can literally visualize in his mind. If he can't get a mental picture of what you are talking about, he won't understand you. If you are unable to find the words to give a visual picture, then you are asking the other person to understand something that you can't explain. That is not fair.

- Try to avoid criticizing your ex-spouse even if she is wrong. People don't like to be judged. Instead, tell your ex-spouse that you have a different idea or perspective about how to handle a particular problem. It will not hurt you to sometimes agree and say to your ex-spouse that she does some things better than you. Agreeing with the other parent when she is right will quickly defuse the power struggle.

- Realize that you don't always have to agree. If parents can "agree to disagree," that is better than trying to beat the other parent down. It is much better for the children not to hear your fights.

- Put the issue in perspective before making a big deal about it. How important is the issue, compared to other things going on in your and your child's life?

- With every power struggle, there is an implied demand. People are sensitive to the notion of fairness. "Why should I bend to your desires if I get nothing in return?" they think. If the other person feels your demands are unfair, he will either fight you or passively back down to your will and get back at you later. If you are making a demand, think ahead of time about what you are willing to give in order to get what you want in return. You could agree to give the other parent more time, provide support for other issues, transport the children to the doctor, help with a household repair, etc.

- When you negotiate, remember that you will not always get every-thing you want. Instead, both of you should get some of what you want. Remember, to get you have to give. What are you willing to give in order to receive?

Power struggles can happen with your ex-spouse and the children. This occurs when you hear "no!" to your request. This could be a request for a change in the parenting time schedule, access to report cards, or asking your child to call. The frustration is an unconscious awareness that your child or other parent saying "no" is more powerful than your demands. Hearing "no!" or listening to nagging is enraging. A fight will surely ensue unless someone backs off or you give in. This is also true when arguing with your ex-spouse. Giving up does nothing more than allow you momentary relief from your frustration. Of course, your child learns that nagging is good and more nagging is even better. This is probably not the lesson you want your child to learn. To break the cycle, you must realize that your persistence will cause your child's behavior to get worse before it gets better. Instead of arguing, try negotiating.

TIP: The person saying no and not the person saying yes has the power.

Don't Let Yourself Be Manipulated

We all know that grinding sensation in the stomach that comes when we feel we are being manipulated. When you have the sensation, the best thing to do is nothing for the time being. Tell the demanding person about your discomfort and state clearly, "I can't give you an answer now. I have to think about what you are asking." Be firm but polite in stating your posi-tion. Don't let the other person talk you into doing something you will later regret. If it is easier, give the person a reason to excuse yourself and leave. Once you are alone, take some time and think about what you want to do. Without the pressure to make a decision, your thinking will be clearer because you have sidestepped a potential power struggle. You can avoid feeling guilty if you do not let people manipulate you into doing something contrary to your values and beliefs. It is you, and not others, who are accountable for your behavior.

Overcoming power struggles is difficult, especially for two parents who already have a history of being unable to resolve differences. Mediation can be helpful, though I have seen this fail when a power struggle is at the heart of the parents' conflicts. Usually, the parent who feels they are losing the power struggle will regain their status by quitting the mediation. After all, the one who says "no" wins. Now, the targeted parent and the mediator are lost. What do they do when one parent asserts their power by doing nothing? Typically, the only thing left to do is to get the alienating parent into court ordered therapy. This is not easy to do unless the parent can be shown how she is hurting the children. There is hope if the parent is either a naïve or active alienator. If the parent is an obsessed alienator, the outlook for making things better is poor. That is why it is important to recognize these problems early and act quickly, before the alienator becomes entrenched in a hostile position.

Avoid Rationalizations

You may have reasons to justify your alienating behavior. Listen to your self-talk. If any of the examples below sound familiar, rethink what you are saying or doing. You can be inadvertently adding to your problems and causing problems for your children.

Typical Rationalizations for Alienating

- "I am the one who makes sacrifices for our children. You don't do a thing to help out."

- "You're a bad influence on the kids. I know that boyfriend of yours stays overnight. What are they supposed to learn from that?"

- "You have no experience in raising children. You didn't even change diapers. How can you take care of the children?"

- "I know what's best for the kids, so do it my way and they'll be fine."

- "It's absolutely ridiculous how much I have to pay for child support. I'm paying an arm and a leg. You get the house and everything, and I get the bills."

- "I can't ask you anything. All we do is fight every time I try to talk to you."

You can be assured that you have been in a power struggle if these rationalizations sound familiar, and heard from an angry voice. Some parents fight for their belief that their way of parenting is best. The quarreling about whose parenting is better causes power struggles that should be avoided. Sometimes parents rationalize their insistence that their way is better by proclaiming, "Children need consistency." Of course, consistency means that their standards, and not the other parent's, are to be followed. The insistent parent wants total control and domination as to how the children are raised. What everyone may be forgetting is that the children live with inconsistency every day and do just fine.

Alienation Backfires in the Long Run

> Why did you lie to me all those years? I went to see Dad last week, and now that I'm older, I can see that he's not half as bad as you always said.

It is important for alienating parents to understand that, when children get older, many have a desire to make some kind of contact with the targeted parent. They are curious to know more about this person they have been told to hate. Once the children are older, perhaps adults, their feelings will temper. They will make their own judgment about the targeted parent based on their personal experience rather than on what the alienating parent has said. In addition, the targeted parent is usually a little wiser and more mature. The targeted parent won't be the same person who had been described years before as an ogre. This now causes a discrepancy in the adult children's minds.

When the adult child comes to believe that the alienating parent has filled their heads with lies, the adult children can feel betrayed and bitter. They feel victimized all over again, but this time by the alienating parent. They may resent the years they lost with the other parent and his or her family. The alienation can taint the children's adulthood as well as their childhood. The impact of what they learn about relationships can adversely affect the spousal relationships of the adult children. Intimacy and trust can become a problem. This goes back to the question: If you can't trust the very person you love, who can you trust? This is only one example of how alienating parents damage the children, perhaps for many years.

No matter what your reasons are for wanting to alienate your children from their other parent, you owe it to them to think long and hard about what you are doing. Understanding possible reasons for alienation does not give you excuses for your behavior. Instead, be honest with yourself and look at your behavior to understand how you can do better.

6

Significant Others

I know you wouldn't want custody if your mother wasn't pushing you.

Grandparents, siblings, in-laws, stepparents, and new romantic partners are all significant others having a vested interest in the conflicts between two parents. The loyalty for the parent and concern for the children creates a perfect breeding ground for alienation because often all the significant others believe they have to take a side, especially when custody is an issue. Obsessed parents recruit unsuspecting others to take on their cause. Grandparents want to support their son or daughter; friends and in-laws have their opinions; and stepparents are always involved because of how custody will affect their lives.

Each parent embroiled in a custody battle or struggling with alienation will seek support and affirmation from friends and family about what they are doing. The problems arise when the significant other wants to take control of the biological parent's decisions or how they should interact with the other parent. They all have opinions. Perhaps most damaging is the significant other's adverse influence on the children during the course of the separation or divorce, with denigrating statements or hostile expressions when the other parent's name is mentioned. Children are not stupid. They know what the looks mean. Though all the attention is focused on the parents and the children, the significant others also have an emotional interest because they have to adjust their thinking and decide what to do with their allegiances.

Siblings

When couples separate, it is not always easy to know what side siblings will take. Sometimes your brother or sister will actually show more support to your ex-spouse than you. There are many reasons for this. Depending who left whom, the sibling may hope that the two of you will get back together. Your ex-spouse and your sibling may have been friends for years before you married, or they may have been fishing buddies or coworkers. Sometimes siblings have their own issues with you or your ex-spouse that stir resentment. Whatever the relationship, siblings and in-laws should not get caught in the fray. Custody, visits, parenting time, and child support are not their issues, and any well-meaning opinions expressed over the divorce can cause more animosity and confusion for the parent having to make serious decisions. Everyone may mean well, but an opinionated sibling doesn't help. The best advice is to remind the sibling to take a low profile, perhaps be your sounding board, and let your sibling and ex-spouse redefine their relationship without your interference.

New Romantic Partners

Dad has a new girlfriend.

New romantic partners can cause problems between you and your children and your ex-spouse, even if they do their best not to meddle. Sometimes the new partner does not want to share you with the children, or dreads the idea of sharing her life with the children. You are probably familiar with mothers saying in frustration, "Who wants a wife with three children?" Or fathers saying, "I don't know if my girlfriend wants to be a stepparent." If you have a significant other, you must keep him or her under control; after all, you will be held responsible for how this person behaves. You must remind the significant other that any nasty comments or cold looks at the mention of the other parent hurts the children and must stop. With a soft voice, you can thank the significant other for his or her support while expressing your concern about what is said in front of the children. Children do not need to hear nasty comments from anyone.

> TIP: You need to set limits and boundaries with significant others early in the relationship, otherwise their intrusions will only get worse.

Introducing a New Romantic Partner to Your Children

How can you introduce your children to your new boyfriend or girlfriend without risking alienation? Your children may feel enormous conflict, a divided loyalty between you and their other parent. Often, they may not know how to feel or react towards you or your friend.

The issue of introducing your children to a new romantic partner can be problematic for parents, the children, and the new partner. The other parent may feel threatened, thinking she will have to compete with the new partner. The new partner may feel like an intruder, and just hope that the children are accepting. Most new partners try very hard to be liked by the children. Parents have to be sensitive to how much time the new partner is around the children. Many people now think living together is acceptable, but parents must remember that their home is also their children's home. Having a friend move in and take over can be a terrible imposition upon the children, who can get angry because the new partner is forced upon them and they have no power to do anything about it.

There are many issues facing children when meeting your new friend; many are the same for both custodial and noncustodial parents. If they like your friend, they may feel guilty, thinking they are betraying their other parent. They may also have to give up the illusion that their parents may someday get back together again. Your children again must face the reality of the divorce. Old memories of the intact family and divorce can set off their grief. They may not be able to tell you how they feel because they do not want to disappoint you.

Judges can attest to the fact that the risk of alienation is greatest when a parent introduces a romantic friend to the children. Parents must take special care to consider how the children will feel about the introduction. You should take a moment and try to empathize how they will feel. The children may not share your enthusiasm. Also, consider their ages and their ability to express their feelings.

> TIP: Introducing a new romantic partner is a common trigger for alienation, particular if the ex-spouse has not yet healed from the hurt or betrayal.

Children learn early that parents will date and have other adult relationships. Some children even encourage their parents to do so. If you are dating more than one person, do not feel you have to introduce all your dates to your children. You will just confuse them. Wait to introduce your friend until you know you are fairly serious about the relationship.

Tips for Making the Introduction More Comfortable

When it is time to introduce your children to your friend, prepare the children ahead of time. When you are alone with them, let them know you are dating and would like to introduce them to your friend. Tell your children a bit about your friend's interests and family. Take time for your children to express their feelings about your dating and your friend. Encourage them to ask questions and express their feelings. Do not make judgments about their feelings. This is your time to intimately exchange feelings and be comforting.

The actual introduction is usually a tense moment for everyone, even when your children are prepared. Scheduling a structured activity like dinner or a visit to a theme park will help everyone feel more comfortable. Structured activities help prevent those uncomfortable lulls in the conversation and give a focus other than on the relationship.

To help your children feel more comfortable, do not pressure them to like or be affectionate towards your friend. Asking your children to "kiss Annie good-bye" before they are ready is offensive. Children, like adults, need control over their personal space. Your children need time to develop their own relationship with your friend without your interference. Allow them to set their own pace. Be patient.

No one—adult or child—wants to feel like a fifth wheel. The fifth wheel is never comfortable. Having children sit in front of a television set while you entertain your friend is not visiting. Instead, it says to your children that they are not important, or at least, less important than your friend.

If you and your friend must physically cling to each other, it is too soon for you to introduce the children. Children feel awkward when they watch a parent hold hands, hug, and kiss a new partner. You may think showing affection to your new friend is cute, but your children will not agree. You and your friend should not act like two high-school lovers in front of your children. Instead, when all of you are together, you should sit closer to your children than to your friend. The closeness will give your child the feeling they are with you and not with the "outsider," your friend.

In addition, remember that visits are for you having time with your children and not your friend. If you believe that your friend must *always* be present, you need to question your intentions and values. Maybe you are not as interested in seeing your children as you should be. Maybe you do not understand the reasons for parenting time and what this time means to your children.

Do not have your friend present during the entire visit. Spend some time alone with your children, especially at the end of the visit. You need time alone to bond and exchange your feelings before your children return home or go on a visit to their other parent. Noncustodial parents must be more cautious than custodial parents about using a babysitter because of the limited time with the children. Noncustodial parents should try to avoid using babysitters. Parenting is your responsibility and rarely should your friend be "watching" your children. This is less an issue for a parent with split custody or living with a grandparent. Use your best judgment when considering going out while the children are in your care.

Noncustodial parents frequently question why they cannot care for the children when the other parent needs a babysitter. That is a good question. Having the other parent watch the children makes a lot of sense for many reasons. It affords the other parent and children bonding time, saves money, and should give the parent confidence that the children are well taken care of. Parents should be encouraged to use each other to babysit. Some parents have this provision written in to the parenting plan or divorce papers.

Having a friend spend the night during a parenting time weekend creates a difficult situation. Some kids don't care; others are troubled. A lot depends on your child's sensitivity. However, your responsibility is to model good values for your children. You must teach your children healthy boundaries in healthy relationships. Having a friend sleep over, and sleep with you, gives your children very clear messages about your values regarding sexual intimacy. Do not be surprise if, years later, your child throws up to you, "Why can't I move in with Jake? You had Rob spend the night with you!" Think hard before having your friend spend the night while your children are in your care. Sneaking around is risky. How are you going to explain your friend if he is running to the bathroom wearing only a bathrobe or underwear? If an angry parent brings this behavior to the court's attention, many courts frown on this behavior and will order that no unrelated adults spend the night while the child is in the household.

Consider your children's feelings before inviting someone to spend the night. Children may (understandably) feel jealous about sharing their time with an outsider. Affectionate or sexual displays will make them uncomfortable. Middle-school age children have a "yuck factor" with most "mushy" behaviors. When they see you being "sexy" with a date, kids' yuck factor triples. Overhearing sexy remarks makes most children cringe. Teenagers almost cannot stand the thought of either of their parents having sex with the other parent or anyone else. Teens in particular need time to adjust to the idea of a parent having sexual feelings with another potential partner. In general, children may feel awkward, embarrassed, confused, or angry about sharing their time with your friend, or having your friend stay overnight.

If you have a good relationship with your ex-spouse, she may be able to give you some idea about how your children will react. If your ex-spouse is angry and believes your friend spending the night will harm the children, she could sabotage your children's future relationship with your friend. You have a problem if your ex-spouse does not share your values about sex or intimacy. You may hear for the first time alienating comments to your children. That is why you might consider talking to your ex-spouse first. If you expect problems and cannot talk with your ex-spouse, you will have to rely on your own judgment. Whatever you do, move slowly. If your friend does spend the night, spend some time alone with your children before they return home. They could feel you have pushed them away in favor of your love interest.

Like it or not, before introducing the children to your friend, you may also need to consider how your ex-spouse will react. Are you going to make your ex-spouse's hostilities worse? You may believe that what you do is none of your ex-spouse's business. In a perfect world, you may be right; in reality, however, you are unfortunately wrong. You must consider your ex-spouse's feelings because it is your ex-spouse who may have to handle the fallout with your children and thus has a right to be prepared. Another consideration is what the ex-spouse will say to the children. This is another provocation for alienation.

For the most part, parents expect their ex-spouses to date and eventually remarry. The problem occurs if one parent is struggling with ex-spousal issues and believes their ex-spouse has introduced the new person to the child too quickly, or the friend was the reason for the divorce. Perhaps the parent has no legitimate reason to complain, but that does not negate the strong feelings when hearing the news that someone else is in the picture. Maybe you need to think twice about whether your timing is appropriate if you anticipate problems with your ex-spouse or you suspect that the children will have to deal with the fallout. You could be moving too fast. All of you need time adjusting to changes. Don't get defensive or angry if the other parent gets upset.

Your new relationship could trigger old wounds or jealousy that interferes with your ex-spouse's support in helping your children adjust. His feelings could influence what is said to your children. Your ex-spouse could target your new friend because of hurt or a sense of loss. Even when an ex-spouse does not want you back, knowing you have a new friend can still hurt. Sometimes feelings can be irrational. Hurt is most intense when the ex-spouse knows the children will meet your friend. He may feel threatened by the mental image that the friend is a competitor for the children's affection. Feeling powerless, the offended parent may strike back with alienating behavior.

It is easy to blame your children's refusal to visit when they know your new friend is present on the other parent. You may accuse the other parent of "brainwashing" the kids or make equally absurd comments such as, "He is just angry because he still loves me." Neither of these reasons may be true. These alienating statements, when directed to the children, often perpetuate the parent's irrational belief that the other parent is the cause of the alienation. The noncustodial parent naïvely believes the children should inevitably feel comfortable with the new friend. This is not always true. Very sensitive or angry children can take a long time adjusting to a new significant other.

Mary and the Bimbo's Story

Mary was adjusting poorly to her divorce. She often felt lonely, believing she would never again find someone to love her. Though she publicly denied having any feelings for her ex-husband, she continued to love him. When asked, she expressed contempt for her ex-husband because he left her for a "bimbo" twelve years her junior. When John introduced their three daughters to his girlfriend, Mary was enraged. She knew, for her children's sake, that she had to control her feelings.

Mary was surprised to learn that John's girlfriend, later his fiancée, was actually an asset to her children. Mary had worried about John being too lax and insensitive to the girls' welfare. John had allowed the girls to "run wild around the neighborhood" without supervision. He had been lax about their hygiene. On occasion, the girls would go without baths and come home without once changing their underwear. Sometimes the girls had slept in the living room with their clothes on. Mary knew that she could do nothing to restrict parenting time. Nonetheless, she had worried every time the children went to visit their father.

When John's girlfriend came onto the scene, Mary noticed an improvement in the girls' appearance after they returned from a visit. The girls were cleaner and appeared more relaxed. They became more enthusiastic and animated when describing the visit. Mary learned from the girls that their father's friend had a young daughter who was usually present during the visit. Mary surmised that John's fiancée was taking an active part in caring for the girls and supervising their play. Much to her surprise, Mary felt more relaxed when the girls had their weekend with their father, knowing that the girlfriend would give the girls proper care.

Significant Others as an Asset

Mary learned an important lesson. She learned to not judge John's fiancée too harshly because the fiancée actually became an asset for both her and the children. Sometimes this happens. Girlfriends can empathize with how the children may feel. Boyfriends can also empathize with children, especially if they have children of their own. The maternal or paternal instinct kicks in when needed. At issue is whether the significant other can speak up if they sense a problem with how the children feel, and the parent's willingness to listen.

Stepparents

Becoming a stepparent is never easy. The family dynamics and parental roles and responsibilities change. Unless the children have a lengthy history with the new spouse, they will be suspicious, apprehensive, and unsure about how to act. They struggle with the issue of getting close to the stepparent and not wanting to betray the other parent. Some issues the new family face must resolve are:

- Children, and sometimes parents, have the irrational belief that people have a limit to how many people they can love or learn to love. Of course, the answer is that children as well as adults have an unlimited capacity to love many people.

- Children should not be pushed to call the stepparent Mom or Dad but instead should be given permission to use a name that is comfortable. Decide whether the child calls the new stepparent by a first name, or Mom or Dad. Keep in mind that the child calling the stepparent Mom or Dad can have a symbolic significance to the other biological parent, while the meaning to a young child is different. For the adult, Mom or Dad means there is a biological bond; for the child, the title implies that this person is important and has a special social significance. Young children do not understand the biological connection because they don't yet understand sex. Parents offended by hearing their children refer to the stepparent as Mom or Dad should remind themselves that the children do not mean to reject the biological parent's status. They are just doing what they think may be socially correct.

- Children should be accepted for who they are. Do not try to make them over to fit your idea of *Ozzie and Harriet* or *The Brady Bunch*.

- Stepparents should not push children to be physically or verbally affectionate. The children will be affectionate when they are ready. Let the child approach you.

- You and your new family need to discuss discipline of your children: who will administer it and how it will be carried out. These can be sticky issues, particularly when parents have different values about what is appropriate discipline or family rules. Children will adjust to differences, providing parents do not put them in the middle of the parents' arguments. Children at an early age learn that they behave differently with different people: for example, one way with a strict teacher; another way with a permissive teacher. Learning to adapt is a good social skill that continues into adulthood.

- Stepparents need time alone with the children to have fun building a relationship. Children can accompany a stepparent to the grocery store or go along on short errands. Children should participate in planning family outings.

- Do not make negative comments to the child about the other parent. Avoid your own alienating behavior.

- Be patient and do not try to rush towards creating the ideal family.

When you are faced with the prospect of a new stepparent in your child's life, do not rush to judgment or theorize in your mind all that can go bad. A new stepparent can be an asset and a valuable addition to your child's life. Be patient and give the person a chance. The new stepparent can be as nervous about your children as they are about him.

> TIP: The new stepparent may be an asset to you and your children. Keep an open mind.

Theresa, a thirty-four-year-old divorced mother of two girls, ages four and eight, expressed her feelings well: "I think my children feel a stronger bond with their stepmother than they do with their father. Cathy pays attention to them while he just sleeps." Theresa recognized the importance of having a positive relationship with her ex-husband's wife because they could calmly talk to each other about what was best for the children. In time, Theresa learned to trust Cathy. Theresa knew that Cathy would not let anything happen to the children. Theresa, like many parents, has learned that a stepparent or an ex's friend can be an asset to her and her children.

Grandparents

I know I agreed to take care of my grandchildren until you got your life together, and I will. I don't think you're ready yet for the responsibility.

Children need and want a loving relationship with their grandparents. This remains true after a divorce. Grandparents strengthen the grandchildren's sense of family by passing on family history, values, and traditions. They give the grandchildren a historical perspective about where they come from and a vision for the future. Since grandparents are close but not in the smaller family unit, they also act as grandchildren's confidantes and buffers for their emotions, and they assist children with developing perspective. Grandparents need to remember these important roles and take care to not cross boundaries and begin their own alienation of one or both parents.

Most grandparents are well meaning, but they can also participate in the alienation cycle—by their own actions, by being pulled into parent's problems, or because of their misguided attempts to help the children. Grandparents can be overly critical of the other parent's values and parenting skills. Because they love the grandchildren, they must fight the temptation to control, to try to dictate how to parent. After a divorce, grandparents may be frustrated because they don't have the same access to the children's other parent to influence parenting.

TIP: Grandparents should not help unless asked.

Grandparents do not always trust their own children to parent competently, and sometimes with good reason. They can be critical of their daughter's parenting, constantly looking over her shoulder, ready to criticize and correct her; or may have learned that their son has been untruthful with them.

Of course, the grandparents say, "We're only trying to help." Well, they should not be helping unless asked. Just as grandparents raised their own children, parents also have a right to raise their children as they choose. You each may have different opinions or values about raising children, but since when did different generations always agree about childrearing?

A parent's right to parent must come before the grandparents' right to parent. Most parents appreciate and enjoy the occasional help with the children. Children like their grandparents around, but parents must have control of when and where grandparents help. Despite their good intentions, grandparents who get too involved may inadvertently demean their children and shake their confidence to parent. Tensions will mount if parents feel the grandparents are an unwelcome intrusion.

A Parent and Children Living with Grandparents

Often after a divorce, parents move with their children to the home of the children's grandparents, who help newly single mothers or fathers take care of the children. Grandparents often take care of the children while the mother or father is working or going to school. Sometimes the grandparents get overly opinionated with issues related to the divorce. They may unknowingly contribute to alienation. Grandparents in this situation must first comply with the court's orders and diligently avoid expressing any animosity about the other parent and in-laws in front of the children. The grandparents and the biological parent must negotiate parenting responsibilities when both are home. Sometimes parents take advantage of the grandparents, expecting them to care for the children whenever they go out and have a good time. Having a grandparent babysit while a parent goes out can be fine but the parent should not abuse or cavalierly take advantage of this privilege. Parents must remain responsible as primary caregivers and role models to their children, regardless of where or with whom the parent and children live. The argument of some young parents—"I have a life too"—doesn't carry much weight in the court when a parent is seen as neglectful.

Grandparents Rescuing a Parent in Trouble

Some parents have serious problems that tempt grandparents to rescue their son or daughter by helping care for the grandchildren. Though noble and sometimes necessary for the grandchildren's welfare, problems may occur when the grandparents become overly assertive and controlling. Though they mean well, these grandparents take over everything. They tell the parents what and when to do whatever needs to be done. Sometimes they create leverage by threatening to withhold financial assistance, or by saying, "If you don't do what I tell you, you can just leave and then I'll be out of your lives. You don't appreciate all that I have done for you." Sometimes grandparents push the son- or daughter-in-law aside, despite that fact that he or she is capable of caring for the children.

When parents invite grandparents to help care for the grandchildren, grandparents must allow the biological parents to retain as much responsibility as possible. Parents and grandparents should understand that this arrangement is supposed to be temporary. Over time, as parents adjust to being sole caregivers, they should take back their parenting duties while the grandparents back off. Grandparents and biological parents must be sensitive in explaining to the grandchildren about what is happening and the temporary living arrangements. At this point, the grandparents could easily cause alienation by attacking the biological parents, especially the absent parent.

When grandparents see problems with their son or daughter and ex-in-law, they should try to remain neutral and let them work things out on their own. Grandparents should not take on all the responsibility for solving the family problems.

Grandparents as the Grandchildren's Full-Time Caretakers

For many reasons, parents might ask the grandparents to care for the children temporarily because they are unable to do so themselves. Typically, the grandparents and their son or daughter agree that the grandparents will take care of the children until the parent wants the children returned. The problem with this arrangement is that, although each side believes they have a time-limited agreement, somehow the terms become twisted. The parent believes she can get the children back anytime she wants, but the grandparents assume they will return the children only after deciding if, and when, the parent is ready to resume parental responsibilities. Many families return to court because the parent and grandparents failed to make their agreement clear about when the grandparents will return the children. This adds serious stress on the relationship for the grandparents, biological parents, and the children.

TIP: A formal written agreement is essential.

If you are considering having your parents take care of your children until you can get back on your feet, you can do a few things to avoid trouble later. First, obtain an understanding in writing, with an attorney's help, which outlines each other's expectations and conditions for when the children will be returned. Such an agreement may not be legally binding unless you file it with the court and a judge signs it.

Second, include a provision stating that you and the other parent can see or visit the children any time you want. If you skip seeing your children or you wait a long time before asking for their return, it will be harder to get them back. The worst thing you can do is not spend quality time with your children or show little interest.

Sometimes the grandparents and children form a strong bond with each other. In this situation, either the children do not want to return to their parent's home or the grandparents set unrealistic conditions for when they are willing to return the children. The parent has no chance of ever getting the children back. When this happens, everyone returns to court. When grandparents list lengthy or ever-changing conditions for returning children, they don't say it, but they really don't ever want to return the children. They like raising the children and wish the parent would just back off.

Sara and Betty's Story

Sara has two children, each from a different father. Her first child was born when Sara was sixteen. She has not seen either father for months and receives no child support. Sara finally admitted that she is a recovering alcoholic and needs to find a job to support her children. No one questions her love for the children, though she raised eyebrows when she said, "I have a life too." In the past, Sara turned to her mother, Betty, whenever she went out to get drunk. Now, Sara has asked her mother to care for the children while she looks for a job and gets her apartment in order. Betty agrees.

Sara spent many months on her own. She found a new boyfriend, who now lives with her. When Sara felt able to resume parenting, she told her mother that she wanted her children back. This led to a big fight because Betty has no confidence that Sara has been sober long enough. Further, Betty does not trust Sara's boyfriend. Feeling very concerned for the grandchildren, she tells Sara, "You don't have your life together enough yet to raise your children." After months of arguing, they have no choice but to go to court.

Finally, if you are planning to have a grandparent care for your children while you get your life in order, you can avoid many future problems if you use a court-ordered mediator or a family therapist to draft an agreement outlining your responsibilities and the conditions when the children would be returned. Utilize a counselor who can monitor how the children are adjusting and give both of you some guidance. You would be amazed at the problems that can occur that you would not have anticipated.

> *TIP: You are giving your parents tremendous power as a gatekeeper when you have them care for your children while getting your life together. They will use their criteria, and not yours, when deciding to return the children.*

Grandparents Being Too Attached

If your parents are willing to care for your children, you should guard against over attachment by your parents. Always keep in mind that you may suddenly want your children back and that it may not be as easy as you think. Be prepared for the possibility that they will refuse your request. To help minimize this risk, there are things you must do:

- Stay actively involved with your children. See them regularly on a regular basis.
- Continue your parenting responsibilities by taking your children to doctor's appointments and attending school conferences and extracurricular events.
- Keep the relationship with your parents strong. Have frequent communication with your parents about how the children are adjusting.
- Encourage the noncustodial parent's visits or parenting time. Unless a court order says otherwise, they are still entitled to spend time with the children.
- Do not engage in your own alienating behavior by blaming the other parent for your problems.
- Ensure that the grandparents understand that you will spend time alone with the children.
- Write up an agreement with the court and your parents and stick to it.

Taking your children out or spending the day with them is good not only for you and the children, but also for your parents. The time alone gives your parents some relief. If your parents know you frequently see your children and are interested and actively involved in their lives, this reduces the risk of their becoming overly attached. If you disappear, then suddenly show up asking for the children, then expect problems.

If you have emotional problems or a substance addiction, your parents may be concerned that you are not capable of caring for your children. Your parents may require you to seek counseling before they feel comfortable with you raising the children. If you refuse, and your parents have reason to believe that you are neglectful or abusive with the children, they should report this to your local children's services agency and consult their attorney. If the children's services agency agrees with them, your parents can volunteer to take temporary custody. This way, everyone knows the process is legal. But in that case, your parents cannot give you your children without a hearing and possibly a recommendation from the children's services agency. Your parents are looking out for you to get you the help you need. However, there is a fine line between the grandparents' rightful concerns and over attachment to their grandchildren. Whatever happens, make it clear to your parents that you intend to raise the children to adulthood. The grandparents will be disappointed, but if the parent's home is stable, the best place for children is with their mother or father.

Why Do Some Grandparents Alienate Grandchildren?

With few legal rights, grandparents may think that getting the grandchildren to reject their parents is the best chance of keeping the children. Grandparents may also want to protect the children from a situation the grandparents sincerely believe to be unsafe. This tactic can ultimately hurt the children, especially when they get older and realize that the grandparents alienated them from their parents.

> TIP: As much as a grandparent may love and support their son or daughter, they should not get involved with the biological parent's arguments. Instead, they should be supportive without taking sides or engaging in their own alienating behavior.

David and Carrie's Story

Eleven-year-old David absolutely refused to have anything to do with his biological mother. Carrie, like many young mothers, got pregnant at a time when she and the father could not adequately care for their son. The father disappeared, leaving Carrie with little money and no help. Carrie's parents, feeling a responsibility towards David, agreed to care for him until Carrie "got on her feet." Over the years, Carrie finished her education and held a responsible job. She made the mistake of not keeping in contact with her son. Her relationship with David became more distant while his relationship with the grandparents grew stronger. Carrie realized that nothing she did to pull her life together would ever be good enough for her parents. They always had excuses about why she could not resume her parental responsibilities. The grandparents argued that David was afraid of his mother. They told David that his mother had physically abused him when he was a baby and blackened his eye; they showed David photographs of the injury. David also believed that his mother once forced his head underwater at a pool. His grandparents acknowledged that Carrie may have been trying to teach David how to hold his breath while swimming. Later, Carrie denied that she had ever held David's head under water, stating, "I have never even been in a swimming pool with him."

David's fear of his mother became very severe. He displayed an attitude consistent with parental alienation syndrome (PAS). During an interview, he asked, upon entering the office, "What chair did my mom sit in?" When he could not be told with certainty, he reasoned that the chair against the wall was safe. He pulled the chair over closer to the desk. He then noticed his mother's name written on a sheet of paper. Without any hesitation, he immediately covered her name with the nameplate on the desk. Later in the interview, he said he did not want to hear the word "Ohio." David had even told his teachers not to mention Ohio in class, because the word reminded him of his mother who lived there, and that was upsetting to him.

It was concluded that the grandparents had caused, or at least reinforced, alienation between David and his mother by instilling false allegations of abuse. Carrie added to the problem, however, by withdrawing from David and making excuses for not seeing him.

Some grandparents blame themselves for the way their own children turned out. Now they want to make amends with their conscience by seeing to it that their grandchildren don't follow the same path. To steer them down the straight and narrow, they may use the absent parent as a negative example, playing up their faults and drumming in the notion that their son or daughter is a bad person. This puts the children in a terrible position. They want to love even an absent parent without anyone's interference. Again, grandparents in this situation should keep their opinions to themselves and let the children have a relationship with both biological parents.

Your parents, as well as your ex-spouse, will have trouble trusting you if you have a history of being a neglectful or irresponsible parent. You will have to prove yourself. Promising to do better is not enough. Your behavior must be predictable: meaning, you do what you say. Rebuilding trust, once it is lost, takes time. The best advice is to behave yourself and be a responsible parent.

George and Missy's Story

Like many couples whose marriage is failing, George and Missy decided to move, believing a new start would save the family. Soon after the move from Ohio to Florida, they realized this was no simple cure for their marital problems. Before their divorce, Missy decided to remain in Florida while George and their son Terry, age five, and daughter, Tracy, age sixteen, returned to Ohio.

Upon their return, George and the children stayed with the maternal grandparents. For a while, all went well, until George decided to move into his own home with the children. The grandparents understood George's desire but felt a loss and emptiness when the children moved out of their home.

In the beginning, the grandparents had frequent visits. Also, arrangements were made for Missy to return from Florida to visit the children. However, this arrangement did not work for long, because Missy's finances prevented her from traveling back and forth. In time, Tracy and her brother felt abandoned by their mother's insistence on staying in Florida rather than returning to Ohio. Since the children could not direct their anger towards their mother, they took their feelings out on the grandparents.

The grandparents saw the children's resentment of their mother grow, especially Tracy's. In turn, they became defensive of Missy's behavior. They made excuses to the children for her decision to remain in Florida and reminded them how much Missy loved them. The children did not accept their arguments. Each time the grandparents reminded the children of their mother's love, the children got angrier. Eventually, the children refused to visit the grandparents because they were tired of their grandmother telling them that they "should be understanding." Their comments made Tracy feel like there was something wrong with her for feeling angry with her mother. Tracy's refusal to visit was the only way she knew to get back at her mother and grandparents. Tracy even refused to accept the grandparents' birthday and Christmas gifts.

The grandparents blamed the children's rejection on George's recent remarriage. George and the children denied the allegation, the children saying they could decide for themselves not to visit. The frustrated grandparents were successful in getting court-ordered parenting time because the children's mother decided to stay in Florida. However, George did not follow the court order. He continued to make it clear to the grandparents that he supported the children's decision about not visiting. He remained passive, waiting to see if the children changed their minds.

Grandparents Must Be Careful about Defending Parents

As can be seen in George and Missy's story above, grandparents must be careful when they defend their son or daughter's behavior to the grandchildren. Children are not stupid. If the children clearly see behavior that is different from what the grandparents tell them, the grandparents will lose all credibility. The grandparents can create problems with the children if they are too pushy and insistent that the grandchildren forgive the irresponsible parent. Children, like anyone, will make up their own minds about how they feel, without anyone's help. They will probably keep their opinions to themselves unless pushed. Rarely have I seen a grandparent successfully defend the biological parent to the children when the grandchildren's experience is contrary to what they are being told. If there is a serious problem with the children's feelings, the biological parent, and not the grandparents, must repair the damage. Otherwise, the grandparents' good intentions could backfire, causing even more problems.

In the complex tangle involving George, Missy, Missy's parents, and the two children, several people had the power to intervene:

- George could have helped by reminding the children that the grandparents had nothing to do with their mother's decision. He could also have told the grandparents that the children were getting angry, and gently suggested they back off and not be so defensive of Missy. Finally, he could have encouraged the children to obey the court order and maintain a relationship with the grandparents.

- The grandparents' defense of Missy was understandable, but they would have had fewer problems if they had been less persistent about it.

- Missy, and not the grandparents, should have defended her decision to live in Florida. She should have maintained verbal and written communication, continued to acknowledge holidays with gifts, and made it a point to visit the children whenever possible.

- Tracy needed to learn to separate her feelings towards her mother from her feelings about the grandparents. Tracy and her brother needed their father's support to have an ongoing and loving relationship with their grandparents, while acknowledging they still feel hurt and angry about their mom's decision.

- The children did need a relationship with their grandparents. Unfortunately, the grandparents became a symbolic extension of the mother and a target of the children's anger. Nevertheless, children need both their mother and father, and both grandparents.

Grandparents Can Be the Alienators Behind the Alienator

Some grandparents actively participate in their adult child's campaign of alienation against his or her ex-spouse; some are even the instigator. Their contribution might include egging on their son or daughter with insinuations and innuendoes against the other parent and inviting their adult child and grandchild to live with them after the adult child is awarded custody. Understandably, grandparents want to support their son or daughter's efforts to get custody if it appears justified. However, grandparents should not use their adult children to satisfy their own desire to raise their grandchildren.

Targeted parents need special help dealing with alienating grandparents because of the risk that any retaliation will backfire. Children usually have a special relationship with their grandparents and any interference with the relationship by the targeted parent will be interpreted by the children as alienating. If you are not careful, your children can actually come to resent you and become aligned with the alienating grandparents. This is when you need a mediator to step in.

To minimize the risk of being victimized by a grandparent's alienation behavior, strive to keep the relationship strong; do not criticize the grandparent or your ex-spouse to the grandparent. You should try to keep strong your children's relationships with the ex-spouse's extended family: the cousins, aunts and uncles. Do not totally withdraw from the children's other family.

A Final Word to Grandparents

Most adults have fond memories of the times spent as children with their grandparents. Your grandchildren should be no different. They need your love. If necessary, you should exercise your rights to seek grandparent parenting time if your state has such laws. You can be an invaluable source of support for the whole family. Just remember to let your adult children do the parenting of their own children unless they ask you to help. But love your grandchildren, and stay involved with them over the years. They will love it.

7

Obstacles to Change:
Parental vs Ex-Spousal Issues

You will never see my girls because of your little lovefest.

Fighting about why he left you, who gets the tax refund, or a mother-in-law's meddling has nothing to do with what's best for your children. Arguments about these issues are common among divorced parents. Exposing the children to these arguments confuses them and increases their fears. You can do a lot to prevent exposing your children to these arguments if you understand the difference between ex-spousal and parental issues.

The confusion between ex-spousal and parental issues is a common obstacle in doing what's best for your children and a major contributor to ongoing dissent between formerly married couples with children. Pain, anger, sadness, inadequacy and all the feelings that go with a failed marriage and divorce don't just go away when your divorce is final. These feelings can fester and influence how you relate to your former spouse for years. When bitterness from the marital relationship bleeds through to interactions about the children, as it often does, you get interactions like Mary Beth's and Stuart's (see chapter 4, "Your Child Comes First").

TIP: There is no timetable for when healing is done.

Ex-spousal issues are emotionally charged topics that have nothing to do with your children or how to raise them. They stem from your relationship with each other and probably contributed to the breakup of your marriage. The more common ex-spousal issues that linger between parents after divorce or separation are:

- A lingering sense of betrayal that dates back to the day you found out your spouse was having an affair
- Anger about having to lower your standard of living (because you must pay child support or no longer can depend on your spouse's income)
- Feeling old and inadequate compared to your ex's new mate
- Memories of being controlled, belittled, abused, or lied to by your spouse during your marriage (and anticipating that you will be again).

When parents have not healed, a simple conversation or a look on your ex-spouse's face can trigger intense feelings. These ex-spousal issues tend to come up again and again, making almost any interaction between ex-spouses a potential battleground.

Parental issues, by contrast, focus on your children's needs and problems: their health, safety, progress in school, adjustment to the divorce, visitation, developmental milestones, and so on. Why is Julie failing math? When will Megan be old enough to date? How will we pay for Sam's braces? Should Pete be involved in two after-school sports, computer classes, and trumpet lessons? Although answering questions like these can still push some buttons and lead to arguments, parents are generally able to discuss them objectively and in a relatively calm, rational manner—unless ex-spousal issues creep into the conversation, creating so much emotional interference that communication virtually grinds to a halt.

TIP: Do not expose your children to ex-spousal issues.

When ex-spousal issues bleed through to discussions of parenting concerns, they distort your perceptions, cloud your judgment, and impair your ability to decide what's best for your children. Nothing gets accomplished. In fact, the feelings aroused by your unfinished relationship business may be so intense (or the ensuing argument so brutal) that you'll never get around to talking about parenting issues, much less resolving them. To avoid this outcome, you must make a continual, conscious effort to separate ex-spousal issues from parental ones. The following exercise can help.

EXERCISE: IDENTIFYING EX-SPOUSAL AND PARENTAL ISSUES

The purpose of this exercise is to help you differentiate between ex-spousal and parental issues. Begin by recalling any topic that triggers your anger, jealousy, grief, frustration, bitterness, resentment, or other strong emotions when talking with your ex-spouse. List these topics on a sheet of paper.

Next, when you're satisfied that your list is fairly complete (you can add more issues at any time), go back over it and write the letter "P" beside the items that pertain solely to the needs, problems, and upbringing of your children.

Then go through the list a second time and write the letter "E" next to items that involve only you and your ex-spouse, not your children. All items should be marked with either an E or a P.

Ex-spousal ("E") issues are never to be discussed in your children's presence. These issues are none of your children's business.

But what about "P" issues? Can't they trigger arguments and cause tension that's bad for children too? Certainly they can. Almost any parent will become defensive when the other parent makes unsolicited comments about her parenting skills. Inflammatory statements, such as "I know more about raising kids than you'll ever know," or "I have to tell you what to do, for the children's sake. You don't know the first thing about parenting," ignite arguments. Tense discussions become full-fledged confrontations.

Go back over the "P" issues on the list. Check those that seem especially explosive. Think about what might make these parenting matters so upsetting or difficult to resolve. Could there be an ex-spousal issue hidden below the surface? What about a fear (losing your children's love, for instance), a desire (protecting your children from unpleasantness of any kind), or a conviction (kids need to go to church every Sunday)?

You can greatly reduce exposing your children to hurtful arguments if you begin by discriminating between ex-spousal and parental issues. Ask your ex-spouse to agree to keep ex-spousal issues from the children and instead discuss these issues out of their presence. Obsessed parents may lack sufficient self-control to keep ex-spousal issues from the children. If this is true, the targeted parent should consciously avoid any ex-spousal issues in earshot of the children. Save the conversations for when the children are not expected to be around to hear. If by chance you are discussing a volatile ex-spousal issue while the children are outside playing, consider asking your ex-spouse to discuss the issue later when there is no chance that the children will walk in during an intense argument. You have to plan out, especially if you must talk with an obsessed parent, even the discussion of parenting issues.

Both of you should use your judgment about parental issues discussed in your children's presence. Your child may be too young to understand, or the issues may be too volatile to be discussed in their presence. This being true, you and your ex-spouse should talk privately. Simply knowing that these underlying currents exist can help you manage your emotions more effectively and work out parental issues more reasonably than you have in the past. If ex-spousal issues are not resolved and continue to interfere with the two of you calmly dealing with parental issues, you may consider getting counseling. Utilizing email or fax is certainly helpful if conversing with your ex-spouse becomes futile or volatile. Remember, what you write, whether on paper or e-mail, can be saved and later used against you; so be careful about what you write.

8

Common Alienating Tactics: Disclosing Inappropriate Information to Children

I have no secrets with my children.

My children have a right to know.

Is honesty the best policy? Your desire to be honest with your children may be commendable if you are sensitive about the nature of the information you share. As discussed in chapter 7 ("Obstacles to Change: Parental vs Ex-Spousal Issues"), there is a difference between ex-spousal and parental information. Ex-spousal information, about the details of the divorce or your life apart from your children, is none of your children's business. They do not need to hear about who had an affair with whom, or the details of your sex life. They may need reassurances about the family finances, but the details can arouse their anxieties. Be reassuring to your children without going into too much detail. Let them know that you may not have the same amount of money as in the past because there are now two households, but they are not to worry. Children may not always understand the significance of what they hear. Though you believe your children are bright and mature, they still do not have the same capacity to understand as an adult. They want to know what is happening with the divorce because they love their parents and fear the future. To reduce any insecurity, children listen for any clue about what their future holds. They listen through walls and eavesdrop on their parents' conversations from the next room. Be careful about the volume of your voice. Respond to your children's fears with reassurance while being discreet about what you say, and being careful not to raise excessive alarm by projecting your own fears onto the children.

TIP: Do not be afraid to tell your child that some issues between Mom and Dad are private and will not to be shared with them.

Parents may assume their children will ask questions if they do not understand something. This is not always true. If your child believes a falsehood, they have no reason to ask for clarification. After all, why should they? Children, like most adults, have difficulty giving up their misperceptions and assumptions. Children may nod in agreement when asked if they understand what they heard. Only later will you learn they did not. To reduce misunderstandings, ask the children to repeat back, in their own words, what they think you said. You can correct misunderstandings if what they repeat is wrong. Just keep in mind that children are more likely to remember inaccurate information than to ask a parent for clarification.

Be suspicious of your own motives if you make frequent public pronouncements about sharing information with the children in the interests of being *honest*. Parents intent on alienating will propagandize their children by selectively giving them information that would support their arguments with little consideration of the other parent. He or she may share the reasons for the divorce, reveal past physical abuse, or declare, "Your father left us to be with his girlfriend." Do you think you can share that information without any bias or inflection in your voice to convey your attitude? It is doubtful.

TIP: Do not show the children the divorce papers.

Showing the children the divorce papers is another common example of a parent sharing information that may not be appropriate. The parent's motivation may be sinister: a desire to get back at their ex-spouse or to be vindicated from the other parent's accusations. Parents will show e-mails, letters, photographs from a cell phone, and listen to audio tapes to make the point that the other parent is no good. However you look at it, this is alienating behavior.

There are occasions when parents have to share information with each other, remembering that similar conversations triggered anger and defensiveness. Discussing medical bills, changes in parenting time schedules, or deciding on how to pay for braces are concerns that parents need to talk over with each other. Sometimes a parent will use the children's presence during the discussion to control the tension level they feel with the other parent. Children may feel trapped when used in this manner and may cope with the tension by trying to isolate themselves with play or become involved in some distracting activity. They act as if they are not listening but, though they appear engrossed in play, they probably are. You must remain sensitive to how the children would feel if they overheard your conversation. Pay attention to what you say in their presence to prevent them from experiencing any unnecessary discomfort.

> TIP: Do not use the children to control the tensions between you and your ex-spouse. If you must discuss sensitive issues and worry about losing control, consider talking to each other in a public place like a restaurant. Everyone is more likely to behave themselves in public.

Sharing information about parenting issues is appropriate. Depending on the child's age and maturity, you can share school reports, medical results, social calendars, letters, and greeting cards. Like so many decisions you have to make, use your best judgment. If you are talking to your ex-spouse within earshot of your children, don't hesitate to gently remind her to be sensitive about what is being said.

Brianna's Story

Brianna, my oldest daughter, was about three at the time when she was sitting on the floor playing with her dolls while my wife and I were watching a story on *60 Minutes* about a rape. I don't remember exactly what the story was about, or the words the commentator was using, other than that he mentioned sodomy. To our surprise, our daughter blurted out, "That would hurt." We were amazed for many reasons. To begin with, we didn't think Brianna would be listening to a television show like *60 Minutes*. Secondly, she obviously understood what was being said, because her response was appropriate. We didn't understand how she would have made the association between sodomy and pain. To this day, I can't explain her reaction. But we did learn some valuable lessons from this experience. First, we can't always protect children from what they will hear on television. Second, children listen when you least expect it. They understand more than we think. Lastly, the experience reminds us to be sensitive to and aware of what is being said around the children.

A responsible parent understands that in many ways they define their children's world. To a great extent we control what they hear, see, and experience. We do this to influence their values, protect them from harm, and assure them that they are loved and admired. We loosen up as they grow older, but that does not diminish our fears. Every responsible parent worries about their teens being exposed to alcohol, drugs, and sex—and do not think that your worries stop when they turn eighteen. Protecting your children is an even more formidable task during a divorce, but a loving parent does not shrink from this responsibility. Parents must protect their children from information that they lack the maturity to understand. We already do this by controlling what they watch on television, who they associate with, censoring their video games and music, and screening their magazines. Divorce papers and the like are no exception.

9

Common Alienating Tactics: Demands and Blame

I expect that I can call my kids anytime I want. They are my children, and no one is going to tell me when I can talk to them. They know I love them.

Demanding parents believe they have rights beyond what is ordered by the court. They are quick to anger whenever anyone refutes or hinders their wants. They often speak with a sense of entitlement and little or no regard for how others feel, or for what schedule and time the court may order. This is especially true for an obsessed parent.

TIP: Never behave in a manner that will cause your attorney to have to defend your behavior in court.

In the portion of a taped conversation below, you can hear this attitude in Megan's father's voice as he demands that she stay on the phone rather than ride her pony. Six-year-old Megan's tears don't even deter him from his insistence. In fact, her father counters Megan's protest by blaming Megan's mother for the fact that she could not ride her pony earlier. This dialogue is an example of alienation and a parent's estrangement.

Megan's Story

Father: Megan, talk to Daddy.

Megan: I want to ride my pony. I just came back from school.

Father: I know you've been home for an hour.

Megan: I want to ride it before it gets dark.

Father: Well, you can ride it in the barn.

Megan: No, I can't. My mom's gonna take the new stalls out. She puts horses out to close the stalls.

Father: Oh, I see.

Megan: The stalls are not that big.

Father: Megan, Megan—you're not going to talk to Daddy?

Megan: I'll call you back!

Father: Well, Daddy'll be in bed by then. I'll be sleeping.

Megan: I'll call you back when I'm done riding. This ain't a good time to be talking.

Father: Well, this isn't a good time for you to be riding your pony.

Megan: Why?

Father: This is going to be the time that I call you from now on.

Megan: Huh?

Father: I'm going to start calling you at five o' clock.

Megan: Mummy, is it five o'clock?

Father: It's after five o'clock. This is when I'm going to start calling you.

Megan: Daddy's going to call me at five every day.

Father: Megan.

Megan: What?

Father: Now, why are you getting upset?

Megan: I want to ride my pony.

Father: Well, Megan, you know how bad you want to ride your pony? You know how bad that is? That's how bad I want to talk to you.

Megan: I want to give you to Grandma.

Father: No, you talk to me.

Megan: Daddy, I want to hang up!

Father: Megan, listen to Daddy.

Megan: What?

Father: Megan, are you crying?

Megan: Yes.

Father: Well, do you think that's fair to Daddy when I call you, you want to go and do something?

Megan:	'Cause I didn't ride my pony last night!
Father:	Well, is that Daddy's fault? That's your Mummy's fault. Because she should have let you ride it, and she didn't so that's her fault.
Megan:	Nuh-uh!
Father:	That's not Daddy's fault, okay? So don't blame Daddy for this, okay? You understand this?
Megan:	Okay.
Father:	It's still daylight out. You'll still get to ride your pony.
Megan:	No, I won't. It gets dark sooner.
Father:	No, it don't. I'm calling now for you to talk to me, okay? And I want you to talk to me, okay? I don't want you to cry; I want you to talk to me. Okay? You understand? Do you understand, Megan? Huh?
Megan:	Yes.
Father:	Now, what did you do in school today?
Megan:	Nothing.
Father:	Don't be upset. Don't you be upset with Daddy, okay? Because remember I told you, me and you are gonna get to go team pen soon. I'm going to come out, and me and you, and we're going to take two horsies and we're gonna go team penning.
Megan:	Hello?
Father:	Hello?
Megan:	Daddy, I'm getting dressed. Hang on for a second.

Now that you have read the script, how do you feel about Megan's father? Was he interested in his needs, or those of his daughter? Was he trying to alienate Megan from her mother? Was he contributing to his own estrangement? I think you know the answers to these questions. What Megan's father fails to see is how he is hurting himself as well as his daughter. He is causing his own estrangement by insisting that Megan talk with him rather than ride her pony. He ignores her tears and instead goes a step further and blames her mother for her not having time to ride. Do you think Megan will see this? She probably couldn't verbalize what is happening, but she knows how and why she feels the way she does.

Cheryl and Larry's Story

Cheryl was protective and concerned about her son's welfare. Jason, age thirteen, had a good relationship with his father, Larry. Larry was an overpowering and demanding parent. He insisted on making phone calls to his son anytime he wanted. He told Jason, "You are old enough to make your own decisions, and you don't have to listen to your mother. If you want to talk to me, you don't have to ask her." Cheryl was angry at Larry for encouraging Jason to violate her authority. She felt frustrated and harassed by Larry's insistence to talk with Jason whenever he wanted. Because the phone calls were upsetting Jason, Cheryl insisted that Larry call before 9:00 pm. She reasoned that limiting the phone calls would allow Jason time to calm down before bedtime. When his father called later in the evening, Jason would toss and turn, trying to fall asleep.

Larry interpreted Cheryl's edict as an attempt to interfere in his relationship with Jason. Jason, like most children, wanted to avoid the entire situation. He would not tell his father anything about how he felt. Larry believed that Cheryl was trying to alienate him from his son when, in fact, Larry was causing his own problems. He did not take the time to empathize with his son's feelings. Instead he blamed Cheryl for controlling their son and interfering with their relationship. Larry made his feelings known to Jason.

Excessive demands by either parent set up a power struggle with no winners. Even if one parent backs off, the other winner has won nothing but animosity. When the children are caught in the middle and pulled in two directions, they too are losers. To help prevent further harm to the children, both parents should take them out of the conversation and instead talk to each other. The children should not be a conduit between the parents.

TIP: The less the children are used to communicate for the parents, the better.

A pushy parent is asking for trouble with the children. Yelling at your child and blaming a parent for your not getting what you want will be seen as selfish and uncaring. Your frustration may be very understandable, because you cannot talk to or see your child when you want to. Your feelings are caused by your powerlessness when you hear "no." Pushing the issue will likely cause the other parent to dig in his heels, adding to your frustration. You may hope that your persistence will beat down your ex-spouse's resistance and cause him to acquiesce to your demands. But do you think this really works for the long term?

The issue for the demanding parent is to back off and remain under control. Speak directly to the other parent; calmly negotiate and reach an agreement. Also, be reasonable. Children do have homework and many times have to quiet down before going to bed. Hearing parents argue does not help prepare for bed. Pause and think about what is best for your children.

TIP: What is best for your child is not necessarily best for you.

10

Common Alienating Tactics: Taught to Fear

If you go and live with your mother, I am not going to see you anymore.

All parents make comments to their children that they later regret. This is more of an issue of estrangement than alienation, but alienation becomes an issue when the other parent uses your comments as ammunition to attack. An alienating parent may frequently remind the children that they have reason to fear their other parent. Sometimes angry parents make hurtful statements that are absolutely meaningless. Parents are notorious for putting spiteful comments in e-mails, trusting that the court or the children will never read them. This is not smart. The other parent, especially if everyone is heading to court, will take your hateful e-mails and letters and use them against you in court. You are fueling the fire for the other parent's alienation when your behavior is upsetting your children and the other parent makes a point of never letting the children's hurt heal but instead frequently reminds them about your hateful behavior. This is an opportunity for the alienating parent to avenge all his hurts.

> TIP: If you engage in estranging behavior, you give the other parent an opportunity to turn your behavior against you to alienate you from your children.

For example, threatening your children that you will never see them again or saying you will find a new family is completely ridiculous. These statements only scare your children and satisfy your own selfish need to vent your anger. Think about how the other parent can use your statement against you. How would you feel if your child took you up on your threat? Whom would you blame? Yourself.

Imagine how life would be if you were accountable for everything you have ever said. When a driver cuts you off with their automobile, you may want to ram your car up their tailpipe. Should the person driving the other car take your threat seriously? When you say to your child, "I could kick your butt!" should they bend over and wait? Though the threat to your children is inappropriate, should they take what you said literally? Of course not. Interpreting these statements literally is irrational and serves no purpose other than creating more chaos. But children do not always interpret your hurtful words the way you think; instead, they may remember your words and hold them against you. Your ex-spouse, too, will have a good memory.

TIP: Assume your child will remember your vindictive comments.

Going through a divorce does strange things to our reasoning abilities. Suddenly, you may start to take threats literally so that your ex-spouse is now accountable for everything that has ever been said between you. Your ex remembers vividly how you said "I never wanted another kid anyway." Or your ex-husband's anger reminds you of the time he said, "Your son is just as stupid as you." Words said to maim your partner, like the effects of acid, still eat into your interactions. In fact, some of your worst comments may be aired in court to characterize you as an abusive parent. It is very difficult to atone later for your words.

I continue to be amazed at how spouses will threaten their ex-spouses with some kind of terrible legal action as if they were experts. Statements such as, "You will never see the kids again!" or "I'll take you for all you are worth!" are signs of immaturity and are destructive in nature. If you are concerned about your ex-spouse's threats, talk to your attorney for advice rather than waste time arguing with your ex-spouse.

Anger

Now more than ever, you should learn how to express your anger and frustration in ways that do not hurt your children or give ammunition for your ex-spouse. Rather than blame someone else for why your child is alienated from you, maybe you need to look at your own behavior.

No one questions that parenting can be trying. However, the way parents express their anger is a burden for many children. This can be an issue for an obsessed parent having trouble controlling the emotions. If your children perceive you as a screamer, they will naturally try to read your mood so they know when to leave the room. The children will listen to the tone of your voice and watch your gestures. If they can't read your mood, they may actually learn to fear you because they can't predict your rage.

Everyone gets angry and frustrated. There are two aspects of anger that especially cause problems: intensity and duration. Below are some common examples of how parents allow these aspects of anger to sabotage their relationship with their children

Intensity

The intensity of a parent's anger can range from a mild annoyance to out-of-control rage. Of course rage is what children fear. Listening to the screams strikes terror of the unknown. Many parents reading this will rule out their having a problem because their image in their mind of child abuse will be more severe than what they believe they have done to their own children. This is a convenient rationalization, but at the same time, it is a fair question to ask: "What is child abuse?" There is no simple answer. Even children's service agencies are criticized for being inconsistent in deciding the difference between abuse and energetic discipline. Rarely will anyone argue that children *should* be injured or bruised. I say rarely because there are parents who believe bruising is okay. We have all heard the tale from an acquaintance of how his father took him out to the woodshed and "whaled his butt." Afterward, he never did whatever-it-was again. The intent of the story is to advocate for harsh discipline. Without entering the debate about appropriate discipline, parents who lose control of their anger are unpredictable and instill fear in their children, and should not blame the other parent when the children don't want to spend time with them. Parents who do this should not be surprised if the other parent uses such behavior to alienate or argue that they are unfit and undeserving of seeing the children. And this may be a valid argument, if the angry parents cannot control their behavior. This is estrangement. Excuses will not make amends.

Duration

Another little-discussed aspect of anger is a person's ability to recover from anger. Some people explode and minutes later they are fine. Others get angry and the anger can burn for hours. What sometimes is amusing is how the slow-to-recover person gets angry at the quick-to-recover for getting over the anger so fast. The quick-to-recover person is accused of being uncaring or insensitive: "How *dare* you feel better before me?"

Of course this is ridiculous. Parents have differing temperaments that influence how they perceive and respond to stressful events. Some people are more sensitive than others. Some are quick to recover from a stressful event while others can take hours. If two people in an automobile narrowly avoid an accident, it is common for them to have different reactions. One person may recover quickly from the near miss and act like nothing happened, while the other individual might continue to be upset for hours. The difference between the two passengers is their nervous systems and different recovery rates to stress.

Your children may want to avoid you if you are slow to recover from your anger. This may be unfair, but children want everything to return to normal as soon as possible after a parent explodes. They live by the simple principle: When uncomfortable, avoid—even if that means a parent. A parent who has trouble recovering from anger would benefit from learning any one of many relaxation techniques.

Children, too, have different recovery rates. Parents can recognize how their children recover from and react to stress at a very young age. Some children are so sensitive that everything bothers them, while other children appear impervious. Sensitive children will have difficulty recovering from their parent's anger and maybe even adjusting to the divorce. They are easily hurt and frightened. Such children exposed to their parent's anger before an exchange may continue to feel the fear for days. The unsuspecting parent is then surprised to learn that they refuse to visit. Now the parent wants to blame the other parent for why the children don't want to visit, when the problem has to do with his own behavior. This is why it is important for a parent to make up after getting angry with the child.

Children can learn to fear a parent after watching how the parent treats others, especially a sibling. An example is Aggie refusing to visit her mother because she has seen her mother slap and denigrate her brother. Though she has never been slapped herself, she feels protective of her brother and reasons that if she refuses to visit her mother, her brother will be protected. She may also learn to fear for her own safety. The unsuspecting mother does not realize that she caused her own estrangement. The other parent can use this to instill added fear in the children. If the children have legitimate reasons to fear a parent, this is not alienation.

How We Communicate Makes a Difference

Every communication has two primary parts: the topic (what we communicate) and the method (how we communicate). The topic might be the parenting time schedule, and the method is the tone of voice, the type of language, and the interruptions while the other person is speaking. Most arguments are not resolved because one or both individuals react to the delivery, not the topic. Thus, the real issue that stirs their emotional exchange is the method of communication, or how one talks to the other, which never gets resolved.

> TIP: When you hear pressured speech in either your own or the other person's voice, expect that neither will listen to the other.

Reasoning with someone who is loud and who communicates with pressured speech is difficult. If you are loud and angry, you always lose the argument because the other person will not listen to what you have to say or will walk away to avoid an argument. Instead of talking louder, which just raises your own frustration, focus on regaining control of your feelings, and suggest that you both step back and discuss the issue another time. For right now, ignore the topic of the argument.

Have you ever noticed that, after a heated argument, you and the other person often can later calmly talk to each other? Sometimes neither of you may even remember what you were arguing about; or, if you do remember, you agree that the issue was no big deal and didn't deserve the attention.

It usually helps to warn the other individual about your intention to back away from the fight when either of you has pressured speech. When backing off, assure the other individual that you will come back to the topic later, when you have had time to think about how to approach the topic and you are in more control of your own feelings. Below are some helpful methods of controlling the conversations.

- Control the tone and volume of your voice. Speak softly.
- If you expect problems with self-control, consider talking in a public place like a restaurant.
- Agree beforehand on the topic and stick to the issue.
- Avoid distractions with other issues.
- Avoid trying to recall the past. This never works, because the past is not the issue. Trying to get the other parent to agree with your interpretation or recall of the past only leads to blame and attacking. The issue is what the two of you are going to do differently in the future.

- Before the conversation, think about how you can accept responsibility for the problem and the solution.

- If you ask for something from your ex-spouse, expect to give up something in return. Exchanging favors must be fair; otherwise there will be resentment. If you ask for a change in parenting time, what are you willing to give in order to get cooperation? Fair exchanges—or giving to get—also works with your children.

- Many conflicts are not resolved because the parents have not agreed to the solution. Do not assume the other parent's passivity means agreement. It doesn't. When you believe you have an agreement, repeat back your understanding of the agreement and listen for the acknowledgment. If you do not have an agreement, keep talking or negotiate until you do.

Learning to negotiate is a difficult skill. The pointers above are intended to give you some idea of how to improve your communication skills. Knowing these will not make you proficient, but it should help. At minimum, you can look back at past conversations and recognize what you could have done differently.

You can prevent much of the risk of alienation and estrangement if you learn to control your anger and give your children no reason to fear you. An obsessed parent will gleefully use your anger against you. They will remind the children of your past behavior and see to it that their fear and hurt never heal, and any chance of atonement will fail. Think in terms of preventing your anger or hurt from becoming an issue, rather than worrying about whether your children will accept your apologies afterward.

Sometimes parents ask, "How do I know I am doing the right thing?" The answer is simple. Do what will reduce your child's anxiety. Be a source of comfort rather than fear or anxiety.

11

Common Alienating Tactics: Harassment

He calls me in the middle of the night, just laughs, and then hangs up.

Many parents complain about being harassed by their ex-spouse. Threats, sudden appearances at the front door, excessive phone calls, and showing up at unexpected locations is considered harassment. Harassment is sometimes subtle and other times explicit. Either way, if your child is aware of and frightened by your behavior, you and your child will become estranged. Further, you are giving the other parent an excellent opportunity to use your behavior to alienate; you play right into his hands ("See what your mother is doing to us?"). The harassing parent often fails to realize how her behavior can scare children, who may feel they are the target of the harassment. Subtle harassment can take many forms:

- Unannounced visits
- Demanding, frequent phone calls at unreasonable hours
- Forcing the other parent to wait to the exact minute before allowing the exchange of the children
- Listening from a telephone extension to your children's conversation with the other parent
- Making incessant demands upon or threats towards the other parent
- Making frequent changes in parenting times
- Insisting upon making excessive phone calls to your children.

The harassing parent typically denies any wrongdoing. They either make excuses for their behavior, blame the other parent, or complain that the ex-spouse is getting what he deserves. They do not see themselves as doing anything malicious. Instead, they see themselves as virtuous and loving parents who only want a relationship with their children. They are blinded by an obsession that the other parent is trying to interfere in their relationship with the children. Unfortunately, they can see neither that their behavior is hurting the children nor their own dysfunction.

Harassment is a vicious form of a power struggle between two people. Children, family members, and ex-spouses are all potential targets for the harasser. The harasser is an angry parent who believes he has been wronged by the ex-spouse's power to keep him from being involved with the children. He may be an obsessed parent who feels entitled to have whatever he asks. He has no tolerance for boundaries or rules that restrict his behavior.

To gain vindication, the harassing parent has an obsessive desire to destroy the other parent's power. Ironically, the harassing parent believes he, and not the ex-spouse, is the victim. Sometimes he is motivated by the desire to resolve ex-spousal pain or by the mistaken belief that he can reconcile with the ex-spouse. This doesn't work.

Harassment can escalate with the parent threatening and intimidating the targeted parent until she feels beaten down and succumbs to the harasser's demands. The harassing parent intimidates to win the power struggle. Sadly, this tactic sometimes works. After feeling beaten down, the victim may surrender to the harasser's demands, complaining, "It just isn't worth fighting anymore." The next step is returning to court.

Harassment is more complex than just one parent repeatedly annoying or attacking the other parent. Both parents believe they have been victimized by the other. Both feel frustrated by their belief that they have no power to stop or influence the other parent's behavior. The hostilities between the parents intensify while the children helplessly watch. The children are torn by not knowing where to place their loyalty. They will lean toward the parent who offers a sense of safety and security.

Most harassing parents assume that the children will sympathize with their position and pull away from the other parent. This is not always true; it depends on the children's perception and interpretation of both parents' behavior. The targeted parent usually tries to explain the harassing parent's behavior to the children. For a time, she may actually make excuses for the harassing parent because she wants to maintain a positive relationship between the child and harassing parent. Other times, the victim tries to gain the child's sympathy and understanding. The net effect is a mix between estrangement and aliention.

Sometimes a targeted parent will actually cause her own alienation from the children if the child sympathizes more with the harasser because of the victim's degrading comments or retaliation. It is to be expected that victims of harassment will get angry and later enraged. However, victims must contain their anger in the child's presence and use that energy to complain to the appropriate authority or their attorney. Both parents are risking alienation because it is difficult to predict which parent will gain the children's sympathy. Sometimes a child will identify with the perpetrator. This can be dangerous. This is how a child can learn that using power and even abusive behavior to get what they want is acceptable.

Harassment can escalate to an intensity that is frightening and even criminal. Harassers have been known to stalk their victims, peep into windows, and break into houses. They make excuses for their behavior, believing they are in the right. For example, a harasser who broke into his ex-spouse's home argued that he wanted to see if she left the children alone while she went out for the evening. He made the excuse that he was looking out for his children's welfare. Instead, his ex-wife and son were home. The two were scared to death when they heard someone climbing through the bedroom window.

Beth's Story

Beth's is a true story of terror that few parents will ever experience. This is her story in her own words. There was some liberty during the editing to clarify her statements. Though her name has been changed, she very much wanted others to hear her saga. She talks about the years after her divorce, her ex-husband's depravity, and the court's failure to protect her and her daughter. Her story begins describing one of many incidents through which her ex-husband tried to strike terror in her heart.

Beth talks about the phone call she received from her ex-husband, Joey. After answering the phone, she heard a gunshot.

> You hear it in the background. The phone dropped. No one was there. I remember hanging up the telephone thinking I would get another phone call back later with some other story [from Joey]. It was a couple hours later when I got the phone call from the police. They wanted to know if I had any contact with Joey that day. I told them about the phone call. The police know where I live. My only protection or at least what I thought was my only way of protecting myself [from Joey] is to make everyone aware of what was going on. To make the police aware. To make sure that everyone had protection

---

orders. I carried them with me everywhere. That was all that I had. It
didn't work.

Beth didn't think Joey had committed suicide, but still she feared
the worst. Joey was found, alive and well, hours later by the police.

It was the police's opinion that he killed himself, or he was
attempting to kill himself. Their concern was that at some point of
desperation, Joey was going to be coming after me to kill me. I was
working at the time, and they told me not to go to work. They told
me to stay home.

All I can remember was that I stayed in the house three days, and
the guy I was dating was staying there during the day. His cousin
stayed with us in the evenings until he had to go to work. The police
found [Joey's] car. [The police] determined from that that I was
probably okay, and I could leave [the house].

One of the things [my boyfriend and I] enjoyed was going out
dancing. So his cousin watched Christy, and we went to a dance club
and had something to eat. [At the club] I went into the girls' bathroom to go to the bathroom, and when I came out of the stall, Joey
was standing there in the bathroom. He just walked right in. I felt
terrified. He acted as if there was nothing wrong.

Joey had no respect for boundaries. Later the police went to Joey's
house and found

. . . handprints of blood all over his house. It went all the way out
the door of his house. He created this scene to be found. I don't
know if he thought I was going to go over there and see [the blood].
I wasn't going. He took something to stab his hand so that he would
have the blood he needed to create this scene.

Beth and her daughter Christy lived upstairs in an old wooden frame
house that was converted into a triplex. She lived on the third floor
believing she would be safe. The terror continued.

When I had my apartment, Joey would break in all the time. If I was
in the shower, he would open up the curtain. If I was sitting on the
toilet, he would walk into the bathroom and just look at me. Three
times I've had the locks changed on my apartment. The bolts were
supposed to go a certain way. I learned that the locks were not
installed the right way. He would get in with a credit card. It was

normal to have someone standing outside the bathroom to make sure
I was okay.

Beth was confused about how Joey was able to get into the apartment. The doors were locked, the windows nailed shut, and she lived on the third floor. The terror continued. She returned to court four times to have the protection orders updated. Joey's behavior continued.

"There were never any consequences given to him for breaking [protection orders]. It just didn't happen." Beth would come home finding the house in disarray, food taken from the refrigerator, and ". . .cookies sitting on a plate in the kitchen where he baked. . . ." Beth said, "there were no signs of breaking in. The police would say that I must have given him a key."

One night Beth was having an intimate moment with her boyfriend on her daughter's bed. Joey appeared out from under Christy's bed. Again she was startled and confused about how he entered her third-story, one-bedroom apartment, where her daughter slept in the bedroom and Beth slept on a pull-out couch. It should have been a safe haven. She explained,

> I had the locks changed and properly installed, and he was still getting in. I couldn't figure out how. He knew the conversations I had in my house. I didn't know how but I thought there was some sort of technology out there where he had a recording device where he was listening to me speaking on the telephone. He would repeat parts of my conversation. He would show up to pick up Christy for visits in my clothes. He would wear my clothes.

Beth was very careful talking to Joey because she was afraid of provoking his violence. She reasoned, "I had a court order saying that I had to be there to exchange visitation with someone that was physically abusing me, but the courts, in their eyes, thought that Christy's visitation and his rights to her visitation was more important than my safety, more important than Christy's safety. But anyway, I thought I was going crazy. It was normal for me to wake up when I was sleeping on the sofa and feel someone staring at me. He would be standing there."

The height of her terror occurred one night when Joey raped Beth with Christy in the next room. She had to struggle to contain her fear and rage so not to wake Christy. The dread of never knowing when he would again appear from nowhere lasted a couple of months until her boyfriend found "a hole in the ceiling." (She had never paid attention to the crawl space after she first moved into the apartment.)

I had never been up there other than when I first moved in, and I put a table up there that I wasn't using. It was like, where does this [crawl space] go? I told [my boyfriend] . . . there was nothing up there. He needed to crawl up there. To crawl up there, the ceiling was so high we had to do one of those back things where you put your back on one side [of the wall] and your feet [on the other side of the wall, and] go up the wall because I didn't have a ladder. There were no steps. That is how you got in and out, you slide a board [covering the crawl space opening] to the side when you crawled up in the hole. Now here [Joey] had—he was living in my attic all that time. He had his bed made. He had a pillow. He had food wrappers. This whole time I thought I was going crazy. He was just up in the attic. That is how he knew everything.

Beth and her grown daughter have gone on with their lives. Beth has remarried and was pregnant at the time of this interview. Joey lives many miles away and continues to obsess over Beth. He was never arrested. Even after the court learned about his behavior, he continued having visits. Now Christy is eighteen so visits are no longer an issue. Beth now at least has the satisfaction of knowing she wasn't crazy.

Beth's story is extreme, but makes the point that harassers can become abusers; they can become criminals. Most parents who harass are not dangerous, even when they are threatening. They become a pain, a nuisance, or an intruder. In the most severe cases, harassers, like abusers, can threaten to hurt or retaliate against you if you tell anyone about what they are doing. They depend on you saying nothing.

> TIP: If you believe you are a victim of harassment, keep a detailed log of times and dates for your attorney or for the police.

If you give into the harasser's demands, you are inadvertently encouraging the harassment. Your best protection and hope in stopping the harassment is to make your ex-spouse's behavior public. Talk to people who care and who are supportive. Beth had the right idea about making the abuse public, but no one believed her because of the absurdity of her story. Talk to your attorney, file a complaint with your local police, or speak to your therapist. Will your ex-spouse get angry? You can count on it. Harassers know that their ability to control and intimidate depends on your silence.

You should never tolerate harassment in any form. Harassers are abusers and may threaten to hurt you if you tell anyone about their behavior. The harasser rarely follows through with the threats. This is not to suggest that harassers cannot be dangerous. Some are dangerous if they have a history of violence and drug and/or alcohol abuse.

Your best protection against the harasser's threats is to report them to the authorities. If you file charges, do not drop them unless you are advised to do so by your attorney or by the prosecutor. After the harasser sees you are serious, they may beg for forgiveness, cajole, and make all kinds of promises. Listening to an abuser can be very confusing, because she will vacillate between promising to change and threatening you. Though she will sound—and perhaps really is, at the moment—sincere, do not take her word for it. Many of these individuals have severe personality disorders that require professional help: help you can't provide.

In addition, when alcohol or drug use is involved, the risks are even greater that you could be hurt. This is even more reason to report the behavior. The problem with harassers and abusers is their lack of control over how they behave. They have more self-control if they know that the police, a probation officer, a therapist, or someone they perceive as having authority is watching or monitoring their behavior. Of course, this is no guarantee, but it helps.

Most parents considered to be harassers argue that they only want to see or have a relationship with their children. In most cases, this is true. A power struggle ensues between the parent who has the power because of the ability to say "no" and the other parent who feels powerless and frustrated.

When the parents cannot resolve these issues, the court orders must be very specific. Court orders saying "liberal visitation" are asking for trouble when parents cannot communicate or work together. Specific court orders do not negate the possibility of parents changing parenting time or visits if both parents agree and work together.

12

The Values War: Parenting Time and Discipline as the Battlefield

How could you expose our children to your slutty girlfriend? We aren't even divorced.

Nowhere is the battle between two parents more apparent than differences in values and parenting. Criticism is fired back and forth with accusations of incompetence and threats that you will never see your children again. All parents want to believe that their children in time will ascribe to their values. Some parents are very traditional while others hold more liberal views. One parent is a despot; the other the Disneyland parent. Each argues that he or she is the better parent.

There are two requirements for working with an alienated child: access to the child and effective parenting. Perhaps well-meaning judges, alienating parents, or significant others will resist access to the children, believing that time heals all and the best approach is to just wait until the child is ready to initiate parenting time. This rarely, if ever, happens. Waiting for the child living in an alienating mother's household to say out of the blue, "Now I am ready to see Dad," thus incurring the alienating mother's displeasure, is asking too much of a child. Again, it just will not happen. For children, it is easier to avoid a possible confrontation than say, "I want to see my dad." (Remember, this example can be also true for the mother.)

Combating alienation will not happen by doing nothing. The parent must have access to the child to repair the damaged relationship. The only exception is having good reason to believe that an unsupervised visitation or parenting time puts the child's safety is at risk. The child's safety—not necessarily the child's happiness—must always be a first consideration.

The Secret of Building a Positive Relationship with Your Children

Both parents can cultivate the power to influence their children without degrading the other parent or causing the children to feel a divided loyalty. Effective parenting begins with the power to influence your children's behavior and values. Threats and excessive punishment can influence your children's behavior simply because they fear you, but compliance because of fear is not long lasting. Rarely does such behavior influence children to become "true believers" in the values you are trying to instill. On the other hand, if your children value your relationship because of what you give them to feel good about themselves, they will more likely ascribe to your values about what is right and wrong. Children should want to obey because they want to please and maintain a relationship with the people they love.

The difficulty combating alienation is your not having any control over what the other parents does or says to your children. You are in a helpless situation, especially if you and your ex-spouse cannot talk to each other. You may ask, "What am I supposed to do when I know that my ex-spouse is saying derogatory things about me to the kids?" The answer to this question is simple but, for some parents, hard to do. You must learn to trust, and continue to build your relationship with, your children. A solid relationship is your best protection against the other parent's efforts to alienate. Although young children are easily influenced by what they hear, their critical parent's words will have less impact when their actual experience with you contradicts those words. Older children are even more likely to make judgments based on personal experience rather than hearsay.

TIP: When a child is telling you a blatant lie told by the other parent, gently confront the child with the truth without suggesting that the other parent is lying. Remind the child that both parents may see things differently. Tell your child, "What is important is your personal experience rather than what you are told by Mom or Dad."

Building a stronger relationship with your children—and anyone for that matter—is a process that begins with a simple concept: People like to be with a person who makes them feel good. Anyone who makes your children feel good about themselves has power. This means more than treating your child to ice cream every night, heaping flattery upon her, or saying yes when your good judgment tells you to say no. It means treating the child over time with respect and love but knowing how and when to establish limits. Other people cannot build the relationship for you. There is no replacement for the time you spend with your children.

Discipline

> *"I don't dare discipline my kids. If I do, they'll run to their mother and complain about what a bastard I am. I'll never see them again."*

Differences in how and when to discipline can accentuate the differences in the parents' values. Parents may differ on household rules, when and how to punish, or what is considered a lack of respect. The statement reflects the fear many parents have about disciplining their children after a separation or divorce. You may have sincere differences of option from your ex-spouse about discipline. The custodial parent, usually the mother, sometimes feels cheated because she thinks she has majority of the responsibility for raising the kids while their father is irresponsible, the "good guy" who can't do anything but show the kids a good time. Mom has to be the bad guy, laying down the law. Dad is sometimes envious of the time his ex-spouse has with the children. Little things like helping the kids with their homework, getting them off to school, and taking them to the doctor are activities many dads would like to do if they had the kids during the week.

> TIP: Children adjust best when both parents work as a team and protect them from adversity.

Behind one parent's envy of the other parent is often insecurity about his own ability to influence the children and to remain loved. This is especially true when alienation is involved. The targeted parent becomes insecure because of his belief that he cannot overcome the damaging influences of the alienating parent's brainwashing, especially when they see the children only every other weekend.

Like all parents, you want to trust your relationship with your children. You want to be able to correct them, discipline, and if necessary, punish them without fearing reprisal. You want to know that your children are not going to run to the other parent and complain every time they do not get what they want. You want your household rules to reflect your values without the threat of criticism or, worse yet, losing your child's affections.

Effective discipline begins with you having a strong and loving relationship with your children. Your children look to you as a model for how to behave. If you smoke, your children will more likely smoke; if you hit and swear, they are more likely to hit and swear; and if you denigrate the other parent, they are more likely to denigrate. Your children learn by observing your behavior. The question for you is, "Do you like what your children see?"

EXERCISE: SHARING THE PRIDE

Your children need to know that you are proud of them. List five reasons why you are proud of your child(ren).

1. _____
2. _____
3. _____
4. _____
5. _____

When is the last time you told your children these reasons you feel proud? If it has been awhile, try sharing your feelings in the next week. Your children need to hear your excitement and pride.

> *TIP: If you are not a warm and fuzzy parent and have trouble expressing love and affection, consider buying greeting cards to convey your feelings. Some parents buy a number of cards and save them for the right time. This is also a good idea for your new significant other.*

Discipline Is Vital to Good Parenting

Let us be realistic. Sometimes children are mouthy and defiant. Sometimes you will answer in anger and say things to your children that should not be said. You are not Mr. Rogers or Captain Kangaroo. You are expected to have rules, and consequences for your child violating your rules. Like all parents, you will make mistakes. You will lose your cool and hopefully next time step back to figure out how better to react.

Striving to improve your children's behavior is a big part of being a parent. When your children fall short of your standards for good behavior, you may feel like a failure. You are not a failure. You simply have to do more parenting. Moreover, no one does it perfectly.

Approaches to discipline vary, and no psychologist can say with certainty that one method is clearly the best for all children. However, experts agree that the goal of all disciplinary measures should be to teach appropriate behavior, respect for others, and self-control. Is your approach accomplishing this goal? Now might be a good time to rethink certain practices, especially if your ex-spouse, a court-appointed psychologist, or anyone else is questioning your parenting skills and ability to manage children without abusing them. This author found in an unpublished study (1993) that an alienating parent's criticism of the targeted parent is extremely common, usually a rationalization for the alienating parent to criticize the targeted parent. The question to be answered with any discipline is whether the discipline achieves the desired results. If not, why continue doing what doesn't work? You must change your approach. If you don't know what to do differently, ask a professional.

TIP: Discipline is a job for both parents.

Children need discipline from both of their parents. They need loving adults to set limits and put on the brakes when their behavior exceeds limits. Without a safety net, children become frightened and insecure unless they feel a parent's presence to keep them from going out of control. The parent does not need to be in the children's physical presence to convey a sense of control. They can feel your presence even if you are in another room. Even though your rules and methods are not identical to those of the other parent, *both* parents are responsible for disciplining children.

Structure is important. Children feel more secure in homes in which the rules and boundaries are clearly defined. They may not always like your rules; they may fight you or blatantly disregard your rules. However, if your rules are fair and consistently enforced, your children will not only adjust to the rules but will feel reassured that you care enough about them to keep them in line. It is possible to provide structure without being draconian. Bend the rules when the circumstances warrant it. Most parents are not as consistent as you may think at following through with consequences.

Why Do Many Noncustodial Parents Hesitate to Discipline Their Children?

Discipline is difficult for many noncustodial parents. They want the parental responsibilities, yet feel threatened by the prospect of estranging the children. The child's words, "I'm going to tell Mommy on you," and the fear that the child will run to the other parent and tell horrendous stories can set the stage for manipulation. The greatest threat is that of false allegations of abuse. Do not let this threat intimidate you from disciplining your children.

What do you do if your angry children exaggerated tales to others that make reasonable attempts at discipline sound abusive or neglectful? This is a fear of many noncustodial parents. You might not only suffer your ex's fury, but quite possibly be investigated by social services at your ex's request. Again, do not let the children intimidate you. If you believe your discipline was appropriate and you maintained self-control, then trust the love and respect you and your children have for each other and do not be defensive. On the other hand, if you lose control and have to defend your punishment, think about getting help. You could lose control again.

> TIP: Do not always believe what your child tells you about the other parent's discipline. Children, like adults, will exaggerate or distort reality when they are angry.

The threat of a false allegation by an obsessed parent is a frightening prospect for any parent. The threat is very real for young children who complain to the alienating parent about being spanked or disciplined. The child's account of the discipline or spanking can be distorted in a manner that later confuses the child into believing that he was abused, when in fact abuse did not occur. Now the child is taught by the alienating parent to fear the targeted parent, who may not even know what is happening. All the targeted parent knows is that the child wants nothing to do with her. If the alienating parent is successful in getting a court order to cut off all contact between the frightened child and targeted parent, the targeted parent is now helpless in preventing any further damage or repairing the relationship. The child is now isolated and dependent upon the alienating parent's influences. The alienating parent has total control to manipulate the child's memories to fit his agenda. The best defense is for the targeted parent to keep the relationship strong with the children and have an intervention to subdue the alienating parent's tactics. This can only happen if the parent has maximum access to the children and the court appropriately intervenes. Isolating the children from the targeted parent diminishes any hope for repairing the damage from a false allegation.

> TIP: Isolating the alienated child from the targeted parent without a reunification plan will only cause further damage.

Many noncustodial parents think, "If I don't criticize or correct my kids, and if I make sure I befriend them and make every visit fun, they won't turn against me." They are in for a rude awakening. Parents are not doing their children any good by being their "best friend." In fact, be careful about being a best friend. Your kids have friends at school and in their neighborhood. They need you to be the parent they can depend on and look up to, especially when they are already confused by the divorce and unsure about how to behave in your presence. Treating your children as best friends tends to cause friction between you and your ex-spouse.

TIP: Resist the temptation to use your children as confidantes and say more to them than is appropriate for them to hear. Doing otherwise will place a tremendous burden on your children.

Don't Let Your Children Manipulate You

Children are expert manipulators. Manipulation is not always bad if no one is hurt. When no one is hurt, manipulation can be a good social skill. When we interview for a new job and present our best foot forward, are we not trying to manipulate the employer's perceptions? Of course we are. Anytime we consciously modify our behavior to influence another for a desired outcome, we are manipulating. The issue is whether the manipulation is damaging like distorting the truth to harm another.

Children will take advantage when they sense that you are uncertain or insecure. In the absence of clear limits, predictable consequences, and consistent parental guidance to feel safe and secure, children instinctively try to gratify their immediate desires. You cannot blame them for trying, but that is not to say that you must yield to their demands. Without malice or much forethought, children will nag, pout, throw tantrums, feign illness, or make it look as if they're about to embarrass you in front of half the population of your hometown if they think that will get them what they want. They have an uncanny ability to threaten you with the very consequence you most fear: public embarrassment.

Feeling powerless and frustrated by what appears to be the children's control, noncustodial parents worry that youngsters will refuse to visit. Custodial parents, on the other hand, fear their children asking to live elsewhere. As a result, they discipline tentatively at best. Some parents make weak threats that the children know will not be carried out. Others let things slide for hours and then blow their stacks; or they inappropriately punish and later feel guilty. To resolve the guilt the parent may "buy back" the child's affection with gifts or special treatment. Do not give in to those maneuvers. You are the grown-up, and your children are counting on you to provide them with structure, stability, and reasonable guidelines for living. Whether you are the parent in charge two days per month or twenty, you need to set aside your fear of being rejected by your offspring and learn to consistently and appropriately discipline them when discipline is called for.

Both custodial and noncustodial parents can be susceptible to their children's manipulations if they think that whatever they do with the children will be outweighed by what the other parent does better. Each fears that the other is more fun, patient, and loving. Either way, the problem is their not trusting their own relationship with the children.

> TIP: A child will have less success manipulating if he or she knows that both parents can calmly talk to each other, to compare stories.

Children who see their parents calmly talk to each other about their welfare are less likely to manipulate them. They know that their parents will compare notes about what they are doing. In addition, there is the added benefit of knowing that the children will be healthier and better adjusted. This mutual dialogue needs to be your goal. It may sound idealistic, but that does not negate the value to your children of seeing the two of you calmly talking.

Sissy and Her Children's Story

Sissy was an extreme example of a parent trying to be a friend to her daughter. She was a thirty-five-year-old mother of a son, Jason, age eleven, and a daughter, Becky, age fifteen. Sissy was enthralled with Becky's friends. She began dressing like a "biker" and "hung out" with Becky's teenage friends in the driveway until late at night. Neighbors began complaining to the police because of the noise. She was often seen riding around the community with a teenage boy driving his family car. Most of the time, Becky was nowhere in sight. When Sissy's husband, Andrew, was out of town on business, Sissy allowed as many as four teenagers to spend the night. Neighbors talked among themselves about all the cars parked in the driveway overnight. They complained to her and Andrew about the noise and the cars speeding down the street. Sissy was angry and contemptuous towards the complaining neighbors.

When Andrew realized that Sissy was not going to change, he felt responsible and concerned for the children. He had no choice but to get a divorce. Initially, Becky lived with her mother and Jason with his father. Sadly, Sissy embarrassed Becky and Jason by continuing to befriend the teenage boys. The children felt protective towards Sissy but were confused because they knew her behavior was inappropriate. Sissy's behavior caused her to lose custody of her children. A year later, Becky learned that her mother had become pregnant by one of her young friends. Sissy decided to keep the child.

How Children Benefit from Discipline

Consistency Helps Children Feel Secure

Children need structure with predictable rules and consequences. Most parents are not very consistent. Everyone gives in at times to their children's nagging, but they keep trying. Your children need to know what you expect from you. They need to see you react to various circumstances in a logical, consistent manner so that they can predict your future responses with a reasonable amount of accuracy and adjust their behavior accordingly. Parents actively alienating have the most difficulty with consistency when it comes to co-parenting issues. The children need to realize that if they do X (misbehave), they can expect Y (a negative consequence). When they learn to trust that Y consistently happens, they will likely refrain from misbehaving to prevent further punishment. The same goes for positive consequences. Children learn that desirable behaviors produce desirable outcomes if parents routinely reward or encourage appropriate behavior. Rewarding positive behavior is more powerful than punishing inappropriate behavior.

EXERCISE: IDENTIFYING REWARDS

For each child, list on a sheet of paper the most effective ways you reinforce or reward the child for positive behavior. What works for one child may not work for another. If you cannot come up with five rewards, you have work to do. You are missing tremendous opportunities to influence your child's behavior into behavior that is more desirable.

Consistency does not require absolute uniformity. You do not have to respond exactly the same way every time your ten-year-old talks back or your six-year-old shows you an arts and crafts project he made. Many parents worry that the children's psychological health depends on *both* parents being consistent in the rules and values. Their worry is unnecessary.

Children learn to discriminate how to behave with each parent. Outbursts that come out of nowhere, rules ignored one minute and rigorously enforced the next, promised rewards not delivered, and other inconsistencies in one person's parenting methods can produce anxious, untrusting, and insecure children. In the above examples, the child cannot predict the parent's behavior, because the parent is unpredictable.

TIP: Children need consistency within parents, not between parents.

Children Learn to Discriminate

Children learn to size up new situations and adjust their behavior according to each set of rules and expectations. They know to behave differently with teacher A, the disciplinarian; and teacher B, the more lenient teacher. To stay out of trouble, they learn to adjust their behavior to suit each teacher's standards. Discriminating between ways to behave is healthy and necessary to survive in the adult world: You will behave differently with your best friend than with your grandmother. The same holds true for your children when they encounter different rules or expectations in each of their divorced parents' homes. In all likelihood, your children are already aware of the discrepancies between your values and their other parent's. They know, for instance, that the consequences for misbehaving will vary depending on which parent catches them.

Differences in the parents' values can be seen before the separation. These differences can influence how a parent parents and influence a parent's ability to bond with the children. Jeffrey's father is a good example of someone who valued making money over spending time with his son. After the separation he paid the price. A parent's values before the separation are likely to remain the same after the divorce. An exception is the father who realizes, after the divorce, the importance of having a loving relationship with the children. He may be accused of being a superdad, implying that his behavior is insincere and manipulative. This change of heart is often sincere when a father now feels the loss of his children. Rather than questioning the father's motivation, it is in the child's best interest to accept the change and encourage improving relationship.

Jeffrey and His Father's Story

Jeffrey's father was a very hard-working and successful physician who believed that his wife caused the impaired relationship with his son through her alienating behavior. Jeffrey did not want to spend time with his father even though his father was only asking for weekend dinners. Jeffrey felt that the conversations were strained and boring. Unable to imagine why his son would feel that way, Jeffrey's father was angry and bitter that his wife did not remind their son of his sacrifices for the family. He had the irrational belief that his wife was responsible for keeping his relationship with their son strong. During a reunification session, the suggestion was made to teach his son how to drive, believing that the interaction would help strengthen the relationship. The father answered, "That is too dangerous. Let his mother teach him." He had no concept about how to build a relationship. He felt that being close to his son was an entitlement because of all that he had done for the family.

Rational Belief: An emotional bond is not an entitlement; it is earned.

TIP: Reward your children for what they do right.

Discipline Defined

Discipline is not physical or mental punishing, as is commonly thought. *To discipline* means to instruct someone to follow a particular code of conduct, or to adhere to a certain "order," or to adopt a particular pattern of behavior and be a follower from example.

Therefore, discipline is more than punishing misbehavior. You also shape character, teach values, and motivate kids to do their best by rewarding what they do right. By praising their accomplishments, encouraging them to try new endeavors, correcting their mistakes without intimating that they are bad, and showing you love them no matter what they do, you help them feel good about themselves. The seeds of positive self-esteem you plant now will serve your children throughout their lives, enabling them to take risks, bounce back from disappointment, make healthy choices, and more. Never lose sight of their positive qualities, their natural exuberance, their compassion, creativity, agility, adaptability, and other attributes. Take the time to admire your children for who they are and to appreciate whatever they do well at their present stage of development. If you do, you will not have to worry about disciplinary measures driving a wedge between you and your children. Your kids will still look forward to seeing you.

A Comparison of Two Families

To help better understand the importance of having a balance between discipline and positive rewards, let us contrast two fictitious families. The Discontents have serious problems with their children, who fight, disobey rules, and isolate themselves from the rest of the family. The children from the Glad family have their typical problems with children growing up. They are mostly well behaved, relish being part of the family, and obey the household rules with minor infractions. So what makes the Glads and the Discontents different?

If you could sneak behind the walls of these two families' homes, you would see differences in how the parents relate to the children. If you could observe one hundred interactions between Mr. and Mrs. Discontent and their children, you could expect that about 70 percent of the interactions were negative or of a corrective nature, while 30 percent were positive. Because of the number of negative interactions, the children find it more comfortable to avoid their parents than to interact with them. The parents, in effect, lose power to influence the children because the parents have become an aversive presence for the children. This is seen with many youth having severe behavior problems. Sometimes adults complaining about the rise in juvenile crime question why these children are not disciplined. The answer is frequently that they *are* disciplined, excessively, to the point of abuse. What is missing are both parents attending every soccer game, someone sitting down with the children to help with homework or a school project, or sitting down together for dinner. Sadly, uneducated parents, poverty, children having children, children "parenting" children, children with mental health problems, and a drug culture all contribute to the problem. There are well-meaning parents who are overwhelmed by the demands of single parenthood or under- or unemployment, who do the best they can. These parents deserve the community's support and assistance.

The circumstances with the Glad family are different. With these parents, 70 percent of the interactions are positive and 30 percent are negative or corrective. Parents like Mr. and Mrs. Glad have the power to help their children to feel valued. The Glads build on the children's self-esteem rather than tear it down. They are active parents who always know their children's whereabouts, know the children's friends and their parents by name, help with homework, attend school conferences and extracurricular activities, and share parenting responsibilities with the other parent. If fathers are absent from the home, the father's presence is still welcomed.

You may ask how Mr. and Mrs. Discontent can ignore the children's misbehavior. They cannot. What they must do instead is make a concerted effort to spend more time that is positive with the children so they can change the proportion or balance of positive-to-negative interactions. Discontents typically ignore the children when they are behaving themselves instead of taking advantage of the opportunity to spend positive time together.

An analogy may help you understand the differences between the Glads' and the Discontents' parenting style. Take a moment to remember a former supervisor or teacher who was very punitive and critical of your performance. While you may have conformed to the individual's demands for fear of being chastised or, worse yet, publicly reprimanded, you did no more than was necessary to survive. However, the real question is, "Would you invite this person to your home or ascribe to his values?" Of course not! Now consider another situation. Hopefully, you have also had a supervisor or teacher who made you feel valued. She praised you and made you feel important. You felt her support or caring when in her presence. Did you want to please this supervisor or teacher? Is it also true that your supervisor was able to discipline or correct you? The answer is yes. You will be more likely to share this supervisor's values or want to socialize with her because of how you value each other. Do you understand the point? Now apply what you have learned to your children, and even your ex-spouse. Everyone will be better off.

Excessive Punishment, and Failure to Use Age-Appropriate Discipline

Avoid Excessive Punishments

Causing bodily harm, isolating children for long periods of time, depriving them of food or water, or causing them to feel degraded and humiliated are all inappropriate and abusive. Many child-rearing experts frown upon any form of physical punishment, under any circumstances. They believe that inflicting physical pain teaches children that it is okay to hit or hurt people when angry. Parents who hit may get short-term obedience, but many experts say that physical punishment breeds future violence and aggression. Besides, there are more effective forms of discipline. Other psychologists see nothing wrong with an occasional controlled smack on the hand or swat on the butt. Control is essential, however. Lashing out in a moment of fury or frustration does not build character. Hitting because you have run out of patience or can no longer contain pent-up emotions is abusive. If you lose control while spanking a youngster, seek help. I am amazed to hear parents say they spanked their children because the child would not stop crying. Do they really expect a child to stop crying while being spanked?

If you must spank, do not use belts, paddles, switches, or other weapons, because you have no way of knowing how hard you are hitting. Because you are not getting feedback on the amount of pain you are causing, you are more likely to injure your child. What's more, the only reason for using these implements is to inflict additional pain, and any parent who sets out to hurt her children needs to examine her motives and take immediate steps to change the way she parents. Threats, especially absurd threats such as, "I'll get new kids who love me" or "You'll never see Grandma again," should never occur. These threats serve no constructive purpose.

Some parents use threats and excessive punishments to scare their children into compliance. But fear is an ineffective teacher. Although it will keep kids in line on a day-to-day basis, they will rarely become true believers to the values you ascribe; in fact, they are more apt to reject or rebel against your values. Because your children are not internalizing your standards and adhering to them for their own sake, you believe you have to continue threatening and punishing to get your message across. This rarely works.

You will be more effective by capitalizing on your natural power to influence children's values and behaviors. That power stems from the strength of your relationship with your children and their desire to please you rather than fear.

Use Age-Appropriate Discipline

Your expectations for how your child behaves and how you discipline must be age appropriate. Punishing a one-year-old for holding his spoon incorrectly is pointless. There is no incentive, threat, or bribe that can make him do what he is not yet developmentally ready to do. Likewise, having a fifteen-year-old sit in a time-out chair because she stayed out past curfew is ludicrous. Time-out is not just a discipline but a tool for helping young children to learn self-control. Grounding or taking away a privilege is a more logical consequence for an out-of-line adolescent. Likewise, sitting down and discussing rules, negotiating penalties, and drawing up behavior contracts works well with teens and older children but not with younger ones who have a limited cognitive ability to plan or anticipate their behavior.

Four Disciplinary Practices That Cause Problems for Divorced Parents

Divorced parents must deal with the same discipline challenges as any other parent, plus a few special issues unique to divorced parents. These problems can lead to arguments and alienation if not handled carefully.

First Mistake: Trying to Impose Your Rules on the Other Parent

Remember the earlier discussion about consistent rules and values between parents? Does it logically follow that "My rules are better than your rules, so let's raise the children my way"? Such a statement may sound absurd, but it reflects how many parents feel. Believing your rules and values are better than the other parent's will cause a power struggle with no winners. After the divorce is final, one parent does not want to be told by the other parent how to raise the children. Doing so causes a lot of resentment.

A parent who alienates generally wants total control and has a strong need to dictate how to raise the children. The parent sincerely believes that his approach to parenting is best. Of course, the targeted parent is not easily convinced. Why should she be convinced? Just imagine how angry and resentful you would feel if your former mate made up a list of rules and disciplinary practices and expected you to follow them. Such an arrangement is unreasonable, unrealistic, and unworkable unless both parents have an excellent working relationship.

If you question your ex-spouse's parenting and you feel you really must say something, tactfully ask your ex-spouse if she would like a constructive suggestion. If she says "no," you should say no more. Saying no means the parent may be too fragile to hear what you have to say. You can prevent a fight by respecting a person's right to say no. Perhaps another day will be better.

You can ask diplomatically. For example, instead of just blurting out unsolicited criticism, try saying something like, "Sandy's really been argumentative lately, hasn't she? She is tough to deal with sometimes. But would you like a suggestion that I have found helpful?" Seeking the person's permission for the feedback gives her more of a sense of control and power. This way, your ex-spouse is less likely to get defensive and feel attacked.

Second Mistake: Letting the Children Run Wild During Visits

Marge and Wally's Story

Marge, the divorced mother of three elementary-school-aged sons, complains that, "after a weekend with their dad, my boys are completely out of control. At his house, they have no set bedtimes or mealtimes. They bathe if they feel like it, wear anything they want to, and don't have to pick up after themselves. Naturally, when they get home from their forty-eight-hour free-for-all, they're not the least bit interested in following my rules. All I hear is 'Dad lets us do this,' and 'Dad doesn't make us do that.' Wally's house is a full-service motel and amusement park. Mine's a prison. He's their pal. I'm the warden. I spend half the week trying to get the boys back on track, and when I finally do, they go on another visit!"

When children are exposed to different family cultures with different rules, they need time to adjust when they return home. It does you no good to blame the other household for the children's disruptive behavior. Blame contributes to, rather than relieves, your frustration. This is a parenting issue.

Children need structure and familiar routines. They need limits and a clear idea of what to expect from you. If you are the noncustodial parent, there is no faster way to make an enemy of your former mate than to impose no structure on your offspring during visits. Moreover, you are deluding yourself believing that your children will respect you. You will lose more control and influence as the children get older.

If you are a custodial parent who struggles to rein in your children after visits with their noncustodial parent, you probably share Marge's frustration. You may picture your youngsters doing whatever they please during those visits and envy your ex's fun, fun, fun relationship with the kids. Or you may resent being cast as the bad guy when you try to settle them down. Perhaps you have started to dread parenting time. If you feel furious at your former mate, it would certainly be understandable. After all, the entire burden of teaching values, socially acceptable behavior, and basic life skills should not fall on your shoulders. On the other hand, if you and your ex-spouse cannot talk, you will have to trust the strength of your relationship with the children to influence their behavior. Consider counseling if you are overwhelmed.

Helping Children Adjust after a Visit

Some children have difficulty adjusting to changes forced upon them by visits. Upon return, they may be restless and unruly. Such behavior is not always the fault of the noncustodial parent. Some children have trouble adjusting to any change. They squawk about going to bed or getting off the couch. Nothing you can do will make them happy. To help lessen the blow, give your children a warning in advance that a change is forthcoming. Let them complain and moan. When the time comes to make the change, be firm but compassionate. You do not have to yell or get upset. Most important, stay calm and remind yourself that you do not have to always be responsible for their happiness. Many parents easily forget that your goal at this point is compliance and not happiness. If you remember this, you will get less upset by your child's whining.

Third Mistake: Being a Harsh Weekend Disciplinarian

Problems can arise when a noncustodial parent believes her ex is a lax disciplinarian and tries to compensate by being extra strict during visits. Whether the strict parent is terrified that the children will grow up to be criminals, or is convinced that constant vigilance and harsh punishments are proof of parental love and competence, she devotes virtually every moment of her parenting time to breaking the children's supposedly bad habits and teaching them to behave properly according to her unusually high standards. In her mind, the urgency of her mission to shape character in the brief amount of time available to her justifies the severe and cease-less disciplinary measures she employs. "Sure, making Joey scrub the entire bathroom with a toothbrush is a little harsh," the harsh parent says, "but letting him become an inconsiderate slob who forgets to wipe out the tub after showering would be worse. This will teach him."

Unfortunately, there is a good chance that this parent's behavior will estrange her from her son. If you try to compress a year's worth of disci-pline into two weekends a month, you're apt to come off as harsh, rigid, hypercritical, and barely human. Your kids could very well learn to hate you. Certain that she is doing what's best for her youngsters, this drill-sergeant type of parent is perplexed and hurt when the children start com-plaining and refusing to visit. Such parents are blinded by their good intentions. They are sure their kids know how much the parents love them ("Why else would I devote so much time to setting them straight?"). They also believe they deserve thanks, not rejection, and accuse their former mate of turning the children against them, when the truth is that they are causing their own problems. They can't see that they are overly critical and punitive, and they get angry when someone points out how the children are reacting or when someone questions their parenting skills. In their eager-ness to raise perfect children, super-strict parents lose sight of the fact that no one, young or old, likes to be around someone who constantly criticizes.

Karl the Weekend Drill Sergeant's Story

Karl took his parenting responsibilities very seriously. He never missed a support payment or an opportunity to be with his kids. Every Friday Karl eagerly picked up his five children, who ranged in age from three-and-a-half to ten. The two oldest children started complaining to their mother about not wanting to visit. "Dad is mean. He calls us crybabies and stupid," said Vince. "He makes us watch the other kids," Jessica reports, "and if they're bad, we get punished." One weekend they both had to write, "I will set a good example for my brothers and sisters" one hundred times. "We couldn't eat supper until we were finished," Vince states. And when Jessica complained, their father took away the sentences they'd already written and made them start over.

The mother, Jamie, was angry and felt protective as her children tearfully described their ordeal. Immediately, she was on the phone with Karl, angrily attacking his insensitivity. Karl counterattacked, feeling defensive and sincere in his love for the children. He claimed that he was strict because of their mother's laxity: "You let them get away with anything." The fight escalated until Jamie threatened to take Karl back to court. She hung up while Karl was still talking. Karl was angry and scared of the threat, but willing to fight her in court.

Karl is out of line with his parenting. He believes the children get no discipline from their mother—and maybe that is true—but he cannot make up for twenty-four days at their mother's with four days of harsh discipline, without paying a serious price with the children. He is being irrational. He probably rationalizes his behavior saying that is how a competent parent should discipline.

Although children need structure and limits and consistently enforced consequences, that's not all they need. And if all they get is rules, restrictions, lectures, threats, and punishments from a parent who can't seem to be anything but harsh and critical, they'll want to avoid that parent. After all, children are not stupid. They will naturally gravitate towards the parent who, through a mixture of encouragement and instruction, helps them feel confident, competent, and good about themselves. Be realistic. You are not going to cram all of your values and discipline into your children during two weekend visits a month. They should leave the visits feeling good about you and the time they spent with you, not thinking, "Boy, am I glad to be outta there!"

Fourth Mistake: Blaming Your Ex-Spouse for Everything Your Child Does Wrong

Divorced parents tend to be quick to blame their ex-spouse for any undesirable changes in their children's behavior. "If you weren't so critical [lenient, busy at work, wrapped up with your new boyfriend, etc.]," they claim, "then Billy wouldn't be fighting on the playground [failing French, wetting his bed, picking on his sisters, and so on]." Naturally, the accused parent feels attacked, denies the allegations, becomes defensive, and retaliates in some fashion.

Always blaming bad behavior on the other parent's parenting or the divorce itself has a similar effect. Believing in these explanations not only blinds you to other reasons your children might be acting up but can also lead to totally unnecessary arguments. You could even end up back in court only to discover that the changes in your child's behavior were typical for his age and not signs of post-traumatic stress or mistreatment by your ex.

TIP: *You must take into consideration the child's age and maturity when teaching values. What you teach a five-year-old will be different from what you teach a ten-year-old.*

You will witness many changes in your child's behavior as she matures. Children mature at different rates. They will go through relatively placid phases during which they are compliant and eager to please, as well as tumultuous stages when they are more often than not moody and defiant. You will tangle with tantrum-throwers, toddlers who say no to everything, argumentative adolescents, and more. In fact, it will sometimes seem that, just when you have adjusted to one set of quirks, your children take on an entirely new cache of bewildering characteristics. That is how children are. A former teacher on child development who influenced my early career choice (and parenting) summed up the issue clearly: "Even under the best of circumstances, kids go a little nuts every six months or so." Coping with their ever-changing needs, interests, and sensitivities comes with the territory of parenthood.

TIP: *Effective parenting is your responsibility, not your ex-spouses'. If needed, attend a parenting class, read a good parenting book or talk to a counselor. Don't let your pride get in the way from seeking help.*

Good Relationships Are Built Deliberately

Building a relationship does not happen by accident. Most effective parents are conscious of what they are doing to strengthen their relationship with their children. They can tell you specific ways they build rapport and let the children know they are loved. The more support and praise you give another person, the more support and praise you will receive in return. This is true for both your children and your ex-spouse.

There is a value for you and your children in improving your relationship with your ex-spouse. Everyone benefits. If your fourteen-year-old son's father helps him with a scouting project, express your appreciation. Let your children's full-time parent know how well behaved they were when you took them out to dinner or how terrific they looked when you came to pick them up for a visit. Making a conscious effort to give credit to the other parent when it's due will improve the co-parenting relationship. Moreover, that will rub off on your children. After all, former mates are human; and like all humans, they are inclined to continue behaviors that are recognized and rewarded. Thus, praising positive parenting brings more of the same and also reduces resentments.

Learning Childhood Development Can Prevent Misunderstandings

Children go through predictable developmental stages. If you learn about those developmental milestones, you will know what you can reasonably expect from children of various ages. Reading books and attending workshops on child development or effective parenting can teach you many things. There are books describing stages of moral development, cognitive development, psychosexual stages, and social development. Your local library or the Internet can lead you to some excellent resources.

The resources will also show you that some problems aren't anyone's fault. In addition to helping you differentiate between behavior that's normal at a particular stage of development and problem behavior that requires special attention, books and courses on child development usually offer sound advice and suggestions for handling special circumstances such as divorce.

Parents are usually good about taking time to learn about their children's development when they are infants and toddlers. However, after the children turn five or six, many parents spend less time learning about their children's development and more time complaining. This is the reason there are so many baby books and few books about older children, particularly about adolescence. When problems start, parents are quick to blame the other parent rather than trying to learn if the misbehavior is typical for their child's age. Trying to learn about a child's normal development can prevent a lot of mislaid blame on the other parent. It is recommended that you get professional help if you cannot get answers from others, and your children's misbehavior persists and begins to cause other family problems.

EXERCISE: RELATIONSHIP BUILDING

The purpose of this exercise is to enhance your sensitivity and awareness of the other parent's strengths as a parent. Time yourself while completing this exercise. When you are ready to begin, write down five examples of what you consciously do to help build the relationship between your children and their other parent. If you have not completed your list in ten minutes, quit. Write the time you took to complete the exercise in the space provided at the end of your list.

1. _____
2. _____
3. _____
4. _____
5. _____

Time: _____

After you finish reading this book, you might want to try this exercise again, listing ten items instead of five. You will be surprised how much faster and more easily you will complete the exercise the second time.

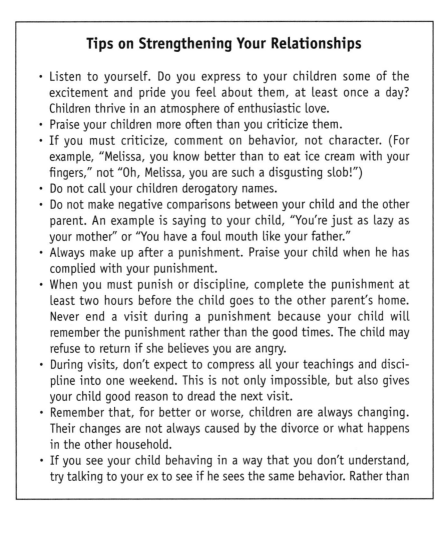

Tips on Strengthening Your Relationships

- Listen to yourself. Do you express to your children some of the excitement and pride you feel about them, at least once a day? Children thrive in an atmosphere of enthusiastic love.
- Praise your children more often than you criticize them.
- If you must criticize, comment on behavior, not character. (For example, "Melissa, you know better than to eat ice cream with your fingers," not "Oh, Melissa, you are such a disgusting slob!")
- Do not call your children derogatory names.
- Do not make negative comparisons between your child and the other parent. An example is saying to your child, "You're just as lazy as your mother" or "You have a foul mouth like your father."
- Always make up after a punishment. Praise your child when he has complied with your punishment.
- When you must punish or discipline, complete the punishment at least two hours before the child goes to the other parent's home. Never end a visit during a punishment because your child will remember the punishment rather than the good times. The child may refuse to return if she believes you are angry.
- During visits, don't expect to compress all your teachings and discipline into one weekend. This is not only impossible, but also gives your child good reason to dread the next visit.
- Remember that, for better or worse, children are always changing. Their changes are not always caused by the divorce or what happens in the other household.
- If you see your child behaving in a way that you don't understand, try talking to your ex to see if he sees the same behavior. Rather than

blaming, speak with concern and a desire to understand the behavior. Decide how you can work together to change the behavior.

- Regularly ask yourself, "How effective is my discipline? Is the discipline producing only short-term results, or is it actually teaching your children to be a more responsible and socially conscious individual?"

Be a Mentor to Your Children, Not Just a Disciplinarian

All parents have an idealized image in their mind of the perfect child. Then there is reality that often falls short of your ideals. As a parent, you must accept your children and offer them loving guidance. The children must believe they are valued for who they are rather than feel inadequate for not living up to your ideals. Children face new and unique situations that they do not know how to handle because they lack maturity and experience to respond appropriately. Because of their inexperience, children make poor decisions that could seem to you to be deliberate misbehavior. This can be confusing for both you and your children.

Parents must be mentors to their children, teachers who lead by example. Take time to explain and interpret confusing and troubling events to your children. Mentoring is an excellent occasion for creating closeness between parents and children. It will help them grow and make sense of the world. Above all, try to set a good example by your own behavior.

Elise and Carrie's Story

Carrie is a usually well-behaved ten-year-old, but today was different. Elise could see from Carrie's expression that something was wrong, but Carrie obviously was not ready to talk. Elise patiently waited until Carrie finally confessed, "Robin and I got into trouble today and we were sent to Mr. Troy's office."

Elise was shocked. "What happened?"

Carrie's voice quivered while she slowly started to explain. "Mom, I didn't know that Robin had taken money off Mrs. Malloy's desk! I didn't see her take it!"

"Carrie, calm down and tell me what happened."

"We were in the lunch room and Mrs. Malloy was coming over to our table when Robin put the money in my hand. Mom, I didn't know what to do! Mrs. Malloy caught me with the money and I didn't take it. Robin gave it to me. We had to go to Mr. Troy's office, and he said he was going to call you. I think I'm supposed to get a detention."

Elise had to make a decision about what to do with Carrie. Should she punish Carrie for having the money, or take this occasion to give her some advice about what she should have done when Robin gave it to her? Elise knew that Carrie needed her understanding and help. Carrie was in a unique situation that she did not know how to handle. She knew she was in trouble and that her friend Robin had done wrong. Wisely, Elise decided that Carrie needed mentoring and help, rather than punishment. She took this opportunity to instruct Carrie rather than punish her, thus strengthening their relationship. How would you have advised Carrie? That is not an easy question.

Give the Gift of Acceptance

Children deserve to be valued for who they actually are and not made to feel inadequate for failing to live up to an ideal that probably came into existence before they did and doesn't account for their uniqueness. This sort of acceptance, along with your loving guidance, is the greatest gift you can give your children. It enables them to grow and develop into healthy, happy, well-adjusted adults.

Janet and Peter's Story

Janet is very conscientious about her parenting. While trying to be sensitive to her children's needs, she expresses strong opinions about what is best for them. "No one gave me the values and self-esteem to make smart choices when I was growing up," she explains. Jane is determined that things will be different for her girls, Valerie, fourteen, and Natalie, ten. Because Janet is a recovering alcoholic, she insists that Valerie attend Alateen. Valerie complains bitterly, but Janet is unyielding. Visits with their father, Peter, had been going well until

Janet learned that Peter had been taking the children to a truck stop for dinner. Janet did not believe the truck stop was a proper setting for her children. "They shouldn't be exposed to the truckers' filthy mouths and see the way those poor waitresses are pinched and harassed," she said. Janet was also upset about Peter keeping *Playboy* and *Penthouse* magazines in his night table drawer, "where anyone could find them." On another occasion, Valerie mentioned to Janet that her father allowed them to watch a movie that Janet knew had an explicit love scene. She was enraged by Peter's lack of morals and sensitivity. Janet lectured Peter on the proper way to raise the children and demanded that he change his ways. When he didn't, she requested the court to limit Peter's visits, firmly believing she was protecting Valerie and Natalie. The court denied her request.

Values

Parents naturally have values or opinions about religion, nutrition, sex education, household rules, neatness, and when and how to punish children. In these and other areas, parents tend to have a strong personal sense of what is right or wrong, and a limited tolerance for anyone who doesn't share their point of view. This is a frequent source of heated conflict between parents. There may be differences in religious beliefs or what is considered safe recreation. One young father made national headlines when he sued for custody because he believed it was wrong for his son to be in day care while the boy's mother attended college courses. I have known mothers who were prepared to go to court because the father allowed their son to listen to heavy metal music, and dads who wanted the mother declared unfit because she hired a babysitter with streaked hair and a nose ring. Their responses may sound like overreactions, but extreme behavior is commonplace when moral or ethical matters are at stake.

Who Has the Right to Judge?

In recent years, we have seen wars fought over moral differences that are fueled by righteous indignation. For example, Janet believed that there was no worthier cause than making sure her children were raised with the right values or sheltered from the wrong values. She sincerely believed that she, and not her ex-husband, was best suited to teach the children proper values. She believed Alateen would give the children proper guidance about alcohol abuse and eating at truck stops would subvert their morals. Unfortunately, Janet's insistence that the children follow her values ultimately backfired, causing them to feel estranged from her and giving her cause to alienate the children from her ex-husband. Janet implied that Peter's values were demeaning towards women and damaging to the children. The girls could see that their mother had a point, but they saw her obsession as vindictive and fanatical. They responded by pulling away from her influence. Since they were unwilling to put their faith in or emulate either parent, as the girls got older they took their cues from other sources: most notably their peers, who seemed to think that smoking and drinking were perfectly acceptable. This was precisely the opposite of the message Janet had wanted to impart to her daughters.

Values Conflicts: A Major Source of Alienation

Values differences escalate into values conflicts when one or both parents believe their values or methods for their teaching children right from wrong are best and expect the other parent to adhere to their moral code. Values conflicts lead to alienation when one parent attempts to convince the children that the other parent's values are wrong, bad, perverse, or even dangerous.

Like Janet and Peter, you and your former mate may have decidedly different opinions on at least one personal values or moral issue. Perhaps you attend church regularly and expect your children to do the same; but your ex-spouse, who places less emphasis on religious training, lets the kids sleep in on his Sundays. Or maybe one of you is a recent convert to low-fat cooking who carefully monitors the children's diets, while the other is a junk-food junkie who considers bologna on white bread, corn chips, and ice cream the perfectly balanced meal. Or your standards of modesty may differ. I have had clients who were appalled because their ex walked around in his underwear or allowed her children into the bathroom while showering. The presumably perverse parties saw nothing wrong with their behavior; in fact, they wondered if their "ridiculously uptight" accusers might be damaging their kids psychologically. Every day we witness in the news adversaries arguing about whose moral code is correct, whether the issue is abortion, stem cell research, or religious teachings, to name a few.

It probably is not news to you that you and your ex-spouse have different values. In some instances, arguing about moral and child-rearing issues may have been reason for the dissolution of your marriage. Those old conflicts often continue with added emotional intensity once you have been through the heartache and upheaval of a divorce. A more recent change in your own or your ex's belief systems may have created new values gaps and new conflicts. Whether you have returned to your Baptist roots or embarked upon a recovery program, embraced a new-age philosophy or gained the confidence to speak up when you disagree with someone, the attitude changes you have made since your divorce can put you and your ex on a collision course. No matter where or how long ago the conflict originated, when deeply held beliefs or strong convictions clash, the ensuing battles tend to be loud and long. They can also be alienating.

> TIP: Exposing your children to arguments over different values or parenting styles is more damaging than having the children adjust to the different values.

Although no one can fault you for wanting your children to grow up with a healthy set of values, criticizing your ex-spouse's values in front of your children or badgering them into agreeing that yours are better is counterproductive. It leads the children to needless anxiety and confusion, as well as a cloudy sense of right and wrong.

Just witnessing your arguments and power struggles over whose beliefs are morally preferable causes children considerable distress. They feel pulled in opposite directions, pressured to choose sides, and miserable about the possible repercussions of their choice. No matter what they do, they will end up disappointing one of you, and young children in particular have a powerful need to please you both.

At some point, your children will make up their own minds about whose standards and values they will follow as adults. But while they are still dependent on you and their other parent to clothe, feed, shelter, love, and protect them, they have no choice but to try to make you both happy (or, at least, make neither of you angry.) The last thing they need is to have either or both of you make them feel bad or guilty for being good by their other parent's standards.

Tips on Values

- Do not expect that you can change your ex-spouse's values. You can't. Values are often passionately held.
- Do not try to convince your children that your ex-spouse's values are inferior to yours. This will cause alienation and confusion.
- Do not expect your children to assert your values in the other household. Doing so will give your child the idea that they are dong something wrong when they are not. Do not put the child in the middle for your own personal agenda.
- There is no harm in exposing your children to more than one set of values as they grow up. They are exposed to different values at their friends' homes, different churches, and every time they turn on the TV.
- Make it clear to your children what your values are and how they are expected to behave when they are with you. Remember, you are a role model. As they reach adulthood, they will choose their own values. The more positive your relationship with your children, the more likely they will be influenced by your values.

It is tempting for targeted parents to retaliate against the alienating parent with defensive allegations and counterattacks when values and standards are questioned. The targeted parent must try to avoid this temptation. Instead of taking the offensive and laying on guilt, acknowledge your children's dilemma. Convey empathy for the confusion or anxiety they are apt to feel. And then, to reduce that anxiety, make your rules and expectations clear. Whether your standards are strict or lenient or somewhere in between, stand firm about what you will or will not accept from your children when they are with you. Assure them that it's okay that they live by different rules when they are with the other parent. You cannot expect that your values will be in sync with your ex-spouse 100 percent—or even 10 percent—of the time. Exposing children to two different moral codes or methods of discipline will not necessarily harm them as long as they are not exposed to your fighting. Once again, have faith in the strength of your relationship with your children. It cannot be emphasized enough that a powerful deterrent to alienation is your children seeing you as a source for building their self-confidence and self-esteem.

13

Common Alienating Tactics: Spying, Secrets, and Using Children as Witnesses

Parents involved in contentious litigation need information to build their case. They frequently look to the child for information. Obsessed parents will coach the children how to spy, gather information to be used against the targeted parent, prepared them how to talk with the attorney and testify in the court. The children can become the unwitting pawns of the obsessed parent's manipulations and goal to cut off the other parent from any relationship with the child.

Gathering Information

Before deciding to gather information, ask yourself, "Why do I need this information? Is the information pertinent for a parental or ex-spousal issue?" If the information has more to do with an ex-spousal issue than the children's welfare, do not expect your children to offer any information. When you ask your children to gather information, you are asking them to lie, deceive, violate a parent's trust, and be disloyal.

There are many ways parents ask children to gather information. Children have been asked to forward private e-mails and look into parents' checkbooks, important personal papers, and phone bills, none of which are any of the children's business. This practice should be avoided or immediately stopped.

> *Sadie, could you look in your daddy's top desk drawer and see how much his car payment is? I need to know for taxes.*

Spying

Would you find your mother's old cell phone? I need to know who is in her address book.

Secrecy and spying are among the most blatant and damaging forms of alienation. Parents who ask the children to keep secrets from the other parent or to serve as spies to gather information are creating in their children a painful conflict whereby they must choose their loyalties between parents. You are asking the children to be deceitful and betray someone they love. Alienating parents have asked their children to retrieve discarded cell phones, tape record the parent, take pictures, obtain phone bills, and instant-message a parent's computer financials and other personal information for learning about the other parent's personal life. New technology has given everyone the ability to spy. This is inappropriate and inexcusable.

The Difference between Casual Questions and Spying

Paul, honey, does Dad ever smoke pot when you're visiting? I'm just curious.

It is natural for a parent to ask their children returning home, "How was your visit?" or "Did you have a good time?" Such questions are harmless, and you should not become paranoid about asking your children innocent questions about visits. There is a difference between these casual questions and asking for specific information. The latter is spying.

TIP: Do not interrogate your child.

Be aware of how your children feel regarding casual questions about the other parent's home. If they spontaneously answer, there is little reason to be concerned. If they appear uncomfortable, you should probably back off from asking any more questions. Sometimes parents ask, "How do I know I am doing right by my children?" Your children's response will answer your question. If they appear anxious, you are probably doing wrong.

Secrecy

Expecting Your Children to Keep Quiet

One of the less malicious forms of alienation or secrecy is asking your children not to tell your ex-spouse what goes on in your home. Such a request may be motivated by the parent wanting to set a boundary between the households rather than having something to hide. Sometimes you may wonder how to keep your child quiet and have any privacy. After all, there are some things that are none of your ex-spouse's business. They shouldn't judge what you do in *your* home, right? Hypothetically, you may be correct, but your belief is unrealistic and can lead to alienation.

Children will talk, especially if they are unhappy about something going on in your home. Expecting them to keep quiet or keep your secrets is unfair and teaches them to lie with your approval. Telling your child, "Don't tell your mom [or dad]," places them right in between both parents. They have to choose their loyalties, which is exactly what they do not want to do.

Instead, you and your children will be better off if you live your life with the belief that you have no secrets, and whatever goes on in your home is open to public scrutiny, including that of your ex-spouse. If you think about it, how much really goes on in your home that anyone cares about? Your children should be free to say whatever they want, without being afraid that they will offend you or violate your trust. They should not have to censor what they say to anyone. If you expect your children to keep their mouths shut, you are taking the risk that you are causing your own estrangement because they may be more uncomfortable with you than with your ex-spouse. However, some children will keep secrets due to deceptive promises and materialistic bribery.

You may feel your behavior is scrutinized by your ex-spouse and the court during a custody dispute. You are probably correct. Both your ex-spouse and the court will pass judgment on any misbehavior that is presented to the court's attention. Feeling scrutinized is uncomfortable, especially if your behavior is questionable. The solution to feeling uncomfortable is simply to behave yourself. Do not live a life that depends on secrets. No one should care about what you do while the children are in your care. It may not always be easy, but you will be amazed how much better you will feel if you don't fear disclosure. How you behave when the children are not in your care is no one's business unless you are involved in an illegal activity.

EXERCISE: MUST MY PRIVATE LIFE BE SO PRIVATE?

Often parents believe that their lives are not only private, but they have to keep certain secrets from their ex-spouse. To help you better understand what actually needs to be a secret, complete this exercise. Below, write down five secrets that your children know about but you don't want your ex-spouse to know.

1. _____
2. _____
3. _____
4. _____
5. _____

Now review your secrets and answer the question, "who cares?" Do these things really have to be a secret, or are you making an issue about something that has little significance to anyone? If you conclude that the issue is important and must be a secret, maybe you need to rethink how you're behaving, and whether or not your children should be exposed to this behavior. You could be putting your children in a very awkward position. Do you think you are causing some alienation?

Why Have Secrets?

Parents want secrets with their children when they have something to hide. A parent is tempted to deceive the other parent when he knows there are values conflicts, or expects the other parent's criticism for how he behaves. Parents wanting to avoid an argument may ask their child to "not tell Mommy." The child now struggles with being either a liar or betraying a parent's trust. The reality is that, in most jurisdictions, a parent can do whatever he wants with their child as long as it is legal, consistent with court orders, or poses no risk to the child's safety. When parents understand this reality, many of the conflicts between the parents will go away.

A frequent complaint against a parent is alcohol and drug abuse. Drinking is a more complex issue because it is legal. A parent cannot expect the court to restrict a legal activity unless it has been shown that the drinker has behaved irresponsibly in the children's presence. Most parents have strong opinions about exposing their children to the use of illicit drugs. Most courts will restrict or ban parenting time if they have reason to believe that the children are exposed to illegal drug activities. However, there are those that believe marijuana should be legal and will smoke a "joint" in front of their children. They see nothing wrong with this practice, but they will ask the children to lie and not let anyone know what they are doing. These parents do not understand the dilemma in which they are placing the children. Again, the children become confused about how they should behave and where to place their loyalties. What values are the children being taught?

Having Secrets and Codes with the Children

Call me on your cell in the middle of the night when your mother is asleep.

Having secrets, special signals, a private rendezvous, or words with special meaning are damaging to your children's relationship with their other parent. It is one of the most blatant forms of alienation. Telling your children, "Don't tell your mother"; "This will be our little secret"; or "When I say 'whimsy,' call me tomorrow," creates an exclusive relationship that psychologically excludes the other parent. The secrecy implies there is something wrong with the other parent that justifies such behavior. The victimized parent is portrayed as not understanding, or as someone who "doesn't want us to have fun." Regardless of the excuses, the results are the same. The children are alienated from the victimized parent while the other parent is characterized as a special person who understands.

Sara and Bobbie's Story

In the middle of the night, Sara went downstairs to get a drink. Looking out from the kitchen window while drinking her juice, she saw a car parked across the street blinking its headlights. Sara recognized the car and the silhouette of the driver: It was her ex-husband, Bob. She couldn't believe her eyes. Sara had always prided herself on bring a rational person, able to stay calm and not get caught up in petty bickering with Bobbie's father. Now she began to understand why Bobbie had been acting strangely lately. For no apparent reason, Bobbie had been withdrawn and "kinda secretive. We use to be able to talk about anything together." Lately, however, Bobbie would just pull away and

---

appear indifferent when Sara tried to talk. Sara could only assume that Bobbie had been going through one of her moods. Now she realized that Bobbie and her father were up to something. Sara felt excluded, pushed away by Bobbie. She was jealous because Bobbie and her father seemed to have something special. Sara ran upstairs, fuming.

Sara was blindsided to learn of the secret rendezvous, and overcome with jealousy by the knowledge that she was excluded from part of Bobbie's life. I suspect that any parent can understand Sara's hurt.

There are many reasons a parent would have secrets or private rendezvous with their children. Sometimes the actions or comments are less obvious than what Sara experienced. The most frequent excuse is that the ex-spouse "will not allow me more time with my children. She would have a fit if she knew the truth about the times I see my children." Sometimes the alienating parent feels powerful for having a special relationship with the children. It is almost like "getting one over" on the ex-spouse. The children become unwitting vehicles for the alienating parent's hostility.

Do not blame your children when you learn they have secrets with your ex-spouse. Without being punitive, ask your children about the secrets. Try to understand how they feel regarding your finding out about the lies. Explain to your children that they did nothing wrong, but that you need to discuss the secrets with their other parent.

When you are alone with your ex-spouse, tell her that you have learned about the secrets. Without attacking or degrading her, explain your concern about how she places the children in the uncomfortable position of having to lie and deceive. Try to understand why your ex-spouse was asking the children to lie. Usually, an ex-spouse will ask the children to keep secrets when she expects that you will get angry about something or try to restrict her activities with the children. Rather than asking the children to keep secrets, see if you and your ex-spouse can come to some agreement about the issue. If you can't reach an agreement, consider taking the children to a counselor or have your attorney discuss the issue with your ex-spouse's attorney or mediator.

TIP: If you have secrets with your children, stop immediately. You are hurting your children because you are teaching them that deception and lies are acceptable behavior.

Roberta and Jerry's Story

Roberta was worried that her ex-husband, Jerry, would allow their son, Bobby, to ride a four-wheeler without wearing a safety helmet. She pleaded with Jerry to make Bobby use the helmet. Jerry was angry by Roberta's intrusion into "my business." He ignored her plea. He resented Roberta, "telling me what to do and having Bobby spy on me." Roberta had Bobby report back to her, telling her if Jerry was having him wear the helmet. Both parents were setting up a power struggle, with Bobby in the middle. Bobby began to feel responsible for the arguments.

Roberta was using Bobby to gather information because of her concern for his safety, but she put Bobby in the middle because of his father's refusal to cooperate. Roberta was correct in her assertion that Bobby should wear a helmet. Since Jerry was ignoring her pleas, Roberta's only choices were to forget the issue, return to court, or teach Bobby proper safety, regardless of whether his father required it. The latter choice is the most reasonable because going back to court is expensive, but she should not ignore Bobby's safety. Unfortunately, this is an example in which sometimes the children have to exercise more maturity and better judgment than the parent.

Using the Children as Witnesses

Will you tell the judge what you told me?

A blatant example of alienation is putting a child in the middle between two warring parents to have the child testify in court against the rejected parent. When a parent decides to seek custody, he realizes he must build a case against the ex-spouse to impugn her competency as a parent. Your attorney will probably ask you how your child feels about a change of custody and if your child is willing to testify. Of course you can only answer the questions by asking your children. This puts you in an awkward position because you must avoid putting your child in the middle and forcing them to publicly reject the other parent. You should only answer the questions if your child has spontaneously expressed a preference without your prodding.

Only the most severely alienated child will ask to go to court. Children, for the most part, want to avoid court and having to publicly testify. In fact, this is most children's fear. Children should not be at court unless authorized by the court. Sometimes a parent's motivation for having children gather information and attend court is not so noble. A noncustodial parent struggling to pay bills may want to know how the ex-spouse is spending his money. Or the custodial parent may have reason to believe that her ex-spouse is hoarding money rather than paying a fair share of child support. Drinking and driving, excessive punishment, allowing the children to engage in dangerous activities, or failure to supervise are all reasons parents may want their children to keep secrets, because they know some courts can restrict or even ban visits. The court's response may pale compared to the other parent's wrath.

TIP: Children should not attend court unless asked by one of the attorneys and authorized by the judge.

For parents to prove an allegation that can have a bearing on the litigation, they often need the children's cooperation to gather information about when and where these questionable activities occur. Some parents may think that if they can prove to the court that their ex-spouse is mistreating or neglecting the children during a visit, they can get a court order to restrict visits to daytime hours or eliminate them altogether. This is a common tactic of an obsessed parent: the parent's desire to gather damaging information is stronger than concern for how this tactic affects the child's relationship with the targeted parent. Such parents may believe the end justifies the means because they are so intent on restricting or eliminating parenting time. The irresponsible parent arguing that they can do whatever they want may deserve a reprimand by the court.

The soliciting parent puts the children in a painfully awkward position because they are asked to betray the other parent's trust. For example, a mother asks the children whether their father is having his girlfriend spend the night. If the allegation is true, and the children are not bothered by the practice, the mother may unintentionally cause her own estrangement. On the other hand, if the children are upset by the girlfriend's presence, they may start feeling estranged from their father. Having to feed their mother information about their father's activities only adds to their discomfort or reinforces their alignment with the alienating parent. Even younger children learn that mother's inquiry has greater significance than just satisfying curiosity.

TIP: If you learn that your child is appearing in court, ask your attorney to prevent the appearance.

Your attorney will typically ask to interview your child before deciding if the child would appear in court. Children are smart and quick to understand the purpose of the interview. Most children know that they are being asked to say "bad things" against the other parent. They will initially be very reserved and uncomfortable. An experienced interviewer will help children feel more comfortable and speak more spontaneously. The severely alienated child may be eager to talk. The risk with very anxious children is the ease with which they can be manipulated, because of their desire to please authority figures. The children's statements during an interview may not be consistent with their testimony, especially if they are scared and cross-examined by an experienced attorney who knows how to interview children. Whatever happens in court, children are not the winners. They know their testimony is intended to reject a parent. After the testimony, everyone goes home without any regard that the children have to face the rejected parent and, at least in theory, maintain some type of a relationship with the parent. This is a very formidable task for children. The child wanting to avoid or not visit the rejected parent is understandable. The alienating parent doesn't share this concern, believing in a higher cause that serves his own selfish interest.

The child severely alienated by PAS is eager to testify. Be very suspicious when you see an overly eager child who shows no reluctance. She will denigrate, exaggerate, and sometimes lie with no regard for consequences or guilt. She is not intimated by the court or the attorney conducting the cross. Look for an obsessed parent standing in the background. The credibility of the child's testimony is questionable.

Most states have criteria for best interest that includes a child's preference as to where he wants to live. The court may need to know the child's preference. The issue before the court is how to get a credible preference without harming the child or risking the child's relationship with either parent.

Judges and attorneys look to the children as witnesses to corroborate the accusations. However, children are not the best witnesses. Their testimony should be corroborated by other sources that are available to testify. This is an appropriate role for a custody evaluator, not a therapist. Judges try to minimize the risk by talking to the child in chambers. Though this helps because the child doesn't have to make a public display, there is still a question about the child's credibility. Judges, like anyone else interviewing a child, want to believe that the child will be more honest with them than anyone else. This is not always true. Counselors and evaluators also share this bias.

Boyfriends spending the night, heavy drinking, smoking in the presence of an allergic child, or using drugs are all arguments that have been used to force an involuntary change of custody. To build a case against the other parent, the alienating parent will draft the children into service to covertly gather information. The process of gathering information may be viewed by the children as a game. Together, they secretly develop strategies for gathering and exchanging information. While the process is occurring, an alienation develops between the children and the targeted parent. Implied in the process is the belief that something is wrong with the targeted parent, while the other parent is there for the rescue.

John and Tish's Story

John used his children to witness to their mother's failure to cooperate with visits. John had custody of the two boys while Tish had custody of their daughter, Rosy. Because of John and Tish's fights, Rosy would refuse to visit her father and brothers. John believed that Rosy's refusal to visit was caused by Tish's manipulation and not by her own choice. He believed Tish was brainwashing Rosy against him.

To prove his point, John would come to pick up Rosy with the boys. Instead of going to the front door himself, John would sit in the car and have his sons go to the door to get their sister. Rosy would have a fit and refuse her mother's prodding to go with her father. Tish felt guilty for what she was doing to Rosy and angry because she knew she was being set up by John. She hated seeing her sons being used, but knew there was nothing she could do about it. John, certain that Tish was keeping Rosy from him, reasoned that he could use the boys as witnesses against their mother to prove her lack of cooperation.

If your children volunteer information about what is going on in your ex-spouse's home, casually listen to what they say. Do not interrogate them by asking numerous questions. Instead, if you are concerned, gently inquire and trust them to tell you if anything significant happens. When they are done talking, don't push.

If your children are upset by what happened while with the other parent, they may spontaneously tell you when they are ready. Do not assume that every time they go with the other parent, something wrong will happen. Your suspicions will only frighten or, in the case of older children, irritate them. Your children must feel comfortable and safe with you before they tell you anything that they believe might upset you. Listen to what your children say without getting upset or making judgments or accusations. Stay calm. Otherwise, you will upset your children, causing them to temper their story.

If your child discloses any information suggesting physical or sexual abuse, listen and gently offer support without overreacting, and report the abuse to the local child protective service agency. If the child is in therapy, contact the therapist, who will probably advise you to contact Child Protective Services. Reporting is the law and the therapist or physician can be prosecuted for failure to report. Interrogating your child could damage any possible future testimony and prosecution.

As discussed in chapter 3 ("False Allegations"), not knowing how to correctly interview your children can give you the wrong impression of what actually occurred. This can be dangerous and lead to false allegations. Parents are not properly trained to interview children. This is why a trained professional is needed to interview the child about the alleged abuse or other serious offenses. You should not ask your children questions about your ex-spouse's behavior that may impugn that parent's character. Satisfying your curiosity is not sufficient reason to risk harming your children's relationship with the other parent.

If your child makes comments about something happening in the other household, listen, but be careful about believing everything that is said. When your child tells you something that is inconsistent with what your ex-spouse has said, do not assume that your child is correct and your ex-spouse is lying. Children can and do lie or distort facts. Your biased desire to believe your child can distort your thinking and later cause a problem between your children and their other parent. If you feel the need, ask your ex-spouse, without losing control, to clarify your confusion about what your child is saying. Don't be quick to pass judgment. Listen to your ex-spouse without blaming or attacking. Later, think about how you want to respond to what you heard from both your ex-spouse and child. You may not have to do anything.

You can prevent problems by not asking your children or your ex-spouse about an alleged incident unless you have good reason to believe something actually happened. Having a vague feeling or sense that something may have happened is not a good enough reason to get everyone upset. Asking your children whether their other parent is using drugs when you have no grounds for this suspicion will raise doubts in your children's minds about their other parent's integrity. Your children may now have reason to feel suspicious and pull away from their other parent. Though you believe your reasons for asking the questions were innocent, you may be alienating your children from the other parent.

Remember, your children's account about events will not always be accurate. This is because of their young age, their biased perceptions, and their limited vocabulary and experience. Younger children will take short-cuts when explaining themselves, because it is easier.

Also, your children may agree with you before they really understand what you are trying to say. This happens frequently with younger children because they are usually more concerned about pleasing you than about being accurate. Asking your children, "Are you telling me the truth?" is meaningless because they will always say, "Yes." Have you known a child to answer that question by saying "no"?

Before pursuing an issue raised by your children, ask yourself whether the issue is important enough to risk problems between you and your ex-spouse. Allegations of sexual abuse are serious and should be reported. If you decide an issue is not important, you can reassure your children and let it pass, while continuing to be vigilant.

14

Health and Safety

Why is it that every time the kids have a runny nose you have to take them to the doctor and tell me I can't see them? You're just making excuses to keep the kids from me.

Parents' first responsibility is to protect their children's health and safety. No one, including the court, will excuse any parent who neglects the children's health or allows them to be put in a hazardous position. Sometimes, however, knowing what is safe takes more than common sense, because parents have different values or ideas about safety and health.

Many health and safety threats are unique for this generation of children. An example is having to teach young children or teens about HIV and AIDS. If you are like most parents, you probably feel strange watching Viagra or condom commercials on television and having to answer your children's questions. Unfortunately, today's children need to know about safe sex and HIV. In addition, our children are also more likely to witness violence in school or on the streets. School officials report an increase in the number of children carrying weapons to school. Hearing about teenage shootings on television causes every parent to wonder about their children's safety. Parents have also developed a pervasive fear about their children being abducted or molested. Amber Alerts remind us of the threats to our children's safety, particularly if we fear that the ex-spouse could abduct our child. School-age children are taught "good touch and bad touch." For many children, they can no longer feel safe in their own neighborhood. They, as well as their parents, have had to become more vigilant, watching for any threat. Parents are caught in the dilemma of needing to alert their children to dangers without making them timid and paranoid.

Simple Decisions Can Get Complicated

Children's age or maturity can make a difference about what they should be allowed to do. A six-year-old riding a bike in the streets is different from a fourteen-year-old doing the same thing. Even the neighborhood in which the parent lives can make a difference. Seven-year-old Billy may be perfectly safe riding his two-wheeler on the dead-end street in Dad's quiet neighborhood, but riding on Mom's busy street would pose a serious threat to his safety. Mom would be expected to use her good judgment about what Billy is allowed to do on her street.

Not everyone will agree about what is safe for children. Dad may see nothing wrong with his ten-year-old riding a dirt bike, while Mom panics over the vision in her mind of her child's bloody body under the mangled bike. Both parents may have strong feelings about what is safe. When the mother tries to say something, the father may resent the intrusion, complaining, "I don't have to do what she tells me. She's just trying to control me the way she did in the marriage." On the other hand, the mother may resent her ex-husband's carelessness and insensitivity to her fears. Now the groundwork is laid for a power struggle to see whose will is stronger.

> *TIP: When you have two family cultures, each may have different values and permissions for the children. Most often, parents can do whatever they want with the children as long as it is legal and consistent with court orders and the children's basic needs are attended to. If you try to assert your values onto the other parent, you could be asking for trouble.*

Overprotective parents are usually seen by targeted parents as being aggressive or overly controlling because of the frequent complaints and harsh judgments about their parenting (Darnall, 1993). Both parents have their own beliefs about how children should be raised. When differences occur, parents must temper their feelings and appreciate the wisdom in learning how to cope with each other's beliefs. There must be room to negotiate and compromise. Otherwise, the children are trapped between the parents' demands and their desire to please both. When children are caught between opposing parents, they are often forced to lie to keep peace. This isn't the message you want to give to your children.

Ray's Story

Ray was angry because he was dragged back to court when his ex-wife complained about his taking their two-year-old son on his motorcycle. He couldn't see where he did anything wrong. His ex-wife could not believe her ears when the judge said that Ray hadn't done anything illegal, as there was no minimum age for a child to ride a motorcycle, providing the child was wearing a helmet. However, the judge agreed with the mother and ordered that the child could not ride on the motorcycle.

Sometimes common sense tells us that some activities are not safe for children even if no law restricts the activity. If you anticipate that this could become an issue between you and the other parent, talk to your attorney about including a restriction in the parenting plan. If your ex-spouse is a gun advocate, you may want the parenting plan to require that your child must have a gun course and be supervised when shooting. Courts will use community standard to judge acceptable behavior.

How sick does Billy have to be before he sees a doctor? When should you cancel a visit because he doesn't feel well? Are you risking our child's health if you smoke cigarettes in his presence or allow him to ride his bicycle without a helmet? Can someone with no experience taking care of children ever really be trusted with children? These are just a few of the health and safety issues divorced parents grapple with that sometimes turn into World War III.

In most states, the custodial parent is responsible for the children's health and medical care. If there is a shared parenting plan or joint custody, the parents are expected to make health-related decisions together. Cooperation is an absolute must; otherwise everyone's life will be miserable. If the parents don't have a shared parenting plan or joint custody, the court usually gives preference to the custodial parent for selecting the children's physician and deciding when and how the children receive medical, dental, and any psychological treatment. This parent, in effect, becomes the medical-care coordinator who delegates, instructs, and communicates the physician's orders to the other parent. Ideally—and for the child's best interest—the two parents can do this without resentment and animosity. This should be a simple and straightforward arrangement, but often it is not.

The Decision-Maker versus the Bill-Payer

A frequent source of resentment is the parenting plan that gives the custodial parent the authority to make medical decisions while the other parent is responsible for paying the medical bills. A problem with this arrangement is that the custodial parent has total control and power to direct the children's health care, while the other parent has a subservient role in making medical decisions but has the legal responsibility to pay the medical bills. This arrangement has a symbolic value for the payer. The payer may feel humiliated by the other parent's authority and demands. The parenting plan obligates one parent to bow to the other parent's controlling demands, otherwise the payer fears that the custodial parent will retaliate by cutting off the flow of information, or worse yet, stop visits. The parent managing the child's health care has the responsibility to select health-care providers that are approved by the insurance or managed care company. Selecting a health provider outside of the network without the other parent's consent is irresponsible and asking for trouble.

To make matters worse, there are instances in which the payer is asked to pay for the child's braces or support treatments that are not a medical necessity but would enhance the child's appearance or health. Another source of conflict is when the bill-paying parent is forced to change health insurance, particularly a change to an HMO that does not include the child's physician or that has higher deductibles. When the bill-paying parent has no money, she can get angry and defensive when accused by the other parent of being selfish or uncaring to the children's health needs. Another concern for the bill-payer parent is the child's reaction upon learning that she has refused to pay for the treatment. Telling the child that you cannot afford the cost does not lessen the child's disappointment and the parent's guilt. If you contribute to the child's disappointment with your negative comments to the child, you are contributing to the alienation. These issues should be worked out between the two of you without involving the children and before major medical decisions are made.

Health

Children get sick. There is little a parent can do about it other than take reasonable precautions to keep the children healthy and care for them when ill. The problem occurs because parents have different opinions about how to keep the children healthy. Some of these opinions, though well meaning, are based on myths or misconceptions, or are not supported by the medical community. For example, many parents continue to believe that children can catch a cold if they get their feet wet or play outside in cold weather. These unfounded beliefs can lead to arguments that are never resolved.

Parents cannot be expected to be medical experts or always know how best to care for an ill child. There are too many differences of opinion about preventative health care and treatment. Even religious beliefs can influence a parent's ideas about good health care. So how do two parents come to some agreement about taking care of their children's health?

Before answering this question, we must begin with the assumption that both parents are equally capable of caring for a sick child. You may not agree. True, some parents are better caregivers than others. But that is not to say that a poor caregiver can't learn to be a better caregiver.

Not all sick children need to see a physician. Children can get colds, skin their knees, cut their finger, or have a stomachache without having to stay home from school or go see their doctor. Parents always make judgments about when to take the child to the doctor or keep their child home.

When Should Visits Be Canceled Because of Illness?

A good guideline for when to cancel a visit because of illness is to use the same standards that you use for deciding when to keep your child home from school. If you are told by your child's physician to keep her home from school or in bed, the same standard could apply to a visit unless the doctor says otherwise. Sometimes the physician will see no problem with the child recuperating at the noncustodial parent's home, if the child remains quiet and rested. Whatever is decided, the physician's orders must be law, and followed by both parents. Children appreciate when both parents can work together on their behalf.

The child's desire to stay at the custodial parent's home to recuperate should have priority over the other parent's desire to care for the child. For the child's sake, the noncustodial parent must trust that the child's expressed desire is not manipulated by the custodial parent. The custodial parent must not excessively use illness to deny the other parent parenting time; to do otherwise will evoke a lot of resentment. If the custodial parent is not available to care for the child, and the other parent is, there is no reason why the noncustodial parent cannot care for the child unless the physician says otherwise.

Both parents should have access to medical information and physician instructions without animosity or defensiveness. The noncustodial parent must be able to converse with the children's physician without any threat of offending the other parent or putting the physician in an awkward position. Cooperation and amiable discussions with the other parent must be your goal. Courts may need to be specific in stating that both parents are to have access to the physician and medical records. This includes mental health records. Otherwise, you can expect to see more animosity and distrust.

> *TIP: The physician's orders are law. If you disagree, get a second opinion. Withholding medical treatment because you disagree can be considered neglect.*

Medication

There is the assumption that both parents are equally capable of administering medication. The custodial parent should be given written instructions that include proper dosage and times when the medication is to be administered. Following the physician's order is critical. If you don't, the court may think you are neglecting your child's care.

When your child goes to the other parent's home, you have the responsibility to give the other parent the doctor's instructions and an amount of the medication that will last the duration of the parenting. You should not expect your ex-spouse to buy the child's medication because you are too stubborn to share. This can be too expensive and impractical if the physician has written a single prescription. Physicians can only prescribe class II medications for thirty days after the child is seen for the appointment. Pharmacies will not duplicate or reissue a class II prescription—for example, the medications frequently prescribed for attention deficit hyperactivity disorder (ADHD)—early, so it is impractical to expect the noncustodial parent to get their own medication. If you are the noncustodial parent, you are expected to continue your child's treatment, including the administration of medication while she is in your care.

One Sick Child with Healthy Siblings

A common alienating tactic that stirs bitter resentment is keeping all the children from going on a visit when only one child is sick. If one child is ill and the others are healthy, there is no reason the healthy children should not go on the scheduled visit. Do not keep all the children from the visit unless all of them are ill or were recently exposed to a contagious disease, seriously enough so that the physician believes that the child may pass the disease to others. Again, if there are any questions about what is best for the children, express your concerns to your ex-spouse and consult the child's physician.

Medical Emergencies

Medical emergencies can happen anywhere and anytime, even when the child is with the most cautious parent. If your child is hospitalized or has a medical emergency, you should assume that your ex-spouse wants to be told immediately. After all, your ex-spouse has as much emotional invest-ment in your child's health and care as you. Nothing gets a parent angrier than feeling excluded from knowing about their child's medical emer-gency. Withholding information will remind your ex-spouse of your power. This is very humiliating, especially when he has to either lie to your child about why he didn't come to see her at the hospital, or tell the unpleasant truth. In addition, your ex-spouse will learn that you can't be trusted. Remember, trust means the ability to predict.

After you have told your ex-spouse of the emergency, he will decide whether to go to the hospital. Sometimes, when the parent fails to visit, this puts the other parent in a awkward position with the child. Now the parent feels obligated to make excuses for the other parent for not coming to visit. This isn't really necessary. Your child may be hurt or disappointed, but it's up to the other parent, not you, to explain why he didn't come to the hosptial. If you are the parent who failed to appear at the hospital, you had better have a good excuse—and it had better not be to blame the other parent. Saying you had to work won't cut it.

Larry and Karen's Story

Larry and Karen were never married. When James was born, Larry assumed that Karen would raise their son while he had regular visits. Larry was a compulsive sort of guy who was thrilled about being a father. He was devoted to his visits, never letting his interests or anything else interfere with time with his son. Shortly after James turned five, Larry and Karen learned that James had severe allergies requiring weekly shots and a smoke-free home environment. The list of requirements provided by the allergist was extensive. Karen was to have plastic covers over James's pillow and mattress, allow no pets or stuffed animals, and give him an air-conditioned bedroom. Unfortunately, Karen was a smoker and very messy. On Friday nights, she had a usual ritual of having friends over to party. When Saturday morning came, the house was filthy and filled with the stench of cigarette smoke. The ashtrays were often full, and the trash can overflowed.

Larry badgered Karen to stop smoking and to clean the messy home. Though Karen tried to keep the house clean, there were piles of laundry on the damp basement floor, a family cat, and clutter scattered about the house. Larry would see the mess when he picked up James. He was angry about Karen's insensitivity to their son's poor health. Larry would enter the home with the eyes and nose of a drill sergeant, smelling for cigarette smoke and looking for dust or anything that violated the allergist's instructions.

Karen naturally became defensive, waiting to be chastised at every turn. She learned to dread Larry's arrival, knowing that she was going to be lectured by "this self-righteous bastard." James watched his father lecture and humiliate his mother. He felt the tension between his parents, believing the arguments were his fault. James, like most children trying to cope with a bad situation, became withdrawn and quiet when his parents were together. Blindly, his parents went on with their power struggle, unaware of how James felt. Larry, feeling that he was getting nowhere, filed for a change of custody. He argued that Karen was neglectful of James's unique medical needs because of her addiction to cigarettes. She argued that Larry was excessively critical and that her home was not a hazard to her son's health. She denied smoking in James's presence, though the dirty ashtrays betrayed her. The case is still not settled.

Differing Opinions About a Healthy Environment

Parents may have different values or ideas about what they consider a proper lifestyle and a healthy environment. Such differences of opinion are frequent sources of conflict. For example, one parent may be a strict vegetarian while the other depends on feeding the children fast foods. Or, as with the example of Larry and Karen, one ex-spouse may ignore the children's severe allergies and smoke cigarettes in front of them. Nonsmoking parents may feel appalled by the smoking parent's lack of sensitivity. These parents have been known to seek a change of custody because they believe smoking is a serious threat to their children's health. Since smoking (including passive smoke) has become a hotly contested issue, I wouldn't be surprised to see it come before the court more often. If this happens to you and you're a smoker, your personal bias may not be enough to persuade the court to allow you to keep custody.

One parent nagging the other about not smoking or eating properly does nothing to help the your ex-spousal relationship. Though you are sincerely concerned for your child's health, your ex-spouse does not have to agree with you. Furthermore, your nagging is not likely to change your ex-spouse's mind. Instead, you are creating a climate of alienation because your children will learn to dread when their parents are together. They do not want to hear your fights. The smoking parent may risk estranging their child.

Many conflicts between parents can be avoided if everyone agrees that the physician will mediate any disputes about the children's health care. For this to happen, both parents must have equal access to the physician and the children's health records. Together you may want to get guidance from your child's pediatrician. You should be sure that your attorney includes in the divorce or custody papers a provision that both parents are to have access to the physician and medical information, and that the physician will have the last word about the children's medical treatment. If you and your ex-spouse find that you cannot agree, there should be a provision that will allow either parent to get a second opinion. Either way, remember that courts have little tolerance for parents who ignore a physician's order. Don't use your children's health as a weapon to get back at your ex-spouse. The only ones you are really hurting are your children.

There were two problems facing James, the boy with severe allergies. His parents had different values about cleanliness, and his mother wasn't sensitive to his allergies. Your children, like James, have little choice but to adjust and survive with the difference in values between you and your ex-spouse. Do not criticize or badger your spouse about whose standards are correct. In time, children will make up their own mind about whose values they will later follow. For now, they have no choice but try to please both parents. Rather than argue with your children, trying to force them into your way of thinking, empathize with their dilemma. Think about how they feel caught in the middle. Consult your attorney to learn your legal options if the conditions become intolerable.

Today's parents are more health conscious. More parents do not want their children exposed to passive cigarette smoke and insist on using booster seats in the car. Recently there has been considerable concern about overweight children and their eating habits. Whether you like it or not, you must follow community standards for proper safety and health care. Otherwise, you are jeopardizing your parenting time or custody.

Safety

Parents do not have to agree on what is a safe activity or environment for their children, providing it is legal and proper safety precautions are followed. Your children should not be without proper supervision in any activity where they are physically or mentally at risk. Some states require children to wear safety helmets while riding their bicycles. If your child is injured and you violated community standards for safety, you will have little defense if you are taken back to court. Remember, regardless of your standards, the judge will use community standards and will usually adhere to the more conservative position when making a judgment about your child's safety. Everyone by now should know the laws about wearing seat belts, using car seats or booster seats, and having children under the age of twelve ride in the back seat. If your children are in an accident, you have no defense for not following proper and usual safety practices.

Calculating Risks

During your children's growing years, there will be many times when you and your spouse have to make decisions about whether your child is mature enough to take on a new risky activity. When toddlers are learning to walk, you will flinch in empathy when they fall and hit their head. Playing outside without close physical supervision, crossing the street, leaving the block to visit a friend, swimming, strolling the mall, going out on a first date, and—oh yes, the fear of all fears, driving—all are examples of activities over which parents may disagree about what is safe. Wise parents know they have to let their children take new risks to mature, although the parents will be sure the children do not get into situations that are over their head.

Making the decision to allow your child to do something new and risky will depend on your child's age and their sense of responsibility. Because there are no rules about when a child should be mature enough to do a particular activity, you have to use your best judgment. This is scary because you can learn later than your judgment was wrong. What can make matters worse is someone looking over your shoulder reminding you were wrong. After a lot of nagging and trepidation, you will finally give in and pray that you made the right decision. If your judgment is to say no to your child, then say no and live with their discontent. That is part of parenting.

Because you have to depend on your judgment to allow your child to do something that months earlier was too risky, it's possible that your ex-spouse will not agree with your decisions. This can create quite a problem, especially because your child may side with the more lenient parent. Differences can become even more apparent when your children starts dating.

Parents should try to work out their differences of opinion if they can do it without fighting and yelling in front of the children. If not, safety can become an issue that serves as a catalyst for a power struggle. The children become victims because they do not know what is the right thing to do. They are pulled between their own desires, having to please the opposing parent, and the fear that they will get into trouble. This is not fair to your children.

Tammy's Story

After months of nagging, Tammy, a rambunctious ten-year-old, was finally allowed by her father to cruise the mall with friends. She couldn't wait to get back home and tell her mother about her new adventure. She felt so grown up and excited! But Tammy didn't get the reaction from her mother that she expected

Her mother was furious. "I don't care what your father says. I told you are not to walk in the mall without your father. I expect you to do what I tell you. If anything ever happened to you, I don't know what I would do." Tammy felt deflated.

Whether you agree with Tammy's mother or father isn't the issue in this example. Both parents had to make a judgment about Tammy's maturity and the risks involved with her walking the mall with her friends. Tammy's father did nothing that was illegal, though some may question his judgment. The problem now is with Tammy. She is trapped between wanting to walk the mall with friends, her father's permission, and her mother's demand to do what she says, suggesting that otherwise she will be in trouble. What would you guess Tammy will do? If Tammy complies with her mother's demand, her father could get angry because his ex-wife is trying to control what she does during his visit. He could take his ex-wife's demand as a criticism of his judgment and parenting. Again, the battle line is drawn and the ground is fertile for alienation unless the parents come to some understanding. One parent mandating the other parent's safety standards will surely cause problems for everyone. Rather than mandating standards, the parents should discuss the issue calmly or accept the idea that both parents have an equal right to set safety standards even if the other disagrees. If the activity is legal and meets community safety standards, the disputing parent must learn to accept that there is nothing she can do. It is important not to trap your child in the middle of your dispute. You cannot expect her to comply with your demands while she is with the other parent.

Another concern you may face is when your child tells you about something you consider dangerous that he did during a visit. Before reacting to what you are told, remember that children, especially younger children, may not understand or communicate accurately, so be cautious before taking what is said at face value. Your child's description of what happened may be unintentionally wrong or distorted. Rather than just reacting and making a rash judgment to restrict or deny visits, make an effort to get an explanation from the other parent. If you get no satisfaction, think about how important the issue is before consulting with your attorney or mediator before considering stopping or restricting visits. Otherwise, you will be asking for a lot of trouble, like having to return to court for contempt.

Rescuing

If you are bored, or if Dad gets angry, call me, and I'll come get you.

A form of alienation is rescuing your child when there is no threat to his or her safety. Rescuing can imply that something is wrong or even dangerous about the targeted parent. The parent may be well meaning, but what message is the child getting? If there is a problem between the child and the other parent, it is the other parent's responsibility to work it out, not yours. On the flip side, if you are the noncustodial parent and you cannot handle your child's behavior and you call the other parent for help or ask for the child to be picked up, think about how the other parent is going to judge your parenting skills. Not good! If you are having a parenting problem that you cannot handle, get professional help or maybe attend a parenting class. You, as well as the other parent, are expected to handle what ever problems arise. Don't ask the other parent to rescue you.

TIP: Do not rescue your children unless their safety is at risk.

You can see that health issues can raise a lot of problems for everyone. When a concern is raised, maintain your calm, empathize with your child's dilemma to please both parents and try to talk out your differences with your ex-spouse. Avoid getting into a power struggle by making demands and accusations.

15

Common Alienating Tactics: Derogatory Comparisons

Your mother is a bitch who is trying to ruin me.

Refraining from making derogatory comments about the other parent in front of the child sounds like common sense. And it is—but it is still the most common example of alienating behavior. For this reason this chapter is written to emphasize a point that any parent should understand without saying.

Examples of alienating behavior are infinite. The most common is a parent making derogatory comments to the child about the other parent or significant other. Derogatory or denigrating comments can range from an offhand, casual comment to damaging accusations that give children reason to fear the other parent. An additional concern is the frequency with which the comments are made to the children. Children will let a casual comment pass without any reaction. But if they hear daily disparaging comments, in time they may believe them. This is particularly true for very young children who have had little experience with the targeted parent. Young children can be easily manipulated because they do not want to believe a parent would intentionally lie. The obsessed parent will try to isolate the children from the targeted parent, making them very susceptible to brainwashing and manipulation. Isolating the victim of alienation is a powerful tool that must be eradicated during reunification. Words become a more powerful weapon against the targeted parent when the child has no or minimal history to refute the allegations. Over time, words reinforce the child's emotional isolation by distorting the child's reality and removing an opportunity to challenge what is said with the child's own reality.

Naïve parents will make casual comments that are rarely damaging. Comments like, "You are acting like your mother," or "You are as bad as your father; can't you pick up your clothes?" A difference between a naïve and active alienator is the intensity and frequency of the statements. Active parents sound angry and will continue to rant for a time. After calming down, they may not say anything but will quietly feel guilty. An obsessed parent will use any excuse to denigrate constantly. They may not always sound angry; instead, they may show a matter-of-fact attitude about their accusations. They cannot say anything nice about the other parent. They may rationalize their behavior by saying, "I am only being honest." Even hearing the targeted parent's name can trigger a nasty retort. Words and persistence are their signature.

Derogatory Comparisons

Calling your child names, making derogatory comparisons between the child and the targeted parent, or making denigrating comments about the targeted parent within the child's hearing are all damaging. Children frequently exposed to name-calling, tirades, and constant false stories to third parties in earshot do not know how to react. They may react with anxiety or anger. Even if they passively sit by watching television, do not assume the comments are not having their impact. Derogatory comments or name-calling can have a cumulative effect on your child's thinking about themselves and the other parent. Older children understand the biological connection with the targeted parent and may not be able to differentiate what they hear about their parent from themselves. Derogatory comparisons directed to themselves and the targeted parent can harm the child's esteem. What are your children to think about themselves if you compare them with a parent you hate? When children hear such comments, they know that you are not paying the other parent a compliment. These statements hurt children in more ways than expected. Your hurt may be understandable, but this is no excuse for hurting your children by retaliating with reckless comments. Stop and think for a moment how they feel.

You must learn to avoid making derogatory comparisons between your ex-spouse and the children. There is no casual comment that does not have the potential to hurt. Not being able to stop the comparisons can be a habit, or it can be caused by your inability to heal from your hurt. If you keep tearing down your child's self-esteem with negative comparisons, in time even your apologies will be no comfort and your children may very well act out in destructive ways in the future.

Name-Calling

You can have a beer. Your mother won't know the difference because she's a stupid psycho.

Children feel uncomfortable when they hear one parent calling the other parent names. Children may not know how to react to what they hear. Should they agree with the name-caller, ignore what is said, or defend the victimized parent? Name-callers would be shocked to hear their child agree with what is said. Imagine your child saying, "Mom, I think you're right. Dad is a bastard. Someone should kick him in the ass for not paying child support." Most parents would be horrified to hear their children make such comments.

Children usually learn to absorb their parent's belittling comments, and they may often parrot the ex-spouse's derogatory words and scenarios. They keep a blank expression on their faces and go on with what they are doing without so much as a flinch. Though they appear uninterested, your children are listening to what you say. They keep their reactions to themselves. Typically, you will not know what your children think or feel about either you or the victimized parent. For this reason, you must be alert to how your children react.

A parent's alienating behavior or comments can backfire. A parent may unintentionally estrange herself from the children because of derogatory comments said about the other parent. Sometimes children feel very protective of the targeted parent. Children who hear their father is a "jerk" or their mother a "bitch" may be very uncomfortable. The derogatory comments may weaken the children's relationship with the accusing parent while strengthening the bond with the victimized parent. Usually the name-caller is unaware that the child is siding with a targeted parent because the child will not speak up to her; sometimes the child doesn't speak up to either parent.

Children of different ages have different reactions to name-calling. Younger children are quicker to believe the disparaging comments, while older children are more skeptical about what they hear. Severely alienated children are true believers without question. A continued stream of disparaging comments will reinforce in the child's thinking that something is seriously wrong with the targeted parent. As children grow older, some children are less likely to be fooled by their parent's comments. Unfortunately, before they reach this age, a teen with an active or obsessed alienator as a parent can have a severely damaged relationship with the targeted parent, and the teen does not have the wherewithal to repair the relationship. Rather than taking derogatory comments at face value, some children learn to use their own experience to form an opinion, though this realization sometimes does not occur until the teen is an adult. This is a more healthy response than passively sitting back and believing everything that is said. This is your child's right, and they usually keep their opinion to themselves. This is why name-calling can backfire.

Rational Belief: A child has the right to draw his or her own opinions based on their personal experience with the parent.

Name-calling is more serious for children already alienated because they are inclined to believe the alienating parent's disparaging remarks to be truth. The comments strengthen the children's erroneous perceptions of the targeted parent. Over time, the child's distorted reality becomes more deeply entrenched, resisting any efforts to change. These children and the accusing parent need therapy, but unfortunately these parents rarely participate because they do not see themselves as having a problem. For the alienating parent the solution is simple, according to their warped mentality: If the targeted parent really cares about the children, he will disappear.

There are occasions when a parent has successfully alienated the child (PAS) and later has had a change of heart, wanting for whatever reason to encourage a caring relationship with the targeted parent. The alienating parent, to his surprise, finds that the child's distorted reality is so entrenched that his prodding to change the child's attitude is futile. This is frustrating for both parents. Professional help, patience, and continued efforts for the targeted parent to rebuild the relationship is absolutely necessary. The once-alienating parent must be firm, not give in to the child's manipulations, and demand that the child continue with visits. The child must understand that visiting is not a choice, and parents must not give in to the child's tantrums. If parents back down and give in to the child's demands, they actually reinforce the resistance and make future changes more difficult for all involved.

TIP: Name-calling and derogatory comments about your ex-spouse must stop. You must learn to take control over what you say in your children's presence.

If you are a chronic name-caller, you need to find a healthier avenue for venting your anger. Maybe a friend or a counselor can help. When times are bad, everyone needs a confidante, whether it is a professional or a friend. Consider getting professional help if your ex-spouse continues to be a trigger for your anger. Otherwise, your children will continue to be torn by your animosity. After all, it is their mother or father you are degrading, someone to whom they are related by blood. That will never change. Some children, when hearing derogatory comments about a parent, will feel the criticism is really directed at them. If mother is called a "bitch," what does that say about her daughter? If father is named a "bastard," what does that say about his son?

Responding to Derogatory Comments

You may learn from your child or other sources about your ex-spouse making derogatory comments about you to your children. You can feel angry and helpless not knowing how to stop the comments. What you should not do is respond to your children with your own alienating comments about the other parent. When you hear the comments, do not get defensive; instead, focus on keeping the relationship with your child strong and positive. Remind your child that people say things they later regret when they are angry. Suggest to your child that she form her own opinion about others based on personal experience, rather than what she is told by others. You can use the example of how she may hear rumors about kids at school that are different from her personal experience, and remind her that she has a right to make up her own mind.

Not calling your ex-spouse names or making derogatory comments to your children is common sense. Maybe after reading this chapter you will be more sensitive to what you say to your children and know better how to respond to name-calling. It doesn't hurt to ignore what is said. Again, you are a role model for your child. Teach them by example.

16

Common Alienating Tactics: Denying Access to the Child

I would like to take you on our family vacation but you have to visit your father.

I don't care if you are only fifteen minutes late. When the court says you are to be here at six o'clock, it means six o'clock, not fifteen minutes later or earlier. Now would you just leave! We have to be somewhere.

Parenting time (or visitation) is important and is frequently the source of dissension between parents. The amount of time children spend with their noncustodial parent is often a barometer of alienation. Those who have regular contact and meaningful relationships with both parents benefit in many ways. This is why courts encourage frequent visits, providing the tensions between parents do not harm the children. Nevertheless, parenting time can be messy. Exchanges from one parent to another and phone calls asking to change parenting time provide the perfect breeding ground for conflicts and power struggles. This is especially true for an obsessed parent who will fight for all she is worth to keep the targeted parent away from the children. The obsessed parent is relentless in sabotaging any contact.

After extensive court battles to gain access, some parents give up trying to see their children. A question asked is, "Why wouldn't a parent want to visit his children?" Dudley (1991) examined the reasons from eighty-four fathers having infrequent or no contact with their children. He learned that thirty-three fathers identified the relationship with their former spouse as the major obstacle, twenty-two described personal reasons (substance abuse, job demands, girlfriends), thirteen said the children were too old or too busy to visit, and the final twelve complained that the children lived too far away. Of the thirty-three fathers whose spouse was the major obstacle, eleven complained about the court's failure to enforce or increase parenting time. Many parents simply ran out of money.

Brainwashing

Brainwashing is an accurate metaphor for understanding severe alienation. To succeed, the alienating parent must isolate the child from the targeted parent, which affords the parent an ability to manipulate the child's mind against the other parent. The child's mind is a palette of colors that can be mixed to satisfy the alienating parent's objectives. The isolated child is a vulnerable victim to the obsessed parent's control and a distorted interpretation of reality. These children do not believe they are brainwashed. Instead, they become staunch supporters of the alienating parent.

Isolating the child is not just restricting or stopping access; isolation is listening to phone calls, causing the child to watch what he says; impeding mail and presents; exposing the child to adults who perpetuate the distorted reality; changing the child's name; keeping the child from others who offer a competing view of reality; telling lies; having secrets; and giving the child reason to fear the targeted parent. In extreme cases, the obsessed parent may abduct the child, change the child's name, and move to an undisclosed location. Abducting parents rationalize their actions by arguing that they are protecting the child from the targeted parent and the system. They have no regard for long-term consequences for the child.

> TIP: The best deterrent to alienation is increasing the child's time with the targeted parent (Clawar & Rivlin, 1991) and significant family members. Conversely, the risk of further damage to the alienated child is reducing or eliminating parenting time with the targeted parent.

For parents, just seeing each other can stir strong feelings that they know must be controlled. The tension grows when the alienating parent begins scrutinizing the targeted parent's words and actions during the preparation for the visit. Sensing the scrutiny, the targeted parent becomes defensive. Both become overly sensitive and ready to pounce on the other. This is the start of the alienating cycle.

Now you need to learn how visits are used to cause or reinforce alienation and what tactics you can use to prevent or resolve these problems before they become insurmountable. Unfortunately, there are a lot ways for one or both parents to use parenting time as a weapon against the other parent. As you will learn, even the children can get into the act and cause problems.

Child Support and Parenting Time

"He doesn't pay his support on time, so why should I worry about his visits?" is the battle cry often heard to justify a parent's refusal to allow the ex-spouse to visit. Courts do not accept this argument. In most jurisdictions, you cannot withhold visits because your ex-spouse is behind in child support. These issues being separate, your must continue to allow visits and discuss with your attorney what to do about the child support.

> TIP: Courts do not equate parenting time with child support.

Because child support is an issue between you and your ex-spouse, your children should not hear about your ex-spouse not paying support, just as your children don't need to hear about other financial problems, such as credit card debt. True, children should have a basic, realistic understanding about family finances—but they need to hear, "We can't afford to buy it," not, "We can't afford to buy it because your father doesn't give us enough money." The children, like you, must face the reality that divorced parents do not usually have the same standard of living as when married. This is reality that both parents must learn to live with.

Implications for Noncustodial Parents

Countless parents ask, "Why should I continue to pay child support if I can't see my kids?" Courts rule against this weak logic because the money is for the children's care, which continues regardless of whether parenting time occurs. The children still need to be fed and clothed. The court views withholding child support under these circumstances as punishing the children rather than punishing the uncooperative parent. Unfortunately, the court does not often exercise effective sanctions against a parent refusing to cooperate with visits. Many states have changed laws that allow for easier sanctions and collection for arrears (being behind in child support). This disparity does not always feel fair. And, though courts can punish parents for nonpayment, the custodial parent often must go through numerous hearings before the court forces the other parent to send the money. So, the cycle continues: one parent (often the father) neglects paying support because he doesn't see his kids; the other parent (often the mother) retaliates by stopping parenting time. There has been some data finding a higher percentage of noncustodial mothers not paying required child support than noncustodial fathers. What percentage of nonpaying mothers is sanctioned by the courts is not known. Court sanctions should not harm the children or the children's relationship with either parent. Parents must realize that parenting time and child support are separate issues, each independent from the other.

States give judges discretion allowing for an involuntary change of custody when a parent refuses to allow parenting time because of alienation. There is no research on how an involuntary change of custody affects the children's adjustment and their relationship with both parents. Dr. Richard Gardner (2001) conducted a study supporting the argument for an involuntary change of custody, but his results are not conclusive. Many courts have disregarded his study. An involuntary change of custody is risky when courts cannot predict a child's adjustment over time when forced to live with the targeted parent. When the new custodial parent receives custody, it is essential for that parent and the children to receive counseling together. The children and parent are likely to have problems integrating into a new family.

Managing Visits

Most cases of alienation involve some problem with parenting time. Parenting time is a commodity that has value for both parents as well as the children. The time spent with either parent is much like a rubber band pulled in opposite directions by both parents until ready to snap. Parents believe someone will win and someone will lose the struggle. Strength has nothing to do with who has the power. Instead, the power rests with the parent or child who says "no" to the visit.

I don't care about your business trip. The court says you're supposed to take Jackie that weekend!

Many problems with visits would be eliminated if parents followed court orders. Obsessed parents frequently ignore court orders, requiring the targeted parent no choice but to return to court. Ideally, changing parenting times for a special activity should be negotiable between both parents. Children should not be part of the negotiation, though their desires should be considered. Children will sometimes ask to schedule changes for their own reasons. In practice, most courts do not care what parents do with visits or parenting time if everyone agrees. Courts only get involved if parents cannot come to an agreement and continue to fight, leading to further litigation. If parents cannot agree on parenting time, the court has no choice but to order a rigid schedule.

> TIP: Courts should avoid using the phrase "liberal visitation" with high-conflict parents and should instead have very specific parenting times when parents have a history of arguing about access.

Parents who rigidly follow the court-ordered parenting time schedule may do so to avoid arguments. The parent's rigidity can also be excessive, to satisfy their own needs rather than those of their children or ex-spouse. As long as both parents cooperate, problems are few. But adherence to the rigid schedule, the parent who says "no!" has the power of the gatekeeper. Many angry and alienating parents abuse their gate keeping power, humiliating the targeted parent.

When one parent makes frequent requests for a change in the schedule, the other parent might give an angry rebuttal: "Why should I let you bring Tracy home late? You wouldn't give me the same courtesy when I wanted more time last month." The rejecting parent may feel power saying "no" to the other parent. Sometimes the resisting parent has good reason to distrust the other parent because history has proven that the other parent will not reciprocate. If you want cooperation with changing visits, plan to give something up in return.

> TIP: Everyone wants a sense of fairness. You can expect the other parent to get angry or resentful if you are a taker and not a giver. Parents must strive to balance the give and take.

Conversely, making excessive requests to change scheduled parenting times disrupts not only the parent's schedule and emotions, but also the child's, and should be avoided. Watching parents argue about changes in the parenting time schedule can remind your children of past fights. They sit silently, hoping neither parent notices their presence.

Children learn to dread the question asked by either parent, "Do you want to visit this weekend?" Children feel uneasy with this type of question because they know they are being asked to choose a side. Either side they choose, someone will be disappointed. It is a no-win situation. The children's desires get lost. The children may even think that parents' fighting is their fault, that they have done something wrong simply because they want to see the other parent. Do you have any memories hearing your parents fight about you? The fights can be scary. To keep peace, the children learn to keep quiet and not ask for any changes in parenting time. They learn that asking for change can trigger more fights. They know they cannot be late returning home or accept offers to go someplace special on a weekend different than one already scheduled. Sadly, the children learn to keep their desires to themselves.

Tips on Changing the Parenting Time Schedule

- If you want to reschedule a visit or bring the children home late, clear it with the other parent before asking your children. Don't get the children excited over a special event that the other parent could veto if she doesn't agree. Don't get your children involved in fights over visits.
- What seems to you like an important reason for changing the schedule may seem unimportant to your ex-spouse. Don't assume that your ex has to agree with your opinion.
- It's okay to ask for your children's input, but not in a way that makes them feel that they must choose one parent over the other. Be aware of how your voice or choice of words can influence your children's feelings.
- Parents and courts can view frequent requests for schedule changes as a harassment or an intrusion in the other parent's life that can stir considerable resentment.
- Do not tempt your children with a fun activity that conflicts with a scheduled visit before getting the okay from the other parent. This is an alienating tactic.

Canceling Visits

I don't want to visit, and you can't make me!

The most common symptom of parental alienation syndrome is the child's unwavering insistence upon not wanting to spend time with the targeted parent for no rational reason. Behind the child's cutting words is often an obsessed alienator who has many reasons for refusing visits. Some of their reasons may sound reasonable, while others are ridiculous. A teen in love would rather be with a boyfriend or girlfriend than see Dad; or perhaps an important ball game conflicts with Mom's weekend. Even good reasons for changing visits should only be an occasional interruption.

The noncustodial parent has good reason to suspect alienation when the other parent frequently cancels visits and offers absurd reasons. The cancellations are a reminder of the noncustodial parent's power over the time spent with the children. Noncustodial parents fear abuse of this power because there is little they can do about it other than file an expensive contempt charge against the custodial parent for failure to cooperate with parenting time. The noncustodial parent must trust the custodial parent's motives and judgment for canceling a visit. You can expect the other parent's resentment when there is a lack of trust. Both parents should do as much as possible to build—or rebuild—trust.

Children Given Choices

Sweetheart, do you really want to visit Daddy this weekend?

Courts differ about how much control a child should have in deciding to visit a parent. Some courts insist that the noncustodial parent's right to have a visit has precedence over the wishes of the child. Other courts argue that when children have reached a certain age, say sixteen, they should know what they want and should exercise greater control over parenting time. Still other courts are vague about the child's power to decide. If the court believes the child should have the right to decide to visit, the court order should say so. Otherwise, the court assumes the child will follow the court order, and both parents should assume likewise. If the court order is vague and causes problems, mediation can help resolve disputes and is less expensive than returning to court.

Courts maintain the position that you should not offer your children choices that are contrary to court orders. Doing so sabotages the court's authority. In fact, many judges will take your defiance as a personal insult. They will reject the argument that you cannot force your children to visit. The court may remind you that children have no choice about attending school. You do not ask your children if they want to attend; you tell them to be up at seven o'clock to catch the bus by eight. So why should your authority be any less in demanding that the child attends parenting time? It can be argued that you should not have custody if you cannot control your child.

TIP: Remember your task as a parent is not to always ensure your child's happiness.

Parents face difficulty about what to do when children start complaining about visits, at the same time the court insisting parents follow the parenting time order. You may want to support your children's wishes although you know you would be in contempt for not enforcing the court order.

Your desire to please your children and your frustration for having to enforce the court-ordered parenting time may incite your anger. Do not direct your anger toward your ex-spouse because of his insistence on seeing the children at the court-ordered time. Maybe you have to face the reality that the other parent is not going to disappear. Seeing his child is his right unless the court says otherwise. If you were the noncustodial parent, you would want the same right. Whether the custodial or noncustodial parent withholds parenting time, both parents feel the same injustice and anger. To avoid the possibility of alienation, do not give your children a false impression that they have a choice about parenting time when, in fact, there is no choice.

TIP: Do not offer your child choices about parenting time when they have no choice.

Placing Blame Where It Belongs

If the kids don't want to see you, what can I do?

Rather than taking responsibility for interfering with visits, many alienating parents place the blame on the children. Do any of these tactics sound familiar to you?

- "It's a shame that the children don't want to visit you." The alienating parent pretends to be a sympathetic harbinger of bad news.
- "My son knows what he wants. I'm not getting involved." This is a passive attempt to alienate. The alienating parent appears neutral and uninvolved, denying any responsibility for the child's behavior.

- "I can't force them to visit! If they don't want to go, that's their choice." The alienating parent professes lack of control over the children's wishes.

- "Nobody, not even the court, is not going to tell my children they have to visit you. They have rights, too." The alienating parent doesn't believe a court order can prevent him from doing whatever he wants. In fact, the alienating parent is often self-righteous in his belief that he is defending her children's rights, so he feels justified in defying court orders. This is very characteristic of an obsessed parent. No one is going to tell an obsessed parent what to do.

The stalemate between parents occurs with the obsessed parent firmly resisting any cooperation with the targeted parent and the court because nothing anyone does or says will change the parent's position. The obsessed parent is angry with everyone, including the court that challenges her authority to make decisions for their children. Isolating the child is the goal. How the targeted parent feels is completely unimportant. The targeted parent now feels helpless because he usually has no access to the child while the alienating parent has made her position clear. It is the perfect breeding ground for alienation. The only recourse for the targeted parent is returning to court. The targeted parent at this point feels beaten down, desperately wanting to believe that the court will hear their case and correct the injustice. What the court does or does not do will influence the defeated parent for years.

Children Sharing Good Times

Mom, I had a great time with Dad!

Children like to talk about having a good time when they return home from a visit. They may be excited about recounting their weekend. Yet hearing their stories about their good time can cause a parent to feel envious of the children's weekend and the relationship they have with the other parent. Though the parent tries to hide the hurt, children are sensitive and may see a disappointed look or the forced smile on the parent's face. They will only share their feelings if they know they are not hurting Mom because they had fun with their dad. Sensing there is something wrong, children learn to be cautious before expressing any more enthusiasm about the visit. They do not want to add to your hurt.

> *TIP: Do not make your children feel bad because they had a good time with the other parent. Watch how you react to their enthusiasm, lest you close communication with them.*

Children react differently when they sense your negative reactions to their having a good time. They could feel guilty, thinking that your pain was their fault. Or, they could get angry, blaming their other parent for hurting you. Whatever the reasons for your reaction, the children should not have to dampen their excitement and miss sharing their good time with you. Expect your children to have a good time during their visit and know they have the right to express their pleasure about a visit without feeling guilty for hurting your feelings.

If you find yourself feeling jealous or hurt by your children's account of their weekend, assure them that you are glad they had a good time. If your child notices your hesitation, take a moment and mentor them about how it is okay for people to have conflicting feelings. Children need to learn that a person can have conflicting feelings: they can feel good about a visit and sad that they couldn't share the fun with you. Give your children support. Let them know that their having a good time on a visit is important to you. Let the children spontaneously tell you about their visit, but do not pump them for information. Mostly listen.

> *TIP: Do not interrogate your children.*

Feeling jealous of the time your children spend with your ex-spouse is miserable. Other parents and mental health professionals will tell you that, like grief and loss, trying to heal from jealousy over your ex-spouse's activities has no fixed deadline. If you fail to heal, and you continue to feel hurt or bitter by your children's accounts of their visit, you should consider talking to a counselor. Your children should not be stifled because you are not healing.

Lynn and Jacob's Story

Lynn remarried and has two stepchildren. Her son from a previous marriage, Jacob, was scheduled to visit his father, Michael, on Labor Day weekend. Lynn felt bitter about the visit because her family had a traditional family picnic on Labor Day weekend. This year, the family decided to have the picnic at Sea World. Lynn knew her ex-husband would refuse her request to change the weekend. Though Lynn did not want her son hurt, unfortunately, her stepchildren teased Jacob about not going with them. Jacob was hurt and disappointed. He no longer wanted to visit his father because he was angry. He instead wanted to go to Sea World. Jacob started complaining to his father about not wanting to visit because "it's boring."

Conflicting Schedules

Dad, I can't go to Disneyland. It's Mom's weekend.

Both parents should know the children's parenting time schedule as outlined by the court. The schedule will allow you an opportunity to plan vacations and spend recreational time with your children. There should be no confusion over where the children are going on any particular week or weekend or for holidays and vacations. If you and the other parent want to change the schedule, no one cares so long as you both agree.

Competing Activities

Parents know how easy it is to entice children to spend time with them. They know that children want to go where they think they will have the most fun. Children will not usually empathize with their targeted parent's loss. A parent dangling a temptation like a trip to an amusement park or the beach will knowingly cause the children to feel torn between wanting to go to a special place and concern over how the other parent will react. Creating temptation is a common alienating tactic. The child may vilify the parent who refuses permission for the outing, while adoring the other parent who holds the promise of doing something exciting and fun.

TIP: Do not schedule competing fun activities when you know your child cannot attend because it conflicts with parenting time.

Jacob's dilemma is common for children of divorced parents. He wants to experience a feeling of family unity by participating in family gatherings and traditions. Even more, Jacob wants to do what he believes will be the most interesting. Lynn could have prevented Jacob's distress by first talking to her ex-husband, Michael, about the weekend. Jacob's father would have had to set aside his feelings and place his child's needs before his own. However, Jacob's father may also have wanted to share a special activity with Jacob for Labor Day. Indeed, sometimes battling parents engage in one-upsmanship, trying to entice their children's loyalty and encourage visits by making offers more exciting than what the other parent offers. Michael may have been more accepting of Lynn's request if she had offered something in return to maintain a sense of fairness. Possibly Lynn could offer Michael an extra day with Jacob in exchange for Labor Day. But both Michael and Lynn must trust that the other will keep his or her word before negotiation can be successful. Both have to have a history of keeping their word.

> TIP: You must be willing to give in order to receive.

Lynn could have been more sensitive about planning such an exciting event on a weekend when Jacob was not home. She could have tried to talk with her husband about planning the activity on another weekend or planned another special activity at another time that would include Jacob. There is no simple answer to this situation that will make everyone happy. Both parents must communicate well before the event to avoid conflicting agendas and consider *all* the children's feelings.

> TIP: Alienation occurs when the offending parent schedules tempting activities that interferes with a visit, straining the relationship between the children and the non-offending parent.

Special occasions require parents to work together by negotiating changes with visits. The parent's animosity should not interfere with the children's desire to attend a special function. After the parents have discussed the request, give your children an opportunity to express their feelings about attending the function without interference or coaxing from either parent. The parents should not get into a fight trying to convince the children what to do. Both parents need to support the children by either negotiating an exchange of weekends or leaving the original schedule alone. For your children to feel comfortable about their choice, parents must set aside their feelings and consider their children. Otherwise, parents again victimize their children.

> I have a date. Why do I have to visit Dad this weekend?

When children become teenagers, they develop social lives independent from their parents. This is a healthy development. Teens can think that visits are an annoyance when it interferes with their social lives, especially when teens fall in love. Almost any teen would rather be with a boyfriend or girlfriend than with a parent, especially if they cannot regularly see their friend because of distance. When the other parent expresses dislike for the boyfriend or girlfriend, or has rules limiting the length of phone calls, making a teen leave for a scheduled parenting time is akin to stripping a toy from a toddler in the midst of a temper tantrum.

Parents need to empathize with their teenager's desires and social needs, and not take personally what appears as a rejection. Sometimes it helps to have a thick skin. The noncustodial parent should be flexible and willing to negotiate with their teenager about visits. If you start fighting about the visit, you may get your visit—but what have you really won if your teen's attitude makes the visit miserable? Most often, a son or daughter can just as easily leave for a date from the noncustodial parent's home. Parents must also be sensitive to teenagers' need for use of the telephone and text messaging. However, children should know that both parents will monitor their son or daughter's activities.

> TIP: Try not to be overly sensitive to your child's nasty or mean comments.

Parents Attending Children's Activities

Courts could prevent a lot of misunderstanding if the court orders were more specific in outlining the parent's rights to attend the children's activities. Many parents would be less confused. Often, the noncustodial parent has the mistaken perception they must have the custodial parent's permission to attend the children's activities. Asking permission can ignite a power struggle between parents. The parent asking may feel humiliated by the very person they resent. To avoid a fight and the humiliation of losing the argument, the noncustodial parent refuses to show up, rather than having to ask permission. Children do not understand this. They may assume that their noncustodial parent does not care about them enough to attend. Now, the children are disappointed by what they perceive as the parent's obvious rejection, even if the rejection is caused only by the custodial parent's refusal to cooperate with the ex-spouse. The noncustodial parent misses the opportunity to see their children perform. Everyone loses, except the alienating parent.

Alienation can be the cause of your child giving no reason they do not want you or a family member to attend one of their activities. Another consideration is the child's age. Young children can sincerely lack the language skills to articulate their reasons. "I don't know" may be an honest answer. True, your child may be too uncomfortable to answer your questions. Be patient and try to understand what your child is feeling. Unfortunately, you also have to contend with a parent who may be reinforcing the idea that their excuses are justified and that your child has the right to exclude you.

The custodial parent must realize their ex does not need permission to attend activities unless restricted by court order. Instead, information should be shared. You can supply the facts—who, what, when, where, and why—without arguing. In fact, giving the other parent the necessary information will prevent arguments. Parents do not need to sit together at the function, but they should remain cordial and cooperative when they are together. Allow the child to experience the support of both parents without conflict.

Court orders outlining parental rights should include a statement encouraging the noncustodial parent's participation in the children's activities. Both parents should have equal rights to attend athletic events, school parties, teacher conferences, graduations, recitals, or scouting events. Courts should not include in court orders any restrictions on attendance, unless one parent has shown reason for the limitations (such as stalking, violence, etc.). When one parent has a restraining or protection order against the other (for example, the order says the father cannot come within fifty feet of the mother) the order must be followed. Consult with your attorney if the restraining order is not clear. Courts could help keep the restricted parent involved with their children's activities by designating a third party to attend the activity with the parent. There must be no confusion about how the restrained parent is expected to behave.

"Mom, Why Can't Dad Come to My Game?"

Children who are not alienated from either parent will want both parents to attend their social activities. They want to show off their talent at sporting events or recitals so they can revel in their parents' applause. Only after the children have experienced alienation or if they have witnessed their parent's public display of hostility will they comment about not wanting both parents to attend. A custodial parent who "forgets" to give the other parent notice of their children's activities, refuses to give information about activities, or demands that the other parent ask permission to attend an event encourages alienation, usually for their own interests.

Noncustodial parents are as eager as custodial parents to watch their children play baseball, sing in a school concert, or have them leave from their home for a date. Both relish the opportunity to witness their children's special day, take pictures, and record the occasion in videos. To squelch unnecessary suspicion and distrust and build meaningful sharing of parenting, parents must tell each other their children's schedules. This allows both parents the opportunity to choose whether or not to attend the activity. Most schools will make notices of activities available to parents, if the parents provide stamped envelopes.

> TIP: If both parents attend their children's event, both are expected to be cordial and well behaved. Do not embarrass the children. Remember, you are role models for proper behavior.

You may think you do not want your ex-spouse to attend your children's activities, and feel their presence is an intrusion into your private life or a hassle you would rather avoid. If you feel this way, you should consider whether you are reacting to your own self-interest or what is best for your children.

Having both parents attend their children's activities can be awkward for everyone. If you anticipate too much tension between you and your ex-spouse, consider attending the school open house at a different time, or rotating the ball games. When both parents attend an event simultaneously, you should expect to sit apart. Parents do not have to socialize with each other, though they must be civil and polite for the children's sake. When your children feel your tension, they will usually feel guilty and ashamed, thinking it is their fault. Do not subject your children to this ordeal. Do not ruin their special event.

> TIP: When you see your ex-spouse at an event, do not think you have the right to get into a heavy discussion about the divorce or whatever else you need to work out. This is not the time or place. You are there to enjoy watching your child and not ruin the event for everyone.

Tips on Managing Activities

- The courts should be explicit in encouraging the noncustodial parent to attend the children's activities.
- You and your ex-spouse should plan your children's social activities together if the activity is expensive or there is the potential for time conflict.
- Do not schedule your children in too many activities. The courts will suspect alienation if numerous activities interfere with scheduled visits. When planning activities, give your child options and prioritize what activities are most important. Either parent can say "no" if the activities consume too much time from schoolwork or parenting time.
- Custodial parents have more power than noncustodial parents because they have physical possession of the children and can say no. However, noncustodial parents should not have to ask permission to attend their children's activities. Otherwise, the other parent has too much power that can be abused.
- Remember, your children's activities are for everyone to enjoy. If need be, put your feelings aside and support your ex-spouse's desire to attend school activities, ball games, or recitals. Your children will feel better having your support.
- Don't let your children dictate who attends their activities. Often children who say, "I don't want Dad to come to my ball game," really mean, "I feel the tension between you and Dad whenever you are together."
- Parents do not have to sit together at their child's functions. Don't expect your children to sit with you during an event if it is not your weekend or the children are not in your care. Parents should be polite and focus their attention on what their child is doing rather than on each other.
- Make a conscious effort to give your children permission to greet the other parent when you both attend the same activity. Children should feel your assurance that they can hug or kiss the other parent in your presence without offending you.
- If the parents live a reasonable distance from each other, there is no reason that your children should not leave for a social activity from the noncustodial parent's home.

Overscheduling Children

> She's got gymnastics or swimming every weekend. You can't expect
> her to visit.

In recent years, parents seem to be doing whatever they can to enroll kids in many outside school activities. Some parents believe healthy, well-rounded children must be very busy. Younger children may start in dance, gymnastics, or karate. Older children are busy with music lessons, soccer, or Scouts. Parents frequently complain about the time spent chauffeuring children from one activity to another. Running to meet the schedules is exhausting.

Overscheduling occurs when one or both parents schedule the children in so many activities that visits becomes impossible or restricted. One mother explains, "I often feel worse for her than for me because I believe she is overextended." Overscheduling can be perceived as an act of alienation.

Parents have been heard to say, "If your father [or mother] really cared about you, he wouldn't expect you to choose between Scouts and visits. He should understand there are times when you are too busy to visit." The statement rationalizes a parent's attempt to alienate. In essence, the parent is saying the child's activities are more important than any relationship the child could have with the other parent.

Most children know when they are involved in too many activities. They complain of feeling tired or will give you a hard time about going to the activity. If you have to nag or cajole your children to attend a specific activity, you may question why their participation is so important. Are you more interested in satisfying your own needs than those of your children? If you hear yourself say, "I know what's best for my children. They will thank me later," you need to question your motives. Maybe you should take a moment and listen to what your children are telling you. It is possible they want to slow down and feel less stress.

Scheduling children in too many activities is usually motivated by parents' unconscious desire to live vicariously and enhance their own self-esteem through the children's successes. They hope for bragging rights to embellish their own sense of self-importance. They appear to others as driven in the quest for their children's success. They are usually the parents who yell the loudest at ball games, are visibly angry when a referee makes a bad call, or are quick to publicly criticize their children for a less-than-perfect performance. Such behavior embarrasses children. These parents believe they are well-meaning, but are confusing their needs with those of the children.

Both parents want their children to be active and well liked by their peers. Noncustodial parents do not want to feel that time with the children takes away from the children's social life. On the other hand, they do not want to be seen as a meddler or a nuisance. This loss of status is demeaning. Instead, the noncustodial parent wants to feel as important in their children's lives as the custodial parent.

You can be active in your child's activities if you choose. To avoid being the fifth wheel with the child, one option is to volunteer to transport your child to and from the activity. True, if your child lives some distance away, the transportation could be time-consuming, but that's the cost of living a distance from your children. Taking over some of the chauffeuring could even give your ex-spouse relief from a hectic schedule. These responsibilities are part of what parenting is all about and are often welcomed by the noncustodial parent.

Precious opportunities are lost when you react by passively waiting to be invited to spend time with your child. Alienating parents rarely see what they are doing, and if they do, they usually don't try to make amends by allowing make-up visits or taking corrective actions. Instead, the victimized parent is usually forced to go back to court and ask that limits be placed on the alienating parent's actions and on the children's activities. Unfortunately, this may give the children the perception that you are the bad guy, especially if the alienator tells the children why they are returning to court. A more effective and less expensive approach is court-ordered mediation, starting with the assumption that the victimized parent is entitled to the standard order of parenting time.

Broken Promises and Trust

But you promised you'd be there!

A problem frequently occurs when parents do not understand that telling their children they will attend an activity is considered a promise. In the children's mind, the parent not attending the activity is the same as breaking a promise. If you tell your children you plan to attend a sports or social event, you *must* live up to your promise. If you don't, you better have a good reason; otherwise, you are creating your own estrangement.

People often misunderstand the word trust. It has nothing to do with liking a person. Trust simply means the ability to predict meaning; you do what you say you are going to do. Parents must teach and demonstrate trust to their children. One way to do this is to keep the promises they have made. If you value trust, the only way to build trust is to be consistent and predictable with your children and your ex-spouse. If you develop a pattern of not keeping your promises and instead are full of surprises, you are heading for big trouble with your children. They learn that your word is meaningless. Worse yet, they think you are a liar. Either way, you are seriously damaging your relationship with your children.

Second, to teach trust, you must admit when you have broken a promise, without excuses. Children do not trust excuses. At first, they may accept your excuses, but over time, their "acceptance" will diminish. If you want to make amends, you must start by becoming predictable, and do what you say you are going to do. You cannot expect your ex-spouse to keep making excuses for you or mend your children's hurt. This is your responsibility. After all, the damage is your doing, not your ex-spouse's doing. If you do nothing to prevent disappointing your child, they will learn to defend themselves emotionally by not caring. That means not caring about *you*. This is a terrible price to pay for something that you have control over.

Roger and Johnny's Story

Roger meant well when he told his son, Johnny, "I'll be at the park this weekend to watch your tennis match." Johnny, sounding almost apologetic, said to his father, "You don't have to, Dad. I know you're busy." Roger persisted in assuring his son that he would be at the match. Late Sunday evening, Roger called to apologize to Johnny. "I'm sorry, Johnny, It couldn't be helped. I got called in to work."

Protesting, Johnny said, "But you promised to come. You said you would be there."

"Johnny, I didn't promise to be there; I said I'd try."

"Yes, you promised! You lied to me! I don't want to see you anymore!" Roger sat there listening to the dial tone.

Roger knew why his son was angry. What happened later came as a surprise. As the weeks passed, Johnny no longer wanted to visit his father. For whatever reason, Johnny's anger was not healing. Possibly his anger is being fueled, perhaps by his mother or someone else close to him. Johnny reasoned that, by refusing to visit, he was punishing his father. This gives

Johnny power. If Johnny's mother remains passive about her son's refusal, she encourages his perception that he is entitled to make these decisions. Johnny learns that his anger is justified and has the right to dictate his father's behavior. This perception is not healthy for Johnny or either of his parents.

Irrational Belief: Remaining passive removes me from any responsibility.

Responding to Your Child's Hurt and Anger

You don't care anyway.

Many children in time will reject a parent who frequently disappoints them by breaking promises or canceling visits. This was definitely true for Roger. His son Johnny retaliates with a rationalization: "Dad never cared; otherwise, he would have come to my tennis matches." He wants to hurt his father by rejecting him.

Johnny's reaction is understandable. Children, like adults, will often silently nurse their hurts. They hold onto the feelings until their hurt turns to anger. Now they share their anger rather than their hurt with such statements as, "I don't want you to come. You don't care anyway." Sadly, Johnny pushes his father away when he really needs his father's reassurance that he cares. Johnny reacts with the only power he knows: rejecting his father.

Johnny should be able to tell his father about his hurt, but should not think he dictates his father's behavior. Such a mistaken belief will cause Johnny, in time, to become more demanding and resistant to both of his parents' authority. When listening to children like Johnny, one usually hears arrogance in their voices, an unhealthy attitude for children. Johnny should not think he has the right to dictate his visitation schedule, or whether his father attends his tennis matches. Both parents can expect Johnny to become increasingly arrogant if they surrender to his demands.

Parents can break this impasse by encouraging their children to share their hurt rather than their anger and to seek reconciliation rather than retaliation. This really works. The next time you get angry; try sharing your hurt, if that is what you are actually feeling. Expressing your hurt, rather than yelling, will get a different reaction from the other person. If you do not immediately get the response you want, be patient and continue sharing your hurt. Parents can model this method for their children, and help them learn that sharing hurt is okay and not a sign of weakness. Share with them how surprised you felt to learn that sharing hurts evokes better responses from others. Be careful not to get defensive or combative when your children share their hurt. Listen and be reassuring. The more your children practice sharing their hurts, the less angry they'll feel, the less they'll feel like retaliating, and the more they'll feel others have really heard them.

TIP: Unjustified anger is a good benchmark that alienation has occurred.

Ideally, if you can talk calmly with your ex-spouse, you might pass along what your child has said and gently suggest that your child would love to hear more supportive comments. Some overzealous parents get overly critical about how his child is playing ball. They take every opportunity during a game to tell the child how to improve their performance. This criticism—and often yelling—drives the kid nuts and takes the fun out of playing. When this happens, the child will frequently complain, saying, "Dad, I don't want you to come and watch me play." The father is insulted and hurt. He immediately thinks that his ex-spouse is behind his child's attitude; he cannot imagine that *his* behavior, not hers, has caused his child to feel this way. He does not understand his own role in causing estrangement.

Surprise Visits

Surprise, I'm here!

There are two fairly common circumstances when parents make a surprise visit. The most frequent occurrence is when a parent decides to come to a sporting event or other special event without either the other parent or the child having any advance notice. All of a sudden you look up and—"Dad's here!" The other circumstance is when the parent hasn't been around in months, or perhaps years, and out of nowhere shows up. Either of these situations can be uncomfortable, but there are ways to deal with such surprises.

Advice to Custodial Parents

As emphasized above, many courts write into the divorce decree a provision stating that either parent has the right to attend any of the children's social or educational activities. If this decree is in your shared parenting plan, you should not be surprised if your ex-spouse shows up. If surprised by your ex-spouse's appearance, do not discuss why he's there during the ball game or open house. This could cause a scene and make everyone uncomfortable, particularly your child. Instead, stay calm, be polite, and discuss it later. Neither parent should threaten the other parent about going to court without first trying to talk with each other, away from the children's presence.

> TIP: Do not threaten your ex-spouse with returning to court if you are angry and only want to retaliate. Threatening to return to court raises anxiety and hostilities. Do not expect cooperation if you make threats.

If it has been years since you have seen your ex-spouse and she suddenly appears at the door, you will certainly be surprised. The most important thing is not to panic. Calmly talk to your ex-spouse, away from the children, about her intentions and try to work out a plan together that will be most comfortable for the children. If the relationship between the child and the absent parent has not been close, your son or daughter may not know whether to hug, kiss, or stand back when initially seeing the parent. It is wise to gently remind your ex-spouse that the children may feel a little awkward about seeing her and not know how to react. Ask the parent to "please be patient." Remember that your ex-spouse still has a right to see the children, unless there is a court order stating otherwise. Even if you are not thrilled to see your ex-spouse and wish she would not complicate your children's lives, remember that you do not have the authority to disobey a court order. If you any have questions, consult your attorney before taking any action. If you are in contempt for disobeying a court order, your attorney will have to defend your behavior, which is a situation you should try to avoid. You are better off going to court being on the offensive than defending a contempt motion.

Advice to Noncustodial Parents

If for whatever reason you haven't seen your children in a while, you shouldn't just show up unannounced. You could make everyone uncomfortable because they don't know how to respond. Your child and ex will be caught off guard. Before doing anything, it is only polite to let your ex-spouse and children know your intentions. If you expect problems or resistance, that is even more reason for not showing up unannounced. Begin by talking with your ex-spouse and, if there are any problems, discuss this with your attorney or mediator if you have one. Whatever you do, do not do or say anything rash. Instead, think ahead of time about what you want to do and how your children will feel.

TIP: You must restrain yourself if you feel attacked or challenged.

It is hard on your children if you have not seen them for a long time and you show up at their door, proclaiming your right to visit them. The custodial parent now has a dilemma. She may know that you are legally justified to see your children, but she also has to be concerned for your children's feelings. She may believe that you and the children should have a healthy relationship and may actually welcome the idea of your re-establishing a relationship with the children. At the same time, she is feeling protective of the children because she is afraid that you will re-establish a relationship, raise the children's hopes, and again disappear. Having disappeared once is good cause to distrust you, even if you think you had good reasons for disappearing. Your ex-spouse will naturally want to protect your children from being hurt again. She may also resent having had to pick up the emotional pieces after you left the last time. She cannot trust you because she has no idea what you will do in the future. All of these concerns are frightening to the custodial parent.

Caught in this dilemma, the custodial parent often does not know what to do. The two of you will need to be patient and take time to rebuild mutual trust. If you have not seen your children in a while and you want to see them again, initially plan short visits until your children get comfortable. Allow your children to have some input in setting the pace for extending the length of the parenting time. When children feel that they have some control, it helps to reduce their anxiety. Because children want to avoid any situation that is uncomfortable, you may have to do a little supportive coaxing.

Have realistic expectations when you see your children for the first time after a long absence. Don't expect your child (or your ex) to be happy to see you; don't expect or ask your children to hug you. Instead, allow them to initiate physical contact. Your children may feel very nervous, which can appear as indifference. Also, your children may feel confused and conflicted, which can appear as anger, especially if they vacillate between feeling happy to see you and hurt over your previous absences. Act cordial and show respect toward your ex, who may feel angry and protective of the child's feelings.

Many children who are not alienated are happy to see the estranged parent after many years. However, if you arrive unannounced, do not expect a warm welcome. At first, your children may be apprehensive because they do not know how to react or what to say. I remember when my father came to see my brother and me after many years; my brother asked what to call our dad. By this time, he was calling our stepfather "Dad," so it felt funny for him to call his biological father "Dad" as well.

After the visit or event, make yourself available if your child chooses to talk to you, but don't insist. They may not want to talk right away, especially in the other parent's presence. Let your child know how much you enjoying seeing them. If you attended one of your children's events, praise their performance. Say good-bye before leaving, but don't make false promises about seeing them later. Instead, tell the children if you plan to talk to your ex-spouse about arranging a visit. Reassure them that you will not disappear again. Remember what was previously said about breaking promises.

Advice to Stepparents and Grandparents

Sometimes stepparents and grandparents are uncomfortable when a biological parent shows up after years of absence. They are threatened because they may need to develop a relationship with the other parent and don't like the idea that "this guy just shows up and thinks he can disrupt our lives. How dare he act as if everything is the same, as if he never left?"

Significant others may have strong feelings, but have few rights to determine what will happen with visits. Remember, the last court order is still in effect unless the custodial parent has returned to court and changed the order. If you have questions, call your attorney. The stepparent needs to sit back and be supportive of the spouse's efforts to work things out. They should not get too involved, especially in talking with the other parent and the children about visits.

Chaos can break loose if significant others, rather than the biological parent, become overinvolved in discussing visits or how to reintroduce the parent into the children's lives. The returning noncustodial parent gets angry, questioning, "Who is this person telling me whether I can see my own children?" This can be a delicate situation because it is easy for the significant other to start alienating the children against the estranged parent.

Many stepparents feel threatened when the biological parent appears from nowhere and claims their right to resume parental responsibilities and, in effect, pushes the stepparent aside. This can be scary. However, stepparents and significant others should remember that, when they have a strong, loving relationship with the children, the children will continue to love them as well as their newfound biological parent. They should not get drawn into the arguments between the two parents. They can be supportive without being a vocal advocate.

What are you to do if your ex-spouse refuses to let you see your children, contrary to court orders? If all your efforts have failed, you may consider filing a contempt charge against your ex-spouse. Though this sounds like a reasonable solution, you must be realistic about what to expect. Sometimes courts are not very effective in enforcing a parenting time order when the other parent does not care about the consequences of her actions. The obsessed alienator may be entrenched in the belief that her position is correct and is consequently willing to defy the court's authority. This causes problems for the court because much of the court's power comes from the perception of authority and the threat of locking up the uncooperative parent. Putting the uncooperative parent in jail is a problem because the children will likely blame you for sending their mother to jail. Then, the children feel more estranged or alienated from the noncustodial parent than ever. The custodial parent, sitting in jail, becomes a martyr for protecting the children. The courts see this dilemma and try to avoid putting anyone in jail. They know that jailing a parent does little to change attitudes or bring families closer. An exception occurs sometimes when the judge decides to send *both* parents to jail to create a crisis that may break the stalemate.

If your ex-spouse is obsessed, do not get into a shouting match, particularly in front of your children. The obsessed parent will use your behavior against you to the children. "See, I told you your father was nuts and can't be trusted." Instead, stay calm, and reassure your children that you will work things out with their other parent. Talk to your attorney, inquire about a new court order requiring sanctions for noncompliance with the court orders, get an order to require counseling or reunification, and, most important, act quickly. The longer the hostilities last, the more difficult it is to reverse course. While you are denied visits, the alienating parent has more time to work on alienating your child. You must have access to your child if there is to be reunification. Waiting for children to spontaneously say to the alienating parent, "I want to see or visit" [the alienated parent] rarely succeeds, especially without support from the alienating parent.

17

Allegations of Sexual or Physical Abuse

"Sweetheart, I know you have a good time when you visit your daddy, but I need to ask you a question. Has Daddy or anyone ever touched your privates?"
"Uh, Daddy touches my pee pee."

Sex Abuse

These are words that every parent dreads hearing: "Daddy touches my pee pee." Immediately the mother is in a panic, not knowing whether to ignore what is heard or to call the attorney the first thing in the morning.

How you handle allegations of sexual abuse depends on whether you are the parent hearing your children's accusations for the first time or the parent being accused. Hearing the allegation of sexual abuse for the first time while a divorce is in process is devastating for both the alleged abuser and the children. The divorce process is thrown into turmoil because the allegations typically have to be addressed before the divorce can proceed. The outcome of the investigation can have a bearing on custody and parenting time.

How Courts Handle Allegations of Sexual Abuse

Courts are becoming more suspicious when allegations are heard for the first time during the divorce proceedings. In years past, the common belief among attorneys, prosecutors, and mental health workers was that children don't lie. The validity of this doctrine is now being challenged. Experts (Kuehnle & Drozd, 2005; Ceci & Bruck, 1995) now recognize that the issue of telling the truth is more complex because of various ways that children can be manipulated and deceived by a parent to think that something bad happened when, in fact, nothing happened.

Manipulation isn't always caused by a sinister parent wanting to get back at an ex-spouse. Well-meaning but frightened parents can unintentionally manipulate or reinforce in the child's mind that something awful happened. Children's perceptions and interpretations can be manipulated by one or both parents, lawyers, and unqualified mental health workers. That is the reason professionals investigating sexual abuse require specialized training. Damaging for everyone is the parent, an unqualified investigator, or mental health worker who uses the allegations to further a personal agenda.

The investigation is typically assigned by the court and conducted by the children's services agency. Every state has an agency responsible for conducting investigations, but they're called by different names. Some families have complained about investigators who come across as friendly and caring and then gathered information that the prosecutor can use against them, leaving them feeling trapped and betrayed. Child protective workers are conflicted because they are investigators but also hold themselves out to the public as wanting to help families. The two roles can be incompatible and lead to mistrust. Some families have felt betrayed by child protective workers. For this reason, always consult your attorney when you first learn that you are being investigated.

The court has a dilemma when someone makes an allegation of sexual abuse: Whose rights have precedence, the alleged victim's or the alleged abuser's? Courts will typically—and rightfully so—protect the alleged victim by asking the alleged offender to leave the residence until the investigation is completed. This is to protect the children's safety from the chance of further abuse and to prevent the children's story from being contaminated by the parent's questions and possible intimidation. The parent remaining with the child is expected to cooperate with the investigative agency and keep the children from the spouse. Parents who do not cooperate with the authorities and allow the accused back into the house can be seen as more worried about their own needs than their child's. The parent is expected to demonstrate a greater loyalty to and concern for the child's welfare than worry for how the spouse feels. If the investigating agency believes that you will not keep the child from the alleged offender, the agency may decide to remove the child, sometimes all the children. The children are usually placed with a relative or in a foster home until the case is resolved. The investigation can take considerable time, resulting in the alleged perpetrator having little or no contact with the child for months. It is in the child's and parent's best interest to encourage a rapid completion of the investigation so the allegations can be properly resolved.

States have varying definitions of sexual abuse. Common among most states is the distinction between sexual contact and sexual penetration. Sexual contact refers to "any contact with intimate body parts including genitals, breast, buttocks, or mouths" (Bensel et al., 1985). Sexual penetration is the insertion of a finger, penis, or an object into the rectum or vagina. When penetration occurs, including oral sex, a charge of rape could be forthcoming.

Most often sexual abuse will be reported to the authorities before the offender progresses to intercourse. Usually the complaint will describe a progressive seduction from seemingly innocent playfulness and touching to not-so-innocent sexual fondling. In some cases, the progression may takes months or even years. A question often asked is, "How far would the perpetrator have gone if they were not caught?" Of course, no one is certain of the answer. The offender will say nothing more would have happened. Investigators and the court will usually assume that it is only a matter of time before the perpetrator would rape the child.

Fixated Offenders versus Regressed Offenders

When most people think about an abuser, they have a picture in their mind of a stranger hiding behind the bushes and grabbing children. Though this happens, it is very uncommon. Most sexual abuse is done by someone who already knows the child and involves fondling. Dr. A. Nicholas Groth (1978) makes a distinction between the fixated offender and the regressed offender.

The primary sexual orientation of fixated offenders is towards children. They typically target their victim and plan their seduction, which can occur over a period of time. They are usually single and like being around children. They can be volunteers, youth leaders, or coaches. It is not uncommon for them to be well liked, even by parents. That is one reason everyone is upset when they learn of the offender's behavior. He is often a person that has earned the trust of others. These are the offenders that most parents worry about. Their prognosis for a favorable response to treatment is questionable. They require psychotherapy, monitoring, and frequently medication.

Regressed offenders prefer same-age adult sexual partners, not children, as their primary sexual orientation. These individuals typically have never had a sexual encounter with a child until a stressful event precipitates a serious temporary lapse of judgment when they sexually offend. Their behavior is more impulsive than premeditated and usually directed towards a member of the opposite sex. After the offending, they feel guilty and ashamed. They know what they did was wrong and will do most anything to convince the victim to not say anything. From this point on, they live with the fear of being discovered. These offenders, once their behavior is disclosed, are responsive to treatment providing they get beyond making excuses and take responsibility for their misbehavior. However, the offense of the regressed offender may not be seen by the court as any different than that of the fixated offender. Both can go to prison for many years.

Recently there are national and state regulations for registering sex offenders. If a parent gets convicted of a sex-related offense involving a minor, their chances for being awarded custody are next to impossible. Getting access to the children is even more complicated. The alleged offender has no choice but to cooperate and hope the allegations get resolved. In the meantime, access will be, if not totally removed, very restricted.

The differences between the fixated and regressed offender were not explained to scare you, or make you an expert. The intent is for you to understand that the issues of sexual abuse and abusers are complex, and a qualified specialist is needed to investigate any allegations. If your family is faced with the revelation of sexual abuse, the entire family may need therapy.

It is natural for you to want to protect your children when you believe their physical or psychological safety is threatened. You will do whatever is necessary to safeguard your children from any perceived threat, even if the threat comes from your ex-spouse. But this is where you have to be cautious. There is a difference between what you think is a threat and what you know is a threat. You need to know rather than just react to what you think; otherwise, you're heading for big problems. If you react to your beliefs by getting angry and threatening the other parent to withhold visits or return to court, he will naturally prepare to retaliate. To avoid this dilemma, first realize that you do not know the reasons behind the allegations. Instead, your interpretation of what occurred may be wrong. Secondly, you may be tempted to ask your children to clarify what happened. Asking for clarification will help temper your emotional reaction to your interpretation, because you now have to listen rather than think. But the risk is you can ruin your child's credibility as a witness if the defense raises the suspicion that you influenced your child's statement. Instead, report the allegation to the proper authorities and let them conduct the investigation.

Sexual Abuse and Divorce

While a marriage is falling apart and a divorce becomes more imminent, there is an increased chance of one parent accusing the other parent of sexual abuse. This is a very real risk with an obsessed parent. Allegations of abuse tend to escalate when an obsessed parent fails to eliminate the targeted parent from the children's lives. Unfortunately, for a very few parents, the risk of sexual abuse increases if the parent is emotionally needy and vulnerable. This is what happens with the regressed offender. Do not misunderstand: this is a very rare occurrence. Occasionally the parent, usually a father, begins to put the child in the role of a surrogate wife or intimate friend. The father begins confiding in his daughter about his hurt and loneliness. In turn, the sympathetic daughter offers her love and comfort. Feeling lonely and insecure, the father begins a slow progressive seductive process of holding, touching, and, in time, sexual fondling. The regressed abuser may, in time, try an overt sexual act. This is very rare, maybe because most regressed offenders get caught before progressing to more intimate sexual contact. This usually occurs in a context in which the parent is trying to be nurturing and kind. What the parent does not realize is the confusion and fear being instilled in the child. Often the offending parent does not believe that he is doing wrong because, in his heart, he does not want to hurt the child. He may rationalize the abuse by thinking that he is not hurting the child because sex is pleasurable. The offender is very wrong; children can hurt for many years to come by such conduct.

> TIP: Do not confuse good intentions with inappropriate behavior. You are probably rationalizing your behavior to make yourself look good at your child's expense.

Stacy and Her Dad's Story

Stacy had just turned seventeen when she learned that she was pregnant. She was confused and scared because she had not had sex with her boyfriend. Unbeknownst to the rest of the family, Stacy and her father had been having intercourse for the past three years. The sexual fondling had begun when Stacy was about four years old. She and her father had kept their little secret through the years, until Stacy knew she had to talk to her mother about the pregnancy. Her mother, of course, was enraged. A complaint was made to the children's services agency, and charges were later filed against her father. Stacy was angry towards her father and the legal system. She complained that the investigator from Children's Services and the prosecutor had lied to her in order to charge her father. She felt that all her power had been taken away by the legal system. Now she is waiting to see if her father will go to prison or be placed on probation. She is hoping for probation because she knows her mother could not financially support the family. Stacy is afraid that she may lose her chance to attend college. She resents her father "for not letting me have a childhood."

Parents must be cautious before making allegations of sexual abuse. An example is a mother who witnessed her seven-year-old son masturbating and then remembered that he and his father had, on one occasion, slept together. At the time, there was no evidence to suggest any impropriety by the father. The mother became frightened and immediately filed a motion to restrict the father's parenting time. Upon inquiry, the court learned that much of the child's behavior was normal and found no reason to believe the child had learned from his father how to masturbate.

This case demonstrates two important points that can lead to alienation: Mistrust can escalate into damaging allegations; and ignorance of normal psychosexual development can stir intense feelings in an unknowing parent. The incident might have been avoided if the mother had understood that young children will explore their bodies and stimulate themselves for pleasure. A proper investigation by a qualified professional could also have prevented the mother from panicking. Instead, she reacted with fear and a desire to protect her son. The mother's motivation is understandable but she must learn to think, control her feelings, and request an investigation from the proper authorities. If you really believe that sexual abuse took place, you are obligated to report it to the children's service agency.

Children are sexual little people from the day they are born. They are curious and able to experience sexual pleasure at any age. Modesty, inhibition, boundaries, values, and guilt are not innate qualities. These qualities are learned, usually vicariously by watching peers, parents, and, of course, television. If you want to be an active participant in what your children learn, you must talk openly and frankly about sex. Your discussions should be age appropriate. They need to know that talking about sex is not taboo but instead an important part of life. For your children to ascribe to your family values, you have to talk with them. They need to feel comfortable coming to talk to you about sex. If they can't, how will they ever be able to come to you and tell you, "Uncle Charlie asked me to touch his pee pee," or talk to you about proper sexual conduct?

Parents' anxiety about talking to their children about sex is more of a hindrance than is any discomfort on the childrens' part with what is being said. Children should learn the proper names of the body. Questions should be answered in an honest and straightforward manner. There is no need to give children more information than they are asking for. Do not push information on them. When they appear bored and distracted, it is time to stop the discussion.

Exaggerating Facts without Malice

It is very difficult to discuss sexual abuse without referencing a gender. Mothers may accuse fathers, fathers can accuse step-fathers, and everyone can accuse a family friend or relative. Though I am using a mother's allegation against a father, do not assume that abuse by a mother or stepparent does not happen. The suggestions for handling an allegation is the same, regardless of the perpetrator's gender.

Children can lie or give an inaccurate account about what happened without being malicious. Very young children can be confused about what is appropriate sexual behavior. Take, for example, a young child who says that someone touched his private parts. The facts may show this was true. The problem now is understanding the context in which this happened, and the intent of the person doing the touching. This is where young children have a problem. They don't understand the importance of intent and context. When a child gives an account about what happened, they may not know that anything was wrong, especially if the touching was pleasurable and not painful. The child may not understand the social significance of the touching until many years later. Children look to parents to put their account into some context and give the act some meaning, right or wrong. The child's account may be accurate, but it's often the parent who ascribes intent to the perpetrator and context to the act. This is where serious alienation can happen. Now the angry mother has every opportunity to embellish the story and nail the alleged offender. What is frightening for the father is not even knowing that anything is happening. Once the allegation is made public, he is labeled and on the defensive. A conviction, or even taking a plea because he cannot afford a proper defense, can have consequences for many years if he is required to register as a sexual offender.

You can't blame a naïve parent for embellishing the child's account of what happened. She is not an expert. She will do what comes naturally: interpret to the child the significance or meaning of what had happened. Now, the risk is if the parent's interpretation of the events is incorrect, or she reacts before hearing the whole story. The parent's reaction, seen and heard by the children, becomes part of the child's beliefs. The parent's reiteration of what is reported can be easily clouded if parents have their own issues as a result of having been sexually abused. So what was originally "Daddy touched my penis" is now "Daddy played with my penis." The latter statement has greater significance for the investigator. The change in the connotation between the two statements may have more to do with the mother's interpretation than an accurate account of what occurred. What is more devastating for the targeted parent is that his child will come in time to sincerely believe his own false or exaggerated allegations after someone has given him an interpretation of intent and context.

If your child initiates concerns about inappropriate touching, you should:

- Listen, do not interrogate.

- Do not ask detailed questions about who, what, when, and where. Leave those questions to the professionals.

- If you suspect physical or sexual abuse, immediately take your child to the hospital.

- Do not delay in taking your child to the proper authorities. The longer time between the incident and the report, the less reliable the memory.

- Do not bathe your child.

- Be supportive and caring, but don't offer any opinions about what may have happened.

What Is Your Child Too Young to Know?

When children are interviewed and judgments made about whether a child was sexually abused, a common criteria used to make that judgment is whether the child has a knowledge of anatomy or sexual behavior that is too advanced or sophisticated for a child of that age. True, there are some things that very young children wouldn't be expected to know. Young girls—say under the age of five or six—would not usually know about erections. Both young boys and girls would know little or nothing about the vaginal canal. Young girls usually think of their vagina as a hole where urine comes from, not an anatomical structure for intercourse or putting something into.

Even these examples are problematic, because we make assumptions about the ages at which children typically learn about their anatomy and sex. The fact is, we don't know. Today's children are exposed to sex and language unlike those of previous generations. This confuses children, because the frequent viewing of sexually suggestive or explicit material gives them a confused sense of what is right and what is wrong. (Television, for example, can be a terrible role model.) Children don't learn what are appropriate boundaries unless they are specifically taught. It is for these reasons that young children can be taken advantage of and sexually abused. Experts do not know at what ages children learn about explicit details of their body or sexual conduct. There are no studies saying whether Susan, age five, should or should not know about erections, oral sex, or intercourse. These are assumptions that child welfare workers or professionals use to support an allegation of sexual abuse.

The breakdown of appropriate boundaries is an issue with sex abuse. Over time the abusive parent becomes almost emotionally desensitized to boundaries, though rational thinking tells the parent that the behavior is wrong. An example is a statement made by a convicted sex offender when asked why he abused his adopted daughter, who had been in his joint care since the age of six months old, and not his biological daughter. He said, "I could never do anything like that to her. She is my daughter." The point the offender made was that the emotional boundary he felt for his biological daughter was different than that with his adopted daughter, even though both had been in his and his wife's care for many years. He acknowledged that he was guilty of the offense but was able to rationalize his behavior, even knowing that it was wrong.

Physical Abuse

No one questions that children should not be physically abused. There continues to be questions (Ver Steegh, 2005), however, about what constitutes physical abuse. Many parents express fear about spanking their children because someone may report them to the local Child Protective Services for abuse. Other than emphatically stating that physical abuse or domestic violence is not tolerated by the court, if you have any questions about your conduct, ask a case worker from Child Protective Services or a mental health counselor. Be aware that a physician, nurse, school employee, or mental health worker who believes you are abusing your child is required by law to report you.

Another aspect of domestic violence frequently overlooked by parents is children witnessing violence even if they are not the physical target. Children do not have to be the victim of a physical assault to be affected. Children who witness domestic violence (Ver Steegh, 2005) can become more aggressive, antisocial, fearful, and inhibited than other children. These children can be traumatized by what they see. There is also a risk that later they too can be a victim of physical abuse. Parents who rationalize violent behavior are ignoring the child's need to feel safe and protected by the nonoffending parent. Physically aggressive parents are also forgetting that the behavior they are modeling for their children is what the children will consider to be appropriate behavior.

Many times we place our children in a dilemma regarding anger. We teach children to not swear, hit, or throw things, but we often never tell them how they *are* allowed to express their anger. Everyone agrees that anger is a natural emotion experienced by all. Their dilemma lies in telling the children what they can't do to express their anger and not telling them what they are allowed to do. They have to guess, and if they guess wrong, they risk getting punished. A parent may chastise a child for being disrespectful without telling the child what the word actually means. Most parents mean, "Keep your mouth shut." The question for the parent to answer is, "How is your child allowed to express anger, and have you communicated this to your child?" This is a good time for mentoring your child. It is best to have this discussion with your child when the two of you are not angry.

Responding to Allegations of Physical or Sexual Abuse

It is horrifying to be accused of sexual or physical abuse, but this occurs too often in divorces. After the allegation, whether you are guilty or innocent, you will be immediately looked upon with suspicion. For many, the assumption still exists that children do not lie and you are guilty until proven innocent. The assumption is wrong. The reasons for this hard attitude are, first, to protect your children's safety; and second, to protect your children's testimony. If the parent is the reported victim, a restraining or protection order can be ordered requiring the alleged perpetrator to keep a distance from the alleged victim.

Every day we hear about abuse, neglect, and even death of children. Hearing these horror stories is enough to scare any parent. It is easy to become overly sensitive to anything we think can pose a risk to our children's safety. Suspicions, or even subtle suggestions, from your child are not reason enough to panic. Before jumping to conclusions and stopping visits or calling the local prosecutor, take a deep breath and think about how to calmly proceed. Though your feelings may be understandable, it doesn't help you or your child if you are hysterical. Take some time to think about what action you are going to take rather than just impulsively acting in a way you may later regret.

If you are accused of sexual abuse, immediately notify your attorney. It is important to act fast because you don't want to waste precious time while the other side is gathering information against you. Ask the attorney if he has had experience in both criminal and domestic law. If not, ask for a referral to a more experienced attorney. You may even ask whom he would hire if he were accused.

When you initially meet with your attorney, you must be completely honest and cooperate to the fullest. Though you are feeling scared and maybe angry, your feelings do not matter. Once the disclosure is made, a series of events will happen. The local children's services agency will conduct an evaluation. You, your children, and their other parent will be interviewed. You may even be asked to submit to a psychological evaluation—which I think is interesting, since psychological evaluations are not valid for identifying a sex offender. If the children's service agency believes they have a strong case against you, they could go to the county prosecutor or district attorney and file formal charges against. In the meantime, your attorney will work with you, review the merits of the investigation, and prepare your defense. This process can takes months and can be very complicated. Without proper legal counsel, you could make a lot of mistakes that will later hurt you in court. Don't make the mistake of thinking that, because you believe in your innocence, you have nothing to worry about. At minimum, you can be spending thousands of dollars for a defense even if you prevail in court.

After contacting your attorney, see about having your child independently evaluated as soon as possible. Have a qualified and respected expert interview and evaluate the apparent validity of your child's testimony. You will need your own attorney to get the evaluation done. However, after the investigation is done, follow the advice of your attorney.

Experts who investigate sexual abuse allegations are not good at telling if the child or parent are lying. For the child to be able to testify, he should be old enough to verbalize what happened, know the difference between a truth and a lie, and distinguish between right or wrong (Schetky & Green,1988). There are no simple questions or techniques that assure honesty and accuracy of what the child and parent are saying because, remember, the child and parent could sincerely believe in the allegations. Children want to believe what their parents tell them. To get at the truth, experts in the field use a complex process for gathering what they hope will be valid and accurate information. The process is time-consuming and, as mentioned earlier, requires specialized training on the part of the investigator. Even this process is not foolproof. That is why you want the most qualified investigators and mental health professionals involved, whether you are the accused or the frightened parent.

Sadly, some parents will need special help because the allegations are true. These parents are encouraged to stop what they are doing and get help. Their excuses and rationalizations do nothing but further victimize the child.

What If the Court Finds the Allegations True?

Very often, convicted sex offenders have to be registered with the local authorities, and get probation or are released from prison on parole. There is no easy way for the other parent to handle this. The convicted parents may want to see their children again. If this occurs, you may need professional assistance to evaluate your children's feelings. It is important that abused children feel some degree of control before deciding what they want to do. If there is parenting time, the court could require supervised visits. You must cooperate with the court order, even if you don't like it. If you have an issue, discuss it with your attorney rather than taking action on your own.

A Word of Caution: Repressed Memories

Repressed memories as a therapeutic tool to discover sexual abuse has lost favor in recent years. "Repressed memories" is not synonymous with "forgetting." Individuals who have been victimized, unless very young at the time of the abuse, will not forget the abuse. They may forget details, but not the totality of the trauma. A repressed memory assumes that all of our history is somehow recorded in our subconscious and, with proper intervention, the memories can be recalled. The recall is thought to be an objective truth and not something manipulated by the therapist, who may have her own agenda. The revelations of abuse are to occur during psychotherapy with the therapist using therapeutic techniques called guided imagery or hypnosis. Part of the treatment, advocated by a very few therapists to help the patient work through any residual feelings from the alleged abuse, was to confront the perpetrator, usually a parent, with a law suit. This has destroyed many families and hurt a lot of innocent people. There is no scientific documentation supporting the validity of repressed memories. This therapy can be dangerous and should not be used as the basis for an allegation of sexual abuse. There have been many ethical complaints and civil suits against therapists who encouraged patients to take legal action against their family members on the basis of nothing more than repressed memories.

TIP: Do not take any action against anyone because of what you learn from a repressed memory.

Bertha and Margaret's Story

Bertha, a particularly vindictive mother, told her daughter Margaret that her father, Sam, had sexually abused Margaret when she was very young. The disclosure may or may not have been true. Most important is that Margaret may have no memory of the incident. If she remembers, her recall of the abuse is probably distorted by time and by what other people have told her. Margaret has little choice now but to trust her mother's story because she would not want to think that a parent who loves her would lie. So Margaret is immediately conflicted between wanting to believe her mother and not knowing how to react towards her father. She wants to see her father but is now afraid of him.

Bertha sees that Margaret is torn and comes to her child's rescue. She tells Margaret that she is not old enough to decide for herself whether she should visit her father. Of course, Sam is unsuspecting and cannot explain the change in Margaret's attitude. Neither Bertha nor Margaret will tell him anything. Instead, Margaret feels uncomfortable, begins to avoid her father, and resists visitation. The alienation progresses as Bertha planned.

Alleging Sexual Abuse to Alienate

It is very frightening to hear for the first time that you are being accused of sexually abusing your child. Everything stops when the accusation is heard. The court's first concern is protecting the child while the investigation is being conducted. Judges frequently stop all contact between the accused and child. There are reasons for the court order other than just protecting the child. The investigators do not want the accused trying to influence the child's testimony. The court may grant the parent supervised visitation while the investigation is conducted. If you are accused, be sure you have an attorney and cooperate with the investigation.

Concluding that a parent is guilty of sexual abuse is very complex. What you believe may not count for much if the court believes you were trying to alienate prior to the allegations. Dean Tong's (2001) experiences with fathers falsely accused of sexual abuse has taught him that obsessed parents will, over time, likely escalate their alienating tactics by raising the bar with false allegations of sexual abuse. Falsely accused fathers typically react and have a different psychosocial history than substantiated abusers. Again, you cannot make definitive conclusions after reading these traits. The reason for describing these indicators is so you stop and think before jumping to conclusions.

False allegations are hard on children because it drags them through the process of investigation and forces them to make public statements that hurt the other parent. A five-year-old female recently had five pelvic examinations at the insistence of her mother, who believes her daughter was raped by the father. All the examinations were negative. Intentional false allegations are malicious, and many people believe should be criminally prosecuted. I agree.

If you are consciously trying to use a false allegation of sexual abuse to get your ex-spouse out of your life, get therapy immediately and think about the cruel long-term consequences of your actions for your children. Whatever your rationalizations or excuses, you are wrong in pursuing a course of action that will destroy people's lives, including your child's. Think about it. Do you want your child to go through life believing she was a victim of sexual abuse, when in fact it never happened? In no uncertain terms, that is abusive.

Reporting Abuse

If you suspect physical or sexual abuse, immediately report the incident to the appropriate child welfare agency. If you see physical evidence of the abuse, take the child to a hospital emergency room for examination. By law, the hospital must report the suspected abuse to the authorities. If you see physical evidence of suspected abuse on your child's body, taking pictures may be helpful. However, be warned that most photographs of bruises do not show up well. Photographs tend to wash out the contrasting colors of the bruises unless you have additional lighting. For this reason, it is best to take your child to the hospital or the authorities to document the bruises.

Parents who know that their former spouse was a victim of childhood physical abuse may worry about whether the former spouse could, in time, abuse their own children. The fear comes from the popular notion that all abusers were also victims of abuse. While it is true that some abusers were also victims, this is not the same as saying that all former victims will abuse their own children. Kaufman and Zigler (1986) conducted a thorough critique of studies assessing the risk of victimized parents abusing their children. They found that the best estimate of intergenerational abuse appears to be between 5 and 30 percent. This is six times the estimated rate of 5 percent for the general population. From their estimates, they concluded that the majority of parents who were abused did not abuse their children.

You should always take your children's accusations seriously, but proceed cautiously. Your first concern must be your child's immediate health and safety. If your child requires medical attention, go to your physician or an emergency room. This is true for both physical and sexual abuse. The abuse needs to be documented by a qualified professional. You are not qualified to assess the validity of a child's allegations of abuse. Do the proper thing and make the report. Children need to be protected, but the alleged perpetrator has a right to a defense before being convicted.

18

Legal and Ethical Challenges to PA and PAS

Parental alienation syndrome is junk science.

By the time you read this book, you probably will have been on the Internet reading about PA and PAS. You will have read the arguments for and against the existence of PA and PAS. The readings may have left you confused, because you know what you have personally experienced, and now you are reading from some authors that what you experience does not exist. You ask yourself, "How can this be?" The answer lies in the limited use of language and in writers failing to fully explain what they mean.

Most parents approaching a court date believe that the truthfulness of their arguments will win over the court. You should be wise enough to know that the court will not accept your testimony at face value. The opposition will try to discredit you and your witnesses. This is the nature of the adversarial system of law. You or your attorney may have hired an expert witness or other witnesses, believing that their testimony regarding the existence of PA or PAS in your case will be enough to support your position. This may be true, but you must know beforehand the ethical considerations and limitations that influence your expert's testimony, and the challenges you may hear during the course of the testimony. With each challenge is a rebuttal or a response that you should understand.

The PAS Controversy

You probably picked up this book because you have some familiarity with parental alienation (PA) and/or parental alienation syndrome (PAS). This book will not resolve the controversy surrounding the concepts. Unfortunately for families and children, PAS has become a political issue. Before deciding to hire an expert witness or going to court arguing the existence of PA and PAS, you need to understand that there are well-respected mental health and legal professionals who do not believe PAS exists, and any suggestion otherwise is tantamount to malpractice. PAS has its detractors. State licensing boards have discussed the use of parental alienation syndrome as a diagnosis. The controversy has been argued ". . . that some believe that the use of such a term [PAS] as a diagnosis is malpractice because 'PAS' does not exist." The point made by this example is that the consequences of using PAS as a diagnosis can be very severe to the psychologist. Any professional using the term should be cautioned to preface their comments by stating that the term is not a diagnosis and to admit, when asked, that PAS has not been validated as of yet. To be safe, the mental health professional should only consider what is written in the *DSM-IV-TR* (*Diagnostic and Statistical Manual of Mental Disorders: Fourth Edition, Text Revision*) or the *ICD* (*International Classification of Diseases*) as a diagnosis. Anything else is a description or a cluster of symptoms that some may consider a syndrome.

Debate about PA and PAS in court is often intended to distract from the point of the testimony; namely, how the child's adjustment is being affected by the parent's behavior. This book will not resolve the debate. Richard Warshak (1999) summarized the issue well, stating, "No study has directly measured the extent to which different examiners with the same data can agree on the presence or absence of PAS. Until such data exist, the reliability of PAS cannot be established through empirical research." In the meantime, there must be agreement about the definitions; otherwise, research is tantamount to comparing apples to oranges. A consensus must be reached regarding the criteria that comprises parental alienation syndrome. Gardner's eight symptoms may not be all-inclusive, or one or more criteria may carry little weight. In the meantime, again—the issue before the court is to identify the pattern of behavior, if it exists, and how the pattern of behavior referred to as PA or PAS harms the children's adjustment and the relationship with the targeted parent.

Opponents of PAS and PA argue that neither exists. It is not clear if the opponents are saying the concept does not exist because the American Psychiatric Association does not recognize them as diagnoses, or if they are saying the pattern of behavior does not exist. The argument opposing the use of the terms PAS or PA is their exclusion from the *Diagnostic and Statistical Manual* published by the American Psychiatric Association (2000). In other words, if the concepts are not in the *DSM-IV-TR*, they do not exist. Granted, neither term is a mental health diagnosis, but this is not to say the behaviors do not exist.

Whether or not the terms are used, no one who has had extensive experience with high-conflict divorce and/or has experienced protracted family law litigation can deny the existence of the behaviors. Critics and proponents agree that a thorough assessment by a qualified provider must take into account the complexities of the family dynamics that include alienating behavior and estrangement.

Admissibility of Evidence

You should expect to hear a challenge when you go to court arguing that you are a victim of parental alienation and parental alienation syndrome. The challenge may come from your own attorney, the opposing attorney, or even the judge. Your attorney, knowing the sentiments of your local jurisdiction, may say to you, "You don't have a chance of winning your argument." The opposing attorney could argue that parental alienation does not exist and that it is "junk science." The judge could completely discount any testimony about parental alienation or parental alienation syndrome, concluding that parental alienation syndrome does not pass the test for admissibility. This decision may confuse you.

What is acceptable to the mental health community and to the legal community is not always the same. We can look at history to see how the mental health community embraced psychoanalytical theory and even client center therapy before the theories were validated. Today, the standards of acceptance are higher, particularly with most of the legal community and some of the mental health community.

There are federal rules for the admissibility of evidence. Rule 702, according to the United States Supreme Court, implies that scientific knowledge or evidence involves scientific evidence based on scientific validity. During the course of your readings about parental alienation syndrome, you may have come across reference to the Frye (*Frye v. United States*, 1923) and Daubert (*Daubert v. Merrell Dow Pharmaceuticals, Inc.*, 1993) standards for admissibility of evidence. The two standards reference federal court decisions about what constitutes scientifically derived knowledge. The Frye standard is less stringent than the Daubert standard and says that a theory can be admissible in the court of law if the theory is "generally accepted in the relevant scientific community." PAS has met the Frye standard in Florida and Illinois (Supreme Court of Illinois, 2004). The Daubert standard is more complex, requiring the theory to be scientifically valid with a known error rate. PAS has not met the Daubert standard, but neither has fingerprinting, many of the widely used personality tests, or eyewitness accounts. Most attorneys do not raise these issues during court proceedings, but if you hear the terms, ask your attorney for an explanation and how it all relates to your witnesses' testimony. There is a trend, in both the mental health and legal communities, to seek testimony that is supported by scientific knowledge rather than an expert's unsupported opinion.

Ethical Considerations

In years past, psychologists were able to testify and stand on the merits of their license and experience to offer acceptable opinions to the court. A few naïve psychologists and psychiatrists have been known to support their testimony, saying that a fact or opinion is true "because I say so." This arrogant attitude is no longer acceptable, and many considered it unethical. Experts must back up their opinions and recommendations with scientifically supported data. An opinion without supporting scientific studies is not acceptable in many courts.

Psychologists are bound to ethical considerations. Each state and the American Psychological Association (2002) have specific standards of conduct when conducting assessments. An assessment can include psychological testing, interviewing, and the gathering of collateral data.

- Standard 2.04: Bases for Scientific and Professional Judgments requires that "psychologists' work [be] based upon established scientific and professional knowledge of the discipline."

- Standard 9.01 (a): "Psychologists base the opinions contained in their recommendations, report, and diagnostic or evaluation statements, including forensic testimony, on information and techniques sufficient to substantiate their findings."

- Standard 9.01 (b): "Psychologists provide opinions of the psychological characteristics of individuals only after they have conducted an examination of the individuals adequate to support their statements or conclusions. When, despite reasonable efforts, such an examination is not practical, psychologists document the efforts they made and the result of those efforts, clarify the probable impact of their limited information on the reliability and validity of their opinions and appropriate limit the nature and extent of their conclusions or recommendations."

- Standard 9.01 (c): "When psychologists conduct a record review or provide consultation or supervision and an individual examination is not warranted or necessary for the opinion, psychologists explain this and the sources of information on which they based their conclusions or recommendations."

The ethical standard of conduct for psychologists has important implications for what you should expect from a custody evaluator or an expert witness. A psychologist's testimony is severely limited if she does not have court-ordered access to all the parties involved in the litigation. When you think about it, this is only common sense. How can an evaluator comment about someone she has never met? She cannot. When the psychologist has limited access to the parties, she must limit her testimony, or report hypothetical statements. The limitations should be explained to the court prior to the testimony. Without both the parents' and the children's participation in the evaluation, the evaluator cannot make any specific recommendations for custody or parenting time.

> TIP: The court is not a place to make a political statement. Your focus is your child's best interest and your child's right to have an unimpeded relationship with both parents.

PAS is Not a Diagnosis

An experienced expert knows the arguments against using PAS as a diagnosis. The opposition will try to discredit the testimony, saying that PAS is not a diagnosis. Technically that is true, for a couple of reasons. Presently, the American Psychiatric Association, which publishes the *Diagnostic and Statistical Manual* (American Psychiatric Association, 2000), makes no reference to PAS. Further, PAS has not been sufficiently validated in peer review articles to support the efficacy of the concept. Proponents of Dr. Gardner's criteria take his eight symptoms at face value, meaning that his symptoms are all-inclusive. Every recognized diagnosis in the *DSM-IV-TR* (2000) has specific criteria defining a diagnosis. Over time, the criteria for a diagnosis may change. Some diagnoses are eliminated from previous *Diagnostic and Statistical Manuals*, and new ones are added.

More important than the label is the cluster of behaviors described. Gardner describes his frequently quoted cluster of behaviors as symptoms.

Experts in the field must acknowledge to the parents and the court the limitations of their testimony about the validity of the symptoms. There are no studies saying that Gardner's eight criteria are all-inclusive or statistically clustered to define a single factor.

> TIP: The label "parental alienation syndrome" is not as important as showing the court a pattern of behavior that demonstrates the damage to the child because of alienating behavior.

An assumption that opponents of PAS make is that only scientifically valid diagnoses are in the *DSM-IV*. This is not always true. The process for the American Psychiatric Association accepting a diagnosis is an involved process and includes a literature review, data analysis, and field trials. Diagnoses and diagnostic criteria change over time as the methods of research become more refined. The identification of a new diagnosis is an evolutionary process that can take years before recognition. Mental disorders do not suddenly appear when the decision is made to make them a diagnosis. The *DSM-II* (1968) originally had 123 pages and the *DSM-IV-TR* (2000) has 886 pages. It would be ludicrous to think that the mental disorders described in the *DSM-IV* did not exist in 1968. Over the years, sometimes diagnoses change because of social changes, research, and recognition of new clusters of behavior that may have a common cause. This can certainly be true with PAS. Only time will tell.

Syndrome?

Opponents argue that the word "syndrome" in parental alienation syndrome implies that the user is making a mental health diagnosis. They argue that syndrome is a misrepresentation to imply a diagnosis. PAS is not a diagnosis because of the word syndrome; yet there are no diagnoses in the *DSM-IV-TR* (2000) that use the word syndrome as part of the diagnosis. Usually the word is relegated to a cluster of behaviors—such as Down syndrome, Tourette's syndrome, battered person syndrome—before they become anointed with a diagnostic label. In the *DSM-IV-TR* (2000), Down syndrome is not a diagnosis. Tourette's syndrome is now Tourette's disorder; and, for treatment purposes, battered person syndrome would be diagnosed as physical abuse of an adult. The word syndrome is dropped when adopted as a diagnosis. The *DSM-IV* (2000) states, "The concept of a mental disorder, like many other concepts in medicine and science, lacks a consistent operational definition that covers all situations." This is very true. That is the reason there is a subjective element to making a diagnosis. Mental health professionals would be the first to acknowledge the lack of consistency in diagnosis between different therapists. With each edition of the *DSM*, there is an attempt to be more specific with the diagnostic criteria, thus reducing error between practitioners. However, the fact is, mental health diagnosis is not yet an exact science. This is also true for identifying PAS.

> TIP: There are no diagnoses listed in the DSM-IV-TR that use the word "syndrome."

There is a distinction between the existence of parental alienation syndrome and a pattern of behavior referred to as parental alienation syndrome. Another argument by some practitioners against using parental alienation syndrome is the belief that the word denotes a medical diagnosis. This is not how syndrome is defined in *Dorland's Illustrated Medical Dictionary* (1965): "A set of symptoms which occur together; the sum of signs of any morbid state; a symptom complex." The *Social Work Dictionary* (Barker, 1995) defined syndrome as "A cluster of behavior patterns, personalities, traits, or physical symptoms that occur together to form a specific disorder or *condition*" (emphasis added). This is similar to the medical definition described in *Barron's* (Giftis, 1996) except *Barron's* does not include behaviors as part of the clinical picture. The *DSM-IV-TR* (American Psychiatric Association, 2000) defines syndrome as "a grouping of signs and symptoms, based on their frequent co-occurrence that *may* suggest a common underlying pathogenesis, course, familial pattern, or treatment selection" (emphasis added). None of the definitions say anything about being a medical diagnosis. What can be argued is that Gardner's symptoms of PAS have not been found to have a statistical relationship defining a single factor. To argue the existence of PAS, four steps should be taken:

- Determine, with collaborative documentation, that the behaviors exist in the child
- Identify that the cause of the behavior is the alienation
- Provide research, not just the experts' testimony, demonstrating how this behavior is damaging to the child. There is considerable research supporting the argument that protracted and high conflict between parents is damaging to children.
- Offer recommendations to repair or minimize the damage to the parent-child relationship.

Parental Alienation

Courts are more charitable about the use of the term "parental alienation" because the word "syndrome" is not attached and does not denote a diagnosis. Parental alienation describes a parent's or significant other's behavior and can be the cause of parental alienation syndrome. To avoid the controversy about the use of the word "syndrome," parental alienation is sometimes used as a synonym for parental alienation syndrome. This is confusing, because the two terms have different meanings. Unfortunately, this does not solve the problem. How do you describe parental alienation syndrome without using the word and getting into trouble with the court and the licensing boards? The answer is describing the specific behaviors, avoiding the use of the word "syndrome," and explaining the limitations of the testimony to the court. These cautions also apply to a written custody evaluation.

PAS and the Gender Gap

Richard Gardner was severely criticized when he asserted that mothers are more likely to be the alienating parent and fathers the victim. Since Gardner's original assertion, the debate has continued, though most in the professional divorce community acknowledge that the gender proportion is more equal than was thought in years past. When an objective evaluation is conducted that is fair and based on objective data, the issue of gender is irrelevant. Both mothers and fathers can be an obsessed alienator or a victim.

An Evaluator's Neutrality

A frequent complaint voiced by parents during an evaluation is the perception that the evaluator has a bias or is on a personal crusade to prove the existence of a preconceived opinion. Unfortunately, this does happen. The American Psychological Association's Guidelines for Child Custody Evaluations in Divorce Proceedings (1994) specifically mandates that "psychologists guard against relying on their own biases or unsupported beliefs in rendering opinions in particular cases." However, do not accuse the evaluator who does not agree with your arguments of having a personal bias. The evaluator's job is to gather data and follow the evidence to a conclusion. He is not to have a preconceived task to prove or disprove abuse, parental alienation syndrome, substance abuse, or any other issue. This is the reason that previous therapists should never make recommendations to the court about custody or visitation. The evaluator has to follow the evidence that will support or refute any conclusions. Notify your attorney if you have reason to believe your evaluator or counselor is not neutral.

PAS and Pathology

Occasionally you may hear the argument that PAS is not a mental disorder because such behavior is normal under very stressful situations. This argument makes no sense when it can be demonstrated that, by this definition, a hateful or an obsessed individual successfully alienates her children— even with false allegations—is being described as normal behavior. A loving parent who has empathy for her children and awareness of a child's need for both parents does not behave that way. Research is very consistent in demonstrating the deleterious effects of high conflict on children. Also, a criterion for all mental disorders (American Psychiatric Association [2000]) is impaired social, occupational, and psychological functioning. The fact that PAS is brought to the court's attention and an impaired parent/child relationship is documented supports the existence of impaired functioning. Alienating behavior and PAS are not normal. The issue is proving the existence of PAS and parental alienating behaviors.

The arguments about the existence of parental alienation and parental alienation syndrome will not abate just because of this discourse. There are efforts to include parental alienation syndrome in the *DSM-V*. There are good arguments for the inclusion, but for this to happen, more research supporting the validity is needed. The issue should not be political, but based on the fact of its existence. We can only hope that the decision-makers for the *DSM-V* do not get caught up in the politics. The sooner the debate over the existence is put to rest, the sooner we can help parents and their children adjust and get on with their lives without distracting delay tactics promulgated by overzealous parents and attorneys. The issue isn't the existence of parental alienation and parental alienation syndrome; the issue is the existence of parental alienation or parental alienation syndrome *in your case*. That is for you to prove and the court to address.

19

Working Successfully with Attorneys, Parent Coordinators, Mediators, and Counselors

"I can't find an attorney that knows anything about parental alienation."

Having never before gone through a divorce or any type of litigation, you may be confused, scared, and totally overwhelmed by all that needs to be done. You are not alone. Litigation opens up a new world to you with rules you may not understand, confusing terminology, and at times very little empathy for what you are going through. You are likely to suffer from sticker shock when you learn the amount of the retainer and the cost of litigation. The "good guy vs bad guy" scenario may quickly put you on the defensive.

This is the nature of the adversary system of law. If it helps, I have never heard a parent say, after facing litigation, "Court was a wonderful experience; I would like to do it again." In fact, the lesson frequently taken away is to do whatever possible to avoid future litigation. This is true for criminal as well as civil cases.

You will learn there are several professionals available who will be a valuable resource for helping you through the tangled web of divorce. This chapter offers useful information about the roles different professions play in the divorce or custody process. You will learn about selecting a qualified attorney who can represent you in court; the role of the guardian ad litems (GALs), parent coordinators, mediators, expert witnesses, investigators, mental health counselors, reunification therapists, and visitation centers.

Right now you may be in a quandary because you have not been served papers, or you don't know the first thing about getting a divorce other than what you hear from friends. Your first step is finding an attorney who will educate you about the process, evaluate your case, and serve as a case manager for all that has to be done. If you suspect you are a victim of parental alienation, do not hesitate to ask your prospective attorney about his background and experience with parental alienation.

When you first encounter the likelihood of a divorce or custody issue, you must begin by thinking over how your case is to be managed. You may begin by finding an attorney, or you may consider representing yourself because of the cost. It is important to get the most qualified person you can afford to be part of your team. Competent representation can make the difference between a workable and dysfunctional outcome. After all, the decisions made in court will affect you and your children for many years to come.

Representing yourself is risky because you don't know the law and court procedures and you are too emotionally involved to sit back and see the whole picture. The court may see your case in a very different light than you do. Your belief that your position is justified doesn't mean others will be convinced. Some courts may be biased against you for representing yourself. Some judges and magistrates are helpful and understanding if your case is simple, but do not count on their help.

Be leery about taking legal advice from well-meaning friends or political activists who have their own ax to grind. In general, I do not recommend anyone representing themselves, because they usually do so for reasons that have nothing to do with getting custody or justice. Representing yourself can become an issue that clouds the real purpose of being in court: access to your children and the opportunity to be an active parent.

TIP: Do not take legal advice from the enemy.

Before deciding to divorce, couples frequently argue and threaten each other about what they are going to do in court. Statements frequently heard are: "You will never see your children again if you don't give me split custody." Or, "I will throw you out of the house if you try to gain custody." The threats are meaningless and should be ignored, because most often the parent issuing them doesn't know what she is talking about. Instead, consult an attorney and learn about your legal rights from someone who knows and has your best interest in mind.

Selecting an Attorney

Most states have a criteria written in administrative law that defines "best interest of the child." Judges have their own biases and their own criteria for deciding a case. They put more weight on some criteria and less on others, making it hard for you to outguess them. In many jurisdictions, anyone with a conviction for domestic violence can pretty much forget about custody. Alienation can become an issue, because many states have a criterion for best interest that includes a parent's willingness to foster and encourage a loving relationship between the children and the other parent. Contrary to that criterion is parental alienation. Because of the complexity of the law and the personalities of the judges, you must select a qualified attorney who knows the local court and judges. Though this is no guarantee of the outcome, it helps to know what you are up against.

Selecting the right attorney involves more than finding someone who will win the case. After the divorce is final, your attorney may continue to be a resource for helping solve future problems between you and your ex-spouse. For this reason, it is important to select the right attorney from the beginning, one who is skilled and who takes an interest in your case. Changing attorneys can be expensive because of the time needed to give an update on your history and explain the merits of your case. Having had many attorneys previously representing you can raise suspicion that you are difficult to work with or you are attorney-shopping. You may want to consider the following guidelines before selecting an attorney. These will give you an idea of what you can realistically expect from your attorney and help reduce some of your frustration and confusion about how most attorneys work.

Tips on Selecting an Attorney

- Always look for an attorney who is experienced in family law. Though the competent attorney's hourly rate is usually higher, by the time the case is completed, her overall costs are usually lower than a less experienced attorney.
- Remember that you are paying for good representation and not specific results. Be suspicious of any attorney who makes promises about the outcome of your case.
- Select an attorney who has a proven track record in the county where your case will be heard. Ask how many divorce cases he has had in the past year.

- Seek the advice of a friend who has had experience with a case similar to your own, and ask for the name of a well-qualified attorney. Friends can be an excellent source of information.
- Ask your local bar association for three names of local attorneys. Keep in mind that the bar association will give you names of attorneys specializing in domestic relations and who have an office close to where you live or work. The names do not take into consideration the attorneys' reputation or competency.
- Be cautious when hiring a big-name attorney for a divorce case. Such attorneys usually specialize in criminal law, are usually expensive, and may show little interest in your case.
- Interview the prospective attorney before deciding to hire her. After all, the attorney will be interviewing you to see if she can work with you, and whether you can afford to pay your bill. Remember, he or she does not have to accept you as a client.
- Look for an attorney who is interested, empathetic, and knowledgeable of the law.
- Remember that your attorney can only represent you on the strength of the evidence, and cannot guarantee that the judge will decide in your favor. Litigation is stressful, even if you are the plaintiff. To lessen the stress, you may want your attorney's reassurance that he will win your case. Though your feelings are understandable, this is not a reasonable or realistic request.

Because you are angry, you may think that hiring a big-name attorney will intimidate your spouse or the other attorney. This rarely happens. Most experienced attorneys know and are not intimated by each other. Any intimidation is usually the client's illusion and not shared by the attorney.

Legal Fees

As previously stated, the least expensive hourly rate is not always the cheapest attorney. Ask the attorney about their hourly fees and what you are getting for the money. Many attorneys will charge for their time on the phone, doing research, or standing in line to file papers. You should know ahead of time what you are paying for so that there are no surprises.

My corporate partners and I once had the occasion to seek legal advice about franchising our clinics. We received estimates from local attorneys averaging around forty thousand dollars in legal fees. We learned from our discussions with these attorneys that they would have to do considerable research to complete the franchising disclosure statements. Not one attorney admitted to being unqualified and referred us to someone else. Because franchising can be complicated for an unqualified attorney, we decided to find a firm in Cleveland with extensive experience in franchise law. Their hourly rate was double the estimates we had received locally, but they did the entire job for around four thousand dollars—or a savings of thirty-six thousand dollars. The lesson we learned was that costs are not always what they appear. This is also true for domestic cases.

TIP: Cheap is not always better.

Most attorneys maintain a running invoice on which they record the time and cost of your phone calls, interviews, consultations, research, preparation, and court appearances. I have no problem with this practice, except that you should know beforehand how costs are determined. Properly preparing a case can be time-consuming. Remember that your attorney may be friendly, but he is in business to make a living. Also, he knows more about contract law than you do.

The agreement between you and your attorney is a contract and should be written to avoid later misunderstanding. Some attorneys will quote you a flat fee for an uncomplicated dissolution or divorce. The attorney may later add costs if the circumstances of the case become more complicated. This is not unusual, especially when a peaceful divorce is later contested. When this happens, you can expect to see a dramatic increase in the fees. Understand beforehand which circumstances could increase the cost of your litigation. Remember, you, and not your attorney, will gather most of the information for your case. You will avoid a lot of disappointment if you understand that you will be doing most of the legwork gathering all the necessary documentation. You know better than your attorney where and how to find the material needed to support your case. If your attorney does the legwork, you will pay dearly for the time.

There are ways that you can save money with an attorney. If you believe parental alienation is an issue, research the subject and be sure your attorney understands the concept. Ask the attorney about your local judges' attitudes regarding parental alienation or parental alienation syndrome. Some states like Florida have a strong line of anti-syndrome case laws (Jamieson, 2007). A clear distinction is made between parental alienation and parental alienation syndrome; however, as mentioned in chapter 18, some jurisdictions object to the use of the word syndrome because the term implies a medically validated diagnosis. You must be sensitive to these issues, thought I disagree with their argument. The different meaning of the terms is important because the differences offer clarity and understanding about how to respond to or treat each condition. Parental alienation is not a diagnosis, but that isn't what is important. What is important is describing the cluster of behaviors identified that are found to hurt children and families. That is the issue. You may consider giving your attorney a copy of this book. Highlight sections that you believe are pertinent.

You save a considerable amount of money if you do your own research and gather documentation supporting your arguments. If you expect your attorney to do all the work, you will pay a fortune. After all, you—and not your attorney—know best about locating the relevant documents. Another source for saving money is researching relevant case law at your local university or library. An example of case law that may be helpful is *Wade v. Hirschman* (Florida 2005) stating that the "Supreme Court upheld the finding that there was evidence of parental alienation of father by mother. The mother failed to cooperate with their parenting coordinator or comply with parenting agreement, mother had violated shared parental responsibility, as evidenced by her unilateral change of child's elementary school and therapist, and mother was in contempt for her actions related to visitation." The Internet can be very helpful if the case law or documents have reputable citations.

Expert Witnesses

On rare occasions, your attorney may suggest hiring an expert witness to testify and present your arguments. Expert witnesses can be expensive because you are responsible for the time they spend conducting research, reviewing your documents, consulting with you and your attorney, writing affidavits, and possibly testifying. Many consultations are in two phases. Phase one is the review of the documents and a follow-up consultation with the parent and the attorney. At this point, the consultant will tell you the limits of the testimony. Phase two is the actual testimony. You should get an itemized statement of expenses for your records. Expect to prepay for travel time, hotel cost, and the testimony. There are ramifications if you do not prepay. The opposing attorney could ask the consultant if he has been paid for his court appearance. If the consultant says "no," the assumption to the court is that the testimony is biased because of the consultant's risk of not being paid if the you dislike the testimony. This is a very real concern for the consultant and should be your concern too.

TIP: You are paying the consultant for his time, not the testimony.

Before you and your attorney decide on hiring a consultant or expert witness, you may want to consider the following:

- What is your goal in hiring the expert?

- Is the consultant independently licensed? Depending on what you are asking from the expert witness, you may want an expert licensed in your state. If you want a court-ordered evaluation, out-of-state consultants have to get approval from the state licensing board to temporarily practice in your state. Each state has different rules, but most are very cooperative and willing to work with the consultant. Most states make a distinction between providing a psychological service that involves an evaluation and counseling, and consultation for educating the court about a specific issue. The consultant is not expected to interview all the parties and will not offer an opinion about custody and parenting time. Making custody recommendations without interviewing the parties is unethical and may even be illegal for an out-of-state consultant. It is the consultant's responsibility to contact the state licensing board and get clarification about what he can legally do in the visiting state. The consultant must be very clear with you about the limits of his role. The purpose of the consultation and limitations are described in an informed consent document provided by the consultant.

- To testify, the consultant must be recognized by the court as an expert on the specific issues presented to the court. If the opposing attorney challenges the qualifications, the decision to qualify the consultant will occur during the hearing by the judge or magistrate. Most judges are liberal in allowing an expert to testify. Your attorney, after reviewing the expert's qualifications, will know if there is a problem before hiring the expert. Most attorneys look for an expert who has experience testifying and who is a good communicator. Expect the opposing attorney to challenge the expert's qualifications and their relevance to the issues before the court. The expert knows she will be asked about education, experience, publications, presentations, and prior court appearances.

- Again, keep in mind that you are paying the consultant for his time and not the content of his testimony. After your consultant studies your case, you and your attorney need a conference to discuss the limits of the expert's testimony or affidavit. After the conference, you and your attorney will decide if the expert's testimony will helpful. If not, the relationship goes no further.

Your Presentation in Court

How you present yourself in court is very important and can make a difference in your credibility. Even the brightest expert who fails to effectively communicate on the witness stand can seriously hurt your case. This is also true for you if you represent yourself (pro se). You must be sensitive to how you dress: neither provocative nor too casual. Consider wearing a smart business suit. Your hair should be neat; don't wear too much makeup; and don't try to make a political statement with your attire. Present yourself as a professional who is confident but not cocky or confrontative. Always keep your composure and follow the judge's directions. These recommendations are applicable whether you are represented by an attorney or by yourself.

TIP: Do not consider representing yourself if you cannot communicate clearly and confidently under stress.

What to Expect from Your Attorney and the Court

The legal system moves slowly. In some jurisdictions, it may take a year to schedule a contested case for a full-day hearing. Typically, the individual who wants the legal proceedings to move slowly is the one who has the most control, because it is easier to slow the legal process down than to speed it up. This is unfortunate, as protracted litigation hurts children and families because everyone is in limbo and can't adjust to whatever becomes the court's decision.

You and your attorney cannot choose who is going to hear your case. Typically the selection of the judge or magistrate is the luck of the draw. After learning who is assigned to your case and their general position on visitation issues, gender bias, and child issues, an experienced local attorney can be greatly beneficial. He will know how best to present your arguments and avoid any issues that may adversely influence your case.

Your attorney will present evidence in a way to support your arguments. The judge then has the responsibility of sorting out the truth and making a judgment on the case. You will lessen your hurt and disappointment if you understand that attorneys are not bound to tell the truth in court the way you understand the truth. An example is an attorney representing a murderer. The attorney may know the client is guilty, but her ethical responsibility is to give a good defense and instill a reasonable doubt in the jurors' minds so she can get an acquittal. The truth, and the defendant's guilt, have little to do with the morality of the defense. This is also true in domestic court. Don't be surprised if the attorney for the other side distorts what you consider the truth. There are two sides to every story, and if you and your ex-spouse agreed on everything, you would not need to be in court.

Try not to take what you hear in court too personally. Instead, help your attorney by being honest and maintaining your self-control. Never place yourself in the position where your attorney has to defend you or your behavior. By maintaining self-control and complying with existing court orders, you allow your attorney to take an offensive rather than a defensive posture. This strengthens your position with the court.

TIP: Behave yourself in court. Do not put your attorney in the position of having to defend your behavior to the court.

Never lie to your attorney. When she learns the truth, she may get angry and feel embarrassed to discover that you lied about the facts surrounding your case. Your attorney can do a better job if she knows everything before going to court, even if the information is embarrassing to you. The courtroom is not the place to begin telling your attorney the truth about the details of your case. You may feel uncomfortable telling your attorney everything relevant to your case, but you have to put those feelings aside.

Many decisions about a case are made in the hallways with the two attorney running back and forth trying to negotiate an agreement. If an agreement can be made, that is great for everyone. But do not allow yourself to be pressured into a decision unless you are in agreement and understand the consequences. Take your time, and have your attorney explain what the agreement means to you and your children. You must take some control over the pace of the events rather than agreeing to something you might later regret. If you can't agree, you will probably return to the courtroom for the another hearing.

Tips on Working with Attorneys

- You naturally feel passionate about your case. Do not feel offended if your attorney does not share your enthusiasm. After all, your case is one of many.
- Do not be outraged if the attorney for the other side distorts what you consider the truth in court. There are two sides to every story.
- Do not make any agreements in court that you cannot live with for a long time. Once an agreement is made and approved by the court, changing it will require legal representation and possibly another court hearing.
- Do not lie to your attorney. He can do a better job for you if armed with all the facts before going to court.
- Remember, you—and not your attorney—will gather most of the information for your case. Otherwise, you will pay dearly for your attorney's time.
- Although you will probably hear things in court that anger you, be honest and maintain your self-control.
- Providing emotional support is not your attorney's responsibility.

Parents frequently complain about their attorney not returning phone calls. Often attorneys consider phone calls from clients a nuisance unless they have new information or it is a return phone call. Clients frequently turn to their attorneys for emotional support. However, most attorneys do not see themselves in the role of counselor and do not feel qualified or comfortable in a supportive role. When clients call to get a status report, attorneys usually have nothing new to say. Consequently, attorneys may avoid taking the call because it is an inefficient use of their time.

Parents want to believe their case is the most important in the world; but remember, most cases are ordinary and do not require special attention. Your attorney has many cases and may ignore your case until the hearing is scheduled and the date is approaching. This may offend you, but a good attorney is busy and has to prioritize his time. The more you help your attorney gathering and organizing the documents for your case, the better. This saves you both time and money.

It is common for parents to make their case a personal crusade. This is evident when they carry boxes of files with documents and are vocal about their quasi-political affiliations. However, realize that, while your attorney cares about your case, he will not necessarily share your passion. Most crusading parents tend towards overkill on the amount and relevance of the information they give their attorney. It is your attorney's job to sort your material and identify what is most relevant to your case. You may not agree with your attorney about what is important but you have to trust his judgment.

> TIP: Do not take it personally when your attorney does not share your excitement about your case and fails to praise your labor.

During the preparation for your litigation, you may develop a laundry list of complaints about your spouse that you believe are important and need to be addressed in court. If you have too many complaints, the court and your attorney may feel overwhelmed. You could be diluting your stronger complaints with what the court may consider frivolous complaints. You and your attorney will need to identify and focus on the stronger issues and ignore the weaker arguments. Let the attorney decide what is best without taking offense.

Mediation

Mediation is a cooperative effort between divided parents and a neutral third person to help develop healthy ways of settling difference about the care of their children. After a history of fighting and an inability to solve differences, mediation may sound like a fantasy, but it does work. Mediation is very effective and plays an important role in helping parents during the divorce. The mediator's role is usually very specific and defined by state law. The effectiveness of mediation, like any other skill, is very dependent upon the qualifications and talents of the mediator.

Most mediators are highly effective in working with parents in low- or moderate-conflict situations. Courts do use mediators to work with high-conflict parents, but there are limits in what mediators can do. Mediation will not succeed if the mediator lacks sufficient training to work with high-conflict parents. Also, many states mandate total confidentiality of the mediating process. This is contrary to what reunification therapy requires.

Unfortunately, having a neutral professional is expensive, time-consuming, and, for many families, not even available within a reasonable physical proximity. However, when it is available, mediation can accomplish a great deal in less time than family psychotherapy and more cheaply than going to court.

A mediator may be a counselor, attorney, or psychologist who has received specialized training in mediation. When looking for a qualified mediator, ask the individual whether he is a member of either the Academy of Family Mediators or your state association. You should be leery of someone who puts out a shingle and calls himself a mediator without documented qualifications and references. Requirements for becoming a mediator vary from state to state. To play it safe, you may want to rely on a mediator recommended by your local domestic court or attorney.

How Does Mediation Work?

Participating in mediation and going to court are not the same thing. Going to court involves one person filing a formal motion or complaint against another. The complainant is saying to the court that there is a difference of opinion between parents that cannot be resolved without the court's help. Both sides present their arguments and evidence to the judge or the referee, who then delivers a judgment.

In mediation, the issues may be the same. How can the two parents work together to make life better for the children? The parents and the mediator meet together to reach agreements on issues involving the divorce and parents working together in the future. The rationale is very sound. Mediation assumes that the children's best interest is better served if decisions are mutually agreed upon rather than dictated by the court. Together, the parents outline their points of agreement and then begin learning ways to work together to settle their differences. This is a give-and-take process in which the mediator may have to remind the parents about what is best for the children. The mediation usually concludes with a written agreement between the two parents. The plan submitted to the court includes only points of agreement.

The conduct of mediators is guided by an ethical code of conduct. The code of conduct may vary in different states. What they report to the court is limited to the signed agreement between the parents. Mediators may ask the parents to agree not to repeat what is said in mediation to anyone else. However, confidentiality is forfeited when mediators have reason to believe that one parent may physically harm someone or there is disclosure of physical or sexual abuse. During the initial session, there should be discussion about the state laws that pertain to confidentiality.

Mediation is a viable alternative to custody litigation and may someday revolutionize how courts decide custody (Warshak, 2001). The process is not a panacea for all the ills that trouble divorced families and their children. For example, there is serious question about whether mediation should be used with a couple with a history of physical abuse. Some mediators argue that a victimized parent can never be on equal footing with an offender. There is a risk that mediation may give the offender an opportunity to continue exploiting the victim. Any agreement is looked upon with suspicion because the court may question whether the victim of abuse was intimidated or entered an honest agreement when face-to-face with the alleged abuser. Mediation has also been found to be less effective with obsessed parents.

Monitors

Courts struggle with getting high-conflict parents to comply with court orders. One way of helping assure compliance is to have someone monitor the parents' behavior. This responsibility can be assigned to a guardian ad litem (GAL), parent coordinator (PC), or special master. Monitoring is no guarantee, but it helps encourage compliance and accountability.

Guardian ad Litem

The rules and qualifications for a guardian ad litem (GAL) vary between states and different jurisdictions. They are typically court ordered and assigned to protect the children's interest. They have considerable power in most courts because they have access to all medical, school, and psychological records without waivers of confidentiality. The GAL is helpful when children do not want either parent to know their preference for custody. It is important to bear in mind that the GAL, after conducting his own investigation, will make a recommendation to the court that could be contrary to the children's wishes. If you think your children's interests are not being served, you may ask your attorney's advice about using a GAL. Be sure that GALs with considerable influence in the court's decisions have training in child development, conflict resolution, domestic violence, and other potentially heated issues that can surface during the litigation. Work with your attorney to assure that the assigned GAL is qualified and has the necessary training for issues you expect to surface.

Parent Coordinators and Special Masters

Many custody or visitation disputes have been successful resolved by simply giving family members an opportunity to tell their side of the story and then offering a little education that puts the issues in a proper perspective. Parent coordinators (PC) and special masters have learned to appreciate the value of parent education because they are believed to be impartial and representing no particular family member.

Courts, families, and the mental health community are looking for viable answers to how to work best with high-conflict families. Recent models proposed are parenting coordination (AFCC, 2006) and collaborative divorce (Testler and Thompson, 2006). Both models have in common the goal of working with families to resolve their disputes for the child's best interest rather than having the court make such decisions. Parents actively involved with making decisions about their children are more likely to comply with their decisions rather than the court orders. Using parenting coordinators (PC) is becoming more common in the number of jurisdictions because of the success of the programs. There is no consensus about the PC's qualifications, though the Association of Family and Conciliation Court's task force (2006) has proposed guidelines and defined parent coordination as

> a child-focused alternative dispute resolution process in which a mental health or legal professional with mediation training and experience assists high conflict parents to implement their parenting plan by facilitating the resolution of their disputes in a timely manner, educating parents about children's needs, and with prior approval of the parties and/or the court, making decisions within the scope of the court order or appointment contract.

The PC is a mental health or legal professional who should have received training in mediation, family dynamics, domestic violence, child development, family law, and conflict resolution. There is yet to be a consensus as to the qualifications of a parenting coordinator. Many states do not have provisions in their laws to use PCs, though some jurisdictions are moving in that direction by assigning a court employee to serve that function. You will find differences between jurisdictions about how these individuals are used. If you anticipate problems with your ex-spouse, you may want to discuss the possibility of using a PC with your attorney.

States vary considerably in how they define the qualifications and roles of mediators, parent coordinators, and special masters. In some states, special master has a more judicial function because they have a limited arbitration power. This is not the case with PCs and mediators. Mediators typically have less formal training or education than PCs. Some states only require a mediator to have forty hours of mediation training before they can put up a shingle.

Visitation Centers

The use of visitation centers has increased in recent years because the centers solve many problems facing families and the court: what to do when parents fight in the children's presence; failure to control their behavior during the exchanges; refusal to cooperate with court-ordered parenting time; or a history of violent allegations. Visitation centers have been a viable answer to these concerns. The courts want a safe and neutral environment for children to interact with their parents. Some centers provide parenting classes, mediation, and limited counseling.

The judge will order parents to a visitation center, sometimes at the attorney's suggestion. The goal of the referral is to encourage a parent/child relationship without the child fearing the parent and without any parental interference. The court or your attorney will give you the necessary information to call the center for an initial appointment. The center will conduct an intake interview in which they explain the fees and the center's rules and coordinate a schedule. The times the parents arrive or leave the center are staggered to prevent parents seeing each other. During a supervised visit, a worker or volunteer may be present in the room while you are playing with your child. The observer will write a report or make notes after the visit. Expect that a report will be forwarded to the court. It is important that you behave yourself, obey the rules, and focus on interacting with your children rather than spend time talking to the observer.

Supervised visits are difficult for a number of reasons. First, you are expected to have a positive interaction with your child while restricted to one room for an hour or longer. Keeping the interaction going that long for any parent is difficult. Children can get bored and conversation becomes strained. This does not help the relationship with your child, because he will blame his boredom on you. The best way to reduce your child's anxiety or discomfort is with a physical activity you both can enjoy. Second, you may feel restricted regarding what you can say to your child or being able to express affection. You should not interrogate your child, ask questions about the other parent, or engage in your own alienating behavior. Finally, most visitation centers will not allow you to give your child gifts or take pictures. This is very painful for most parents.

Regardless, you must follow the center's rules; otherwise you risk hurting your case with the court.

Parent Education

Mandated parent education is an effective tool to ward off parent conflicts and facilitate a child's adjustment to divorce (Garrity & Baris, 1994). Brandon (2006) reports from a sample of 9,876 participants that parent educational programs enhanced their appreciation of the importance of both parents communicating and supporting the children's relationship with the other parent. You may want to ask your attorney about getting a court order for both you and your spouse to participate in a parent education program. Usually the cost is very reasonable and requires only two or three evenings of your time. On balance, you can save money for legal fees and, most importantly, head off a lot of animosity that hurts your children. Unfortunately, most programs do not directly address parental alienation. Though you can bring up these issues during the discussion, do not expect parent education to solve long-term hostilities, especially with an obsessed parent. That is not the function of these programs, which are more preventative than curative.

Counselors

Sometimes there are family or personal problems that have preexisted or that appear during the arduous task of a separation or divorce. A parent or child with a mental disorder or substance addiction, or who is physically abusive or obsessed, will require therapeutic intervention with a counselor, social worker, psychologist, or psychiatrist. Members of your legal team are not equipped to treat these types of problems. If these concerns arise during the team's involvement in your case, listen to what they say and heed their advice.

Deciding Whether You Need Counseling

You may wonder whether you would benefit from counseling. A little guidance should help. Most people start counseling to get relief from psychological or emotional pain. Everyone has days where they feel depressed, on edge, or anxious. Having these feelings does not mean you need therapy. Therapy is helpful when, for whatever reason, you do not bounce back or recover from your psychological pain, or your persistent pain interferes with your daily functioning. You have good reason for getting professional help when you are missing work, no longer enjoying pleasurable activities, drinking more, using drugs, have trouble controlling your anger, or withdrawing from friends and family.

Your hurt and anger from the divorce should heal in time. For most people, a divorce will cause major changes in their life; however, these changes should not cause enduring problems. For some, healing is a slow process, hindered by the ongoing relationship with the children and ex-spouse. If you are not healing or you do not like how you are behaving, do not be too proud to say, "I need help." Divorce is a unique experience with unique problems. This is especially true when you have children. There are many different reasons to consider counseling:

- You are unable to separate your ex-spousal role from your parental role.

- You may have reason to believe you are either an active or an obsessed alienator because you cannot control your behavior or what you say to either your children or the other parent.

- You spend too much time thinking about your divorce and feelings of betrayal by the system.

- Your depression and anger are becoming more severe.

- You drive by your old house, hoping for a glimpse of your ex-spouse or children.

- Your thoughts about making your next phone call to your ex-spouse or the children are interfering with your work. Your ex-spouse complains about your endless phone calls, which you cannot seem to stop yourself from making. Though you believe your phone calls are justified, you know the calls are causing problems, particularly with your children.

- You believe your anger and frustration are justified, but others you trust frequently criticize you for bothering your ex-spouse and the children. You may have quiet moments when you question your own behavior, wondering if you are harming your children.

- You have increased your use of drugs or alcohol.

- You are becoming more afraid and angry because of your ex-spouse's incessant harassment. You are questioning your ability to continue coping with the pressure.

- Sometimes you think you are unfairly taking your frustrations out on your children. You are afraid of losing control and becoming abusive.
- You are missing work because you don't feel like working.
- You are withdrawing from your friends and family.

If any of the above statements are true for you, you are no different from most others who have felt the pain of rejection, loss of a loved one, or a major disappointment. You probably didn't think you had to run for the nearest therapist or take a drug to numb your senses. Instead, you most likely found support from a confidante or a trusted friend. And you probably reminded yourself, "I know I will feel better in time." How many times have you said this to yourself? You say it because it is true: You *will* feel better in time. Sometimes, years later, what was once a painful memory can become a peaceful and even comforting memory. You may have had this experience with an old boy- or girlfriend. You must learn to trust your capacity to heal.

> *TIP: Have a trusted friend to be your confidante.*

> *TIP: Do not overburden your friends with your problems. There needs to be a balance between talking about yourself and attending to your confidante's needs.*

However, if you decide you need more than time in order to heal, do not be too proud to ask for help. Schedule an appointment with a local psychologist, clinical social worker, or family therapist. There are local organizations that sponsor workshops or groups for people adjusting to their divorce. Your local help hotline or crisis center can help you find a qualified referral. Other good sources for a referral are the family court, friends who have had an experience similar to your own, or local support or advocacy groups like Parents Without Partners, ACES, or Fathers for Equal Rights.

Choosing a Counselor

A therapist should not be offended if you ask for their qualifications and fees. After all, they will ask about your ability to pay the bill. Therapists should have at least a master's degree in counseling, social work, or psychology. Most—but not all—states license therapists, social workers, counselors, and psychologists. Most professional therapists are not specifically qualified or trained to work with divorced families having problems with high-conflict or alienation. They should have specialized training in domestic law, family therapy, cognitive behavioral therapy, and/or conflict resolution. They should also understand parental alienation syndrome, if that is an issue.

There should be chemistry between you and your therapist. Sometimes this takes time and patience. Establishing a rapport is a process; do not give up on the therapist if it does not instantly happen. To do a good job, the therapist may have to tell you some things you do not want to hear. This is particularly true if you have been alienating your children. On the other hand, if your gut instinct is that the therapist is off-target and consistently puts you down or makes you feel more depressed, do not think, "This guy has a Ph.D., so who am I to argue with him?" Trust your instincts and look for another therapist. There is a therapist out there who can help you and your children. Don't give up or wait too long to get the needed help.

Epilogue

Divorce Casualties: Protecting your Children from Parental Alienation, Second Edition is the first of two books. A second book, soon to be published, will emphasize repairing damaged relationships and reunification therapy with the alienated children and alienating parent. *Divorce Casualties* (1998) helps identify alienating behavior and provides guidance on preventing alienation. It was most gratifying to hear from hundreds of parents who had read the original *Divorce Casualties* say how much they learned about how to improve their own behavior. This is a much healthier attitude than finding more reasons to blame the other parent. Their enthusiasm kept my passion alive to share what has been learned about parental alienation and parental alienation syndrome since the first edition. It is always scary writing a second edition, not knowing if the second will be as successful and helpful to families as the first.

There are probably many questions left unanswered. Many of these questions will be addressed in the next book. Some of the topics to be addressed in the next book are: eradicating obstacles to reunification; motivating the unmotivated parent; reunification therapy with the alienated child; changing an alienating parent's attitudes and beliefs; and spontaneous reunification. While *Divorce Casualties* focuses on prevention, the next book will focus on repairing the relationship between the targeted parent and the severe alienated child. You may question why this material is not in this edition. The reason is that the draft of the second edition had over 700 pages, considered too long for a book of this nature. I agreed with the publisher that the draft should be divided into two books. The second book, which will complement the first, will be out in 2009.

One of the most frequent questions asked is: what do I do when I have to interact with an obsessed parent who is intent on destroying my relations with my children? There are no simple answers but I want to leave you with these suggestions:

- Don't give up on your children.
- Keep your anger and hurt under control. Losing control only fuels the alienating parent's behavior.
- Don't retaliate with your own alienating behavior.
- With your attorney, be sure the court continues to support your parenting time. The only legitimate excuse for terminating parenting time is allegations of abuse or threats to the children's safety. If falsely accused of abuse, you must cooperate with the investigation and insist on supervised visits rather than no visits. Always first consult with your attorney.
- Don't stop trying to pick up your children for your parenting time. If the other parent refuses, keep showing up unless the court order says otherwise. This may be painful and frustrating, but do it anyway.
- Don't get hostile toward your ex-spouse in your children's presence. This will only make matters worse and give your ex-spouse more ammunition to attack you.
- Keep a log of your activities.
- Focus on keeping a positive relationship with the children positive.
- Don't pump your children for information.
- Don't wait to intervene until you start having problems. Many times problems with alienation start when you or your ex-spouse begin the introduction of a new romantic relationship. If there is a problem, contact your attorney or a parent coordinator.
- Get a court order requiring you and the other parent to get family therapy if problems persist. The therapist will need to determine if the child or children need deprogramming or reunification therapy. The therapist providing reunification therapy must be a different therapist than one working individually with the parent or child. The reason is to prevent distrust between the parent, child, and the therapist.
- The alienator and his or her supports (spouse and extended family) may need to be part of the therapy and be educated about alienation and their role in the problem. At this point, the therapist must be able to engage the significant others in trying to resolve the alien-

ation. A new spouse and grandparent can destroy any progress that the parents and child make in therapy.

- Monitor your own behavior so you do not begin alienating. Know the symptoms described in the previous chapters.

- Try understanding the other parent's argument without getting defensive. Do not get the children involved in the dispute.

- Never violate court orders and expect your attorney to defend your behavior. You always want to be on the offensive, not the defensive.

- The court may have a mechanism, like a guardian ad litem, parent coordinator, or court staff member, to monitor the parent's compliance to the court orders. The court must have sanctions for the parent's refusal to cooperate.

Dealing with an obsessed alienator can be one of the most difficult and painful experiences you will encounter. You feel powerless, knowing that the consequence of the destructive behaviors can last for years. What is most important is not adding to the problem. Remember, prevention is necessary because reversing parental alienation can be difficult but not hopeless.

I hope that as you put this book down, you have specific thoughts about what you can do to strengthen the relationship with your children and have learned new ways of reacting to the alienating tactics from an attacking child and parent. Regardless of the problems, your children need you. You need to be there for them when they are sick, when they marry, and when they have your grandchildren. What you have is very special and cannot be replaced with a better job, a new marriage, or a fancy cruise. Do not give up on them.

Appendix: Parental Alienation Scales (PAS)

The Parental Alienation Scales (Darnall, 1993) are to give you additional insight about how your behavior may contribute to alienation. The scales are for educational purposes only and *are not to be used as a diagnostic tool.* For the more statistically minded parent, the mean scores and standard deviations may help you better understand the meaning of your score.

Complete Form N if you do not have custody of your children. Complete Form C if you have custody. If you have split custody, the primary residential parent should complete Form C. If the parents split the time 50/50, both parents should complete Form C.

Form N (noncustodial parent): The mean score for 90 noncustodial parents who completed the inventory is 88.5 with a standard deviation of 17.6. (Do not worry if you do not understand what a standard deviation is.) If your total score is two or more standard deviations, or greater than 124, you need to seriously look at your behavior. You could be causing significant alienation. Go back and look at the inventory items that you score either a four or five and consider what you can do to reduce the risk of you contributing to the alienation.

Form C (custodial parent): The mean or average score for 100 custodial parents is 79 with a standard deviation of 15. If your total score is two or more standard deviations, or greater than 109, you need to seriously look at your behavior.

The inventory is not intended for you to diagnose yourself or the other parent. Even if your score is below the cutoff score, do not assume you cannot improve your behavior or attitude. The inventory is not to place blame. Remember, there is no perfect parent, only parents who strive to do better.

Parental Alienation Inventory: Form N (for noncustodial parents)

Rate each item by putting the number in the box that most accurately describes how **frequently** you behave in the manner described by the item. If you have more than one child, answer each item as to how the item relates to your oldest child. You must answer all items.

Number 1   Never
Number 2   Rarely
Number 3   Sometime
Number 4   Most of the time
Number 5   All the time

1. I make negative comments to my children about my ex-spouse. _____
2. I argue with my ex-spouse about the scheduled visitation. _____
3. I ask my children about my ex-spouse's personal life. _____
4. I miss buying my children Christmas and birthday presents. _____
5. I have accused my ex-spouse of drinking or drug abuse. _____
6. I remind my children about the lack of money because of the divorce. _____
7. I remind my children that one day they can come and live with me. _____
8. I have secret rendezvous with my children. _____
9. I have asked my children whom they want to live with. _____
10. I have asked my children to keep secrets. _____
11. I schedule secret phone calls. _____
12. When my children call and complain, I feel I must go and pick them up. _____
13. I dislike my children visiting their grandparents. _____
14. I have shown my children legal papers. _____
15. I have canceled visits. _____
16. For whatever reason, I have not returned my children's clothes after a visit. _____
17. I believe my ex-spouse to exaggerate my children's medical problems. _____
18. I feel frustrated because my ex-spouse will not listen to what I say. _____
19. I refuse to talk to my ex-spouse. _____
20. I feel that my ex-spouse lets our children run wild. _____
21. I have good reasons for being critical of my ex-spouse. _____

22. I still cringe when my children talk about having a good time with my ex-spouse. _____
23. I am paying child support. _____
24. My children have a good reason for not wanting to live where they currently are. _____
25. I am often too busy to visit my children. _____
26. I remind my ex-spouse I will take him or her back to court. _____
27. I return my children home late. _____
28. I call my ex-spouse names in front of my children. _____
29. I remind my children that there are things they do not need to tell the other parent. _____
30. I suggest to my children that they tell their other parent they want to live with me. _____
31. I believe that my children are not disciplined by their other parent. _____
32. I believe that my ex-spouse should follow my rules. _____
33. I give my ex-spouse advice. _____
34. My life is private. There are some things I do not want my children to tell their other parent. _____
35. I feel I must listen to my children's phone calls. _____
36. I have trouble keeping promises. _____
37. I make up my own rules rather than listen to the court. _____
38. I don't believe the court has a right to tell me what to do. _____
39. I feel very angry towards my ex-spouse. _____
40. I wish my ex-spouse would just disappear. _____
41. I believe my ex-spouse is a poor parent. _____
42. I believe my ex-spouse uses the children to get back at me. _____
43. My children have good reasons for wanting to live with me. _____
44. I do not believe my ex-spouse really loves our children. _____

Total Score _____

Parental Alienation Inventory: Form C (for custodial parents)

Rate each item by putting the number in the box that most accurately describes how frequently you behave in the manner described by the item. If you have more than one child, answer each item as to how the item relates to your oldest child. You must answer all items.

DIVORCE CASUALTIES

Number 1   Never
Number 2   Rarely
Number 3   Sometime
Number 4   Most of the time
Number 5   All the time

1. I make negative comments to my children about my ex-spouse. _____
2. I argue with my ex-spouse about the scheduled visitation. _____
3. I ask my children about my ex-spouse's personal life. _____
4. For whatever reason, I deny visitation to my ex-spouse. _____
5. I have accused my ex-spouse of drinking or drug abuse. _____
6. I remind my children about the lack of money because of the divorce. _____
7. I deny my ex-spouse access to school grades or medical records. _____
8. I will not give my ex-spouse the children's schedule of social activities. _____
9. I have asked my children whom they want to live with. _____
10. I have asked my children to keep secrets. _____
11. I schedule secret phone calls. _____
12. When my children call and complain, I feel I must go and pick them up. _____
13. I dislike my children visiting their grandparents. _____
14. I have shown my children legal papers. _____
15. I have canceled visits. _____
16. I will notify my ex-spouse if my children have a medical emergency. _____
17. I believe my ex-spouse exaggerates my children's medical problems. _____
18. I feel frustrated because my ex-spouse will not listen to what I say. _____
19. I refuse to talk to my ex-spouse. _____
20. I feel that my ex-spouse lets our children run wild. _____
21. I have good reasons for being critical of my ex-spouse. _____
22. I still cringe when my children talk about having a good time with my ex-spouse. _____
23. I resent it when my ex-spouse shows up at my children's school functions. _____
24. I feel my children have good reason for not wanting visits from my ex-spouse. _____

25. When my ex-spouse is late picking up the children for visitation, I will not allow them to go. _____
26. I remind my ex-spouse that I will take him/her back to court. _____
27. My children are too busy to have regular visit. _____
28. I call my ex-spouse names in front of my children. _____
29. I believe that my children are not disciplined by their other parent. _____
30. I believe that my ex-spouse should follow my rules. _____
31. I give my ex-spouse advice. _____
32. My life is private. There are some things I do not want my children to tell their other parent. _____
33. I feel I must listen to my children's phone calls. _____
34. I have trouble keeping my promises. _____
35. I make up my own rules rather than listen to the court. _____
36. I don't believe the court has a right to tell me what to do. _____
37. I feel very angry towards my ex-spouse. _____
38. I wish my ex-spouse would just disappear. _____
39. I believe my ex-spouse is a poor parent. _____
40. I believe my ex-spouse uses the children to get back at me. _____
41. I believe my children have good reason for wanting to live with me. _____
42. I do not believe my ex-spouse really loves our children. _____

Total Score _____

References

Amato, P. R. (1993). Children's adjustment to divorce: Theories, hypotheses, and empirical support. *Journal of Marriage and the Family.* 55: 23–38.

Amato, P. R. & Rezac, S. (1994). Contact with residential parents, interpersonal conflict, and children's behavior. *Journal of Family Issues,* 15, 191–207.

Amato, P. R. (1996). Explaining the inter generational transmission of divorce. *Journal of Marriage and Family,* 58, 356–365.

American Psychiatric Association (1968). *Diagnostic and Statistical Manual II of Mental Disorders.* (2nd ed.). American Psychiatric Association, Washington, DC.

American Psychiatric Association (1987). *Diagnostic and Statistical Manual III of Mental Disorders.* (3rd ed.). American Psychiatric Association, Washington, DC.

American Psychiatric Association (2000). *Diagnostic and Statistical Manual-IV-TR of Mental Disorders.* (4th ed.). Text Revision. American Psychiatric Association, Washington, DC.

American Psychological Association (2002). Ethical principles of psychologists and code of conduct. *American Psychologist,* 58, 377–402.

American Psychological Association (1994). Guidelines for child custody evaluations in divorce proceedings. *American Psychologist,* 49, 677–680.

Association of Family and Conciliation Courts: Task Force on Parenting Coordination (2006). Guidelines for Parenting Coordination. *Family Court Review, 44:1,* 164–181.

Baker, A. J. L. (2007). *Adult children of parental alienation syndrome: Breaking the ties that bind.* New York: The Norton Professional Book.

Baker, A. J. L & Darnall, D. (2006). Behaviors and strategies employed in parental alienation: A survey of parental experiences. *Journal of Divorce and Remarriage.* 45:1/2 97–124.

Baker, A. J. L & Darnall, D. (2007). A construct study of the eight symptoms of severe parental alienation syndrome: A survey of parental experiences. *Journal of Divorce and Remarriage.* 47:1/2, 55–76.

Bala, N. & Schuman, J. (2000). Allegations of sexual abuse when parents have separated. *Canadian Family Law Quarterly,* 17, 191–241.

Barker, R. L. (1995). *The social work dictionary.* Washington, DC: National Association of Social Workers Press.

Baris, M. A., Coats, C. A., Duvall, B. B., Garrity, C. B., Johnson, E. T., & LaCrosse, E. R. (2001). *Working with high-conflict families of divorce: A guide for professionals*. Northvale, New Jersey: Jason Aronson, Inc.

Bensel, R. W., Arthur, L. G., Round, L., and Riley, J. (1985). *Child abuse and neglect*. Reno, Nevada: Juvenile Justice Textbook Series.

Berg, B. & Kelly, R. (1979). The measured self-esteem of children from broken, rejected, and accepted families. *Journal of Divorce*, 2, 363–369.

Blank, G. K. & Ney, T. (2006). The (de) construction of concept in divorce litigation: A discursive critique of "Parental alienation syndrome" and the alienated child." *Family Court Review*, 44(1) 135–148.

Braiker, B. & Dy, C. (2007). Just don't call me Mr. Mom, *Newsweek Magazine*. October 8, 53–55.

Brandon, D. J. (2006). Can four hours make a difference? Evaluation of a parent education program for divorcing parents. *Journal of Divorce & Remarriage*, 45(1/2) 171–185.

Bruck, M., Ceci, S. J., & Hembrooke, H. (1998). Reliability and credibility of young children's reports. *American Psychologists*. 53(2) 136–151.

Cassidy, J. (1999). *The nature of the child's ties*. In J. Cassity & P. R. Shave (Eds.) *Handbook of attachment: Theory, research, and clinical applications* (3–20). New York: Guilford Press.

Ceci, S. J. & Bruck, M. (1995). *Jeopardy in the courtroom: A scientific analysis of children's testimony*. Washington, D.C: American Psychological Association.

Chatav, Y. & Whisman, M. A. (2007). Marital dissolution and psychiatric disorders: An investigation of risk factors. *Journal of Divorce & Remarriage*, 47(1/2) 1–13.

Clawar, S. S. & Rivlin, B.V. (1991). Children held hostage: Dealing with programmed and brainwashed children. American Bar Association.

Collaborative Divorce Newsblog (2007). *American Bar Association ethics opinion confirms collaborative law is ethical mode of practice* 10.31.07, www.collaborativedivorcenews.com/2007/10/american-ethics-opinion.

Cummings, E. M. and Davies, P. T. (1994). *Children and marital conflict*. New York: Guilford Press.

Darnall, D. C. (1993). The content validity of parental alienation. Unpublished raw data.

Darnall, D. C. (1998). *Divorce casualties: Protecting your children from parental alienation*. Dallas Texas: Taylor Publishing Company.

Darnall, D. C. (Forthcoming). *Beyond divorce casualties: Reunifying the alienated family*. Lanham, Maryland: Taylor Trade.

Daubert v. Merrell Dow Pharmaceuticals, Inc., 509 U.S. 579, 113 S. Ct. 2786, 125. L. Ed. 2nd 469 (1993).

Dorland's illustrated medical dictionary (24th edition). (1965). Philadelphia: W. B. Saunders Company.

Dudley, J. (1991). Increasing our understanding of divorced fathers who have infrequent contact with their children. *Family Relations*, 40, 279–282.

Dunne, J. and Hedrick, M. (1994). The parental alienation syndrome: An analysis of sixteen selected cases. *Journal of Divorce and Remarriage.* 21(3/4): 21–38.

Eddy, B. (2006). *High conflict people in legal disputes.* Canada: Janis Publication

El-Sheikh, M., Harger, J., and Whitson (2001). Appraisals of marital conflict and children's adjustment, health, and physiological reactivity. *Developmental Psychology, 37,* 875–885.

Emery, R. E. (1982). Interparental conflict and the children of discord and divorce. *Psychological Bulletin, 92,* 310–330.

Faller, K. & DeVoe, E. (1995). Allegations of sexual abuse in divorce. *Journal of Child Sexual Abuse,* 4(4), 1–25.

Forehand, R., McCombs A., Long, N., Brody, G., & Fauber, R. (1988). Early adolescent adjustment to recent parental divorce: The role of interparental conflict and adolescent sex as mediating variables. *Journal of Consulting and Clinical Psychology,* 56, no. 4, 624–627.

Frye v. United States 293 F. 1013 [DC, Cir., 1923].

Garrity, C. B. & Baris, M. A. (1994). *Caught in the middle: Protecting the children in high-conflict divorce.* New York: Lexington Books.

Gardner, R. A. (1985). Recent trends in divorce and custody litigation. *Academy Forum (a publication of the American Academy of Psychoanalysis),* 29(2): 3–7.

Gardner, R. A. (1998). *Parental alienation syndrome.* (2nd ed.). Cresskill, New Jersey: Creative Therapeutics.

Gardner, R. A. (2001). Should courts order PAS children to visit/reside with the alienated parent? A follow-up study. *The American Journal of Forensic Psychology,* 19(3): 61–106.

Gardner, R. A. (2002). Parental alienation syndrome vs. parental alienation: Which diagnosis should be used in child custody litigation? *American Journal of Family Therapy,* 30(2) 101–123.

Giftis, S. H. (1996). *Law dictionary* (Barron's Legal Guides). New York: Hauppauge.

Groth, N. (1978). *Sexual assault of children and adolescents.* Lexington, Massachusetts: Lexington Books.

Guidubaldi, J., Perry, J., & Nastasi, B. K. (1987). Assessment and intervention for children of divorce: Implications of the NASP-KSU nationwide study. *Advances in Family Intervention, Assessment, and Theory,* 4: 33–69.

Gunsberg, L. & Hymowitz, P. (2005). *The handbook of divorce and custody: Forensic, developmental, and clinical perspectives.* Hillsdale, NJ: The Analytic Press.

Herman, S. (2005). Improving decision making in forensic child sexual abuse evaluations. *Law and Human Behavior,* 29(1), 87–120.

Hetherington, E.M., Cox, M., & Cox, R. (1979). The development of children in mother-headed families. In D. Reiss & H.K. Hoffman (Eds.) *The American Family: Dying or developing.* New York: Plenum Press.

Hetherington, E. M. (ed) (1999). *Coping with divorce, single parenting, and remarriage: A risk and resiliency perspective.* Mahway, NJ: Erlbaum.

Hetherington, E. M., Cox, M., and Cox, R. (1985). Long-term effects of divorce and remarriage on the adjustment of children. *Journal of the American Academy of Child Psychiatry,* 24, 518–530.

Hodges, W. F. & Bloom, B. L. (1984). Parent's report of children's adjustment to marital separation: A longitudinal study. *Journal of Divorce,* 8(1): 33–51.

Hoffman, D. (2007). American Bar Association ethics opinion confirms collaborative law is ethical mode of practice. *Collaborative Divorce Newsblog.* Retrieved December 25, 2007, from http://www.collaborativedivorcenews.com/2007/10/american-bar-association-ethics-opinion.

Jacobson, D. S. (1978). The impact of marital separation/divorce on children: II Interparent hostility and child adjustment. *Journal of Divorce,* 2(1) 3–19.

Jamieson, C. D. (2007). *How to prepare a champagne case on a beer bottle budget.* Power point presented at Parental Alienation Awareness Organization conference.

Johnston. J. R., Kline, M., & Tschann, J. M. (1989). Ongoing postdivorce conflict: Effects on children of joint custody and frequent access. *American Orthopsychiatric Association,* 59(4), 576–592.

Kaufman, J. and Zigler, E. (1987). Do abused children become abusive adults? *American Journal of Orthopsychiatry,* 57(2), 186–192.

Kelly, J. B. (2000). Children's adjustment in conflicted marriage and divorce: A decade review of research. *American Academy of Child and Adolescent Psychiatry,* 39(8) 963–973.

Kelly, J. B. & Johnson, J. R. (2001). The alienated child: A reformulation of parental alienation syndrome. *Family Court Review,* 39(3), 249–266.

Kuehnle, K. & Drozd, L. (2005). *Child custody litigation: Allegations of child sexual abuse,* Volume 2. New York, NY: Haworth Press.

Lampel, A. (1986). Post-divorce therapy with high-conflict families. *The Independent Practitioner,* 6(3): 22–26.

Long, N., Slater, E., Forehand, R., & Fauber, R. (1988). Continued high or reduced interparental conflict following divorce: Relation to young adolescent adjustment. *Journal of Consulting and Clinical Psychology,* 56(3) 467–469.

Mackey, W. C. & Immerman, R. S. (2007). Fatherlessness by divorce contrasted to fatherlessness by non-marital births: A distinction with a difference for the community. *Journal of Divorce & Remarriage,* 47(1/2) 111–134.

Poole, D. A. & Lamb, M. E. (1998). Investigative interviews of children. Washington, DC: American Psychological Association.

Porter, B. & O'Leary, K. D. (1980). Marital discord and childhood behavior problems. *Journal of Abnormal Child Psychology,* 80, 287–295.

Rothenberg, M. A. & Chapman, C. F. (2000). *Dictionary of medical terms for the nonmedical person: Fourth edition.* Hauppauge, New York: Barron's Educational Series.

Sarrazin, J. & Cyr, F. (2007). Parental conflicts and their damaging effects on children. *Journal of Divorce & Remarriage,* 47(1/2) 77–93.

Schetky, D. H. & Green, A. H. (1988). *Child Sexual abuse: A handbook for health care and legal professionals.* New York: Brunner/Mazel Publishers.

Schepard, A. I. (2004). *Children, courts, and custody: Interdisciplinary models for divorcing families.* New York: Cambridge University Press.

Slater, E. J. & Haber, J. D. (1984). Adolescent adjustment following divorce as a function of familial conflict. *Journal of Consulting and Clinical Psychology,* 52(5), 920–921.

Sobell, L. C. & Sobell, M. B. (2003). Using motivational interviewing techniques to talk with clients about their alcohol abuse. *Cognitive and Behavioral Practice,* 10, 214–221.

Sorensen, E.D. & Goldman, J. (1990). Custody determinations and child development: A review of the current literature. *Journal of Divorce,* 13(4) 53–67.

Supreme Court of Illinois (2004) *In re Marriage of Norma Perez Bates, Appellant, and R. Edward Bates, Appellee.* No. 97059. (212 Ill.2d 489, 819, N.E.2d 714).

Testler, P. H., and Thompson, P. (2006). *Collaborative divorce: The revolutionary new way to restructure your family, resolve legal issues, and move on with your life.* New York: Regan Books.

Tong, D. (2001). Elusive innocence: Survival guide for the falsely accused. Lafayette, LA: Huntington House Publishers.

Trocmé, N. & Bala, N. (2005). False allegations of abuse and neglect when parents separate. *Child Abuse & Neglect,* 29, 1333–1345.

Turkat, I. D. (1994). Child visitation interference in divorce. *Clinical Psychology Rview,* 14(8), 737–742.

Ver Steegh, N. (2005). Differentiating types of domestic violence: Implications for child custody. *Louisiana Law Review.* 65: 4, 1389–1431.

Visher, E. B. & Visher, J. S. (1982). *How to win as a step-family: Second edition.* New York: Brunner/Mazel.

Wade v. Hirschman, 903 So2d 928 Florida Supreme Court (2005).

Wallace, H. (2002). *Family violence: Legal, medical, and social perspectives.* Boston, MA: Pearson Education.

Wallerstein, J. S. & Kelly, J. B. (1980). *Surviving the breakup: How children and parents cope with divorce.* New York: Basic Books.

Wallerstein, J. S., Lewis, J., & Blakeslee, S. (2001). *Second changes: Men, women, and children a decade after divorce.* New York: Mariner Books.

Warshak, R. A. (1999). *Parental alienation in the courts.* Dallas Texas, Clinical Psychology Associates.

Warshak, R. A. (2001). *Divorce poison.* New York: Harper Collins Publishing.

West Virginia. (2008). *Crimes against the peace: Falsely reporting child abuse.* Chapter 61, Articles 6 §61-6-25.

Wood, C. L. (1994). The parental alienation syndrome: A dangerous aura of reliability. *Loyola of Los Angeles Law Review.* 29, 1367–1415.

Index